KW-552-504

This edition of *Children First* supersedes all others and should be the only one in use.

It is the reference point for practice detail.

An Roinn Leanaí
agus Gnóthaí Óige
Department of
Children and Youth Affairs

Ch... Na... ice for... n an... of (...

INSTITUTE OF TECHNOLOGY, CARLOW
This book must be returned by the latest
date stamped below.

Damage to or loss of books will be charged to the borrower.
FINES FOR OVERDUE BOOKS - 10c PER DAY.
INSTITUTE OF TECHNOLOGY, CARLOW.
Kilkenny Road, Carlow, Ireland.

children first

2011
DEPARTMENT OF CHILDREN AND YOUTH AFFAIRS

66891

Copyright © Minister for Children and Youth Affairs, 2011

Department of Children and Youth Affairs
43-49 Mespil Road
Dublin 4

Tel: +353 (0)1 647 3000
Fax: +353 (0)1 667 0826
E-mail: contact@dcya.gov.ie
Web: www.dcya.ie

Published by Government Publications, Dublin

ISBN 978-1-4064-2589-5

LIBRARY I.T. CARLOW
ACC. NO. 66891 DATE 9/12/11
CLASS NO. 362.709415 PRICE €5.00
VENDOR OPW 111400

All rights reserved. No part of this publication may be reproduced, stored in a retrieval system, or transmitted, in any form or by any means, electronic, mechanical, photocopying, recording or otherwise, without the prior permission in writing of the copyright holder.

For rights of translation or reproduction, applications should be made to the Head of Communications, Department of Children and Youth Affairs, 43-49 Mespil Road, Dublin 4, Ireland.

Contents

Minister's Foreword

The Department of Children and Youth Affairs has a number of responsibilities, obligations and duties in relation to the youngest citizens of our country. Paramount among these is ensuring their safety.

No childhood should be shattered by abuse. No young life should be lived in the shadow of fear. While it is not possible to prevent all violence, nor possible to guarantee that no child will ever be harmed by neglect or aggression or exploitation or predation, it is our duty to do everything in our power as a Government and as a society to prevent such harm.

This begins by ensuring that children are safe and protected in all aspects of their lives – where they live, learn, pray and play. This *Children First: National Guidance for the Protection and Welfare of Children* and the accompanying *Child Protection and Welfare Practice Handbook* set out clearly how child protection must be placed at the core of any organisation working with children. The documents detail what is to be done to protect children, how it is to be done and who are the key people in each organisation to do it.

This combination of the *Children First: National Guidance* 2011, as the comprehensive reference document, and a practical handbook to key actions for front-line practitioners will deliver a sound footing for national consistency in our approach to child protection.

These changes and the creation of a dedicated National Child and Family Support Agency, for the provision of family support and child protection services, will result in greatly enhanced protection for children.

Ultimately, it is our intention to update all available guidelines to take account of the new National Agency, its functions and duties, and to reflect the best of practice from Ireland and internationally. The new roles and responsibilities will be supported by the *Children First: National Guidance* and a substantial implementation programme, training and audit of compliance and impact to ensure national application of best practice.

Guidelines cannot eradicate evil. Audits cannot prevent exploitation. Our task is not to delude ourselves that every malign aspect of humanity can be removed; rather, it is to ensure that children are protected from the badness in society. Where we fail, where abuse occurs despite our best efforts, our task is to make sure that the abusers are caught, punished and prevented from re-offending, and to make sure that those who facilitated the crime, either by commission or omission, are held to account.

We intend to enact legislation so that all people who are working with children will have a statutory duty to comply with the *Children First: National Guidance*. This is a significant step forward in the protection of children from abuse. It will result in more effective interagency cooperation and will provide for a more consistent and strong system for the protection of children.

Frances Fitzgerald, TD
Minister for Children and Youth Affairs

PART I:
Key Messages

Key Messages

The aim of the *Children First: National Guidance* is to promote the safety and well-being of children. Parents and guardians have the primary responsibility for the care and protection of children. Many parents from time to time require support and help from the State in carrying out their parental role.

Some parents, for a range of reasons, are not able to provide proper care for their children. These families need more intensive assessment, support and direct interventions to ensure the safety and well-being of their children. People working with children and the wider public should know that early action by them is very often the best way to protect children and to enable a family to stay together. Professionals also have an important part to play and their actions need to reflect the principles and objectives of the Child Care Act 1991 and of this national guidance.

Professionals and others working with children need to pay particular attention to the needs of children who may be at risk of abuse. Research tells us that children whose parents misuse drugs or alcohol are more at risk of neglect or maltreatment. Parents who have a learning disability or mental illness may need particular support in carrying out their parenting role.

Research indicates that most abuse occurs in the family home. Children may be abused by persons other than those living in the immediate family. This may happen where a child is in contact with a relative, a family friend or acquaintance, or a person whose professional or voluntary activity brings them into contact with a child. In all instances, the best interests and safety of the child must be prioritised.

Good practice at the front line is based on clear policies and principles. The Government's policy underpinning this *Children First: National Guidance* is:

- the welfare and safety of children, which is central to all Government policy;
- the promotion of and support for family life;
- the use of the minimum necessary intervention, in a timely way, to keep children safe;
- agencies working together to help children reach their full potential;
- agencies working together to provide safer and more effective services;
- the State and civil society working together to promote children's welfare.

This national guidance sets out the particular statutory responsibility of the HSE Children and Family Services and An Garda Síochána when they are alerted to concerns about the welfare and safety of a child.

The broader group of health, educational and other professionals and organisations, including voluntary groups, whose work brings them into contact with children and families also have a responsibility to be aware of the signs, symptoms and possibilities of neglect and abuse. They need to share their concerns or seek advice from the HSE, make a formal report and cooperate in whatever way possible, including attending at meetings, in order to share information and contribute to good decision-making. In an emergency situation, the Gardaí should be informed of children at risk.

The wider community of relatives, friends, and neighbours are well placed to be aware of a child's welfare and need to know how to respond to ensure the most effective steps are taken to protect a child.

As a member of the public, if you have concerns about a child but are not sure what to do, or if you are worried about a child's safety or welfare, you should contact your local HSE Children and Family Services (*see HSE nationwide contacts in Appendix 2*).

Professionals and those involved in organisations working with children who have concerns about a child but are not sure what to do should discuss these with the *Children First* designated person in your organisation or contact the HSE Children and Family Services for advice (*see Appendix 2*).

If you think a child is in immediate danger and you cannot contact the HSE Children and Family Services, you should contact the Gardaí at any Garda station.

1. Principles, Aims and Use of the *Children First: National Guidance*

1.1 Key principles of best practice in child protection and welfare

1.1.1 The key principles that should inform best practice in child protection and welfare are:

(i) The welfare of children is of paramount importance.

(ii) Early intervention and support should be available to promote the welfare of children and families, particularly where they are vulnerable or at risk of not receiving adequate care or protection. Family support should form the basis of early intervention and preventative interventions.

(iii) A proper balance must be struck between protecting children and respecting the rights and needs of parents/carers and families. Where there is conflict, the child's welfare must come first.

(iv) Children have a right to be heard, listened to and taken seriously. Taking account of their age and understanding, they should be consulted and involved in all matters and decisions that may affect their lives. Where there are concerns about a child's welfare, there should be opportunities provided for their views to be heard independently of their parents/carers.

(v) Parents/carers have a right to respect and should be consulted and involved in matters that concern their family.

(vi) Factors such as the child's family circumstances, gender, age, stage of development, religion, culture and race should be considered when taking protective action. Intervention should not deal with the child in isolation; the child's circumstances must be understood within a family context.

(vii) The criminal dimension of any action must not be ignored.

(viii) Children should only be separated from parents/carers when alternative means of protecting them have been exhausted. Re-union should be considered in the context of planning for the child's future.

(ix) The prevention, detection and treatment of child abuse or neglect requires a coordinated multidisciplinary approach, effective management, clarity of responsibility and training of personnel in organisations working with children.

(x) Professionals and agencies working with adults who for a range of reasons may have serious difficulties meeting their children's basic needs for safety and security should always consider the impact of their adult client/patient's behaviour on a child and act in the child's best interests.

1.2 Aims of the *Children First: National Guidance*

1.2.1 The *Children First: National Guidance* is intended to assist people in identifying and reporting child abuse and neglect and deal effectively with concerns. It emphasizes that the needs of children and families must be at the centre of child protection and welfare services, and that the welfare of children is of paramount importance. It highlights the roles and responsibilities of the HSE and An Garda Síochána, which are the two agencies with statutory responsibility for child protection. It also offers guidance to agencies and community and voluntary organisations (e.g. religious/faith sector, sporting organisations, etc) that have contact with or provide services to children.

1.2.2 Society has a duty of care towards children and everyone should be alert to the possibility that children with whom they are in contact may be being abused or at risk of being abused. This national guidance is designed to encourage people to report concerns or suspicions to the HSE Children and Family Services.

1.2.3 The national guidance is also intended to provide a framework to support interagency cooperation and the strengthening of multidisciplinary responses to child abuse and neglect. Effective child protection will be best achieved where the national guidance and local procedures are underpinned by comprehensive training, supervision and support services for children and their families.

1.3 Use of the *Children First: National Guidance*

1.3.1 Consistent with the principles of *Children First*, every organisation, both public and private, that is providing services for children or that is in regular direct contact with children should:

(i) ensure best practice in the recruitment of staff or volunteers, which includes Garda vetting, taking up of references, good HR practices in interviewing, induction training, probation and ongoing supervision and management;

(ii) ensure that staff members or volunteers are aware of how to recognise signs of child abuse or neglect;

(iii) develop guidance and procedures for staff and/or volunteers who may have reasonable grounds for concern about the safety and welfare of children involved with the organisation. **These procedures should not deviate from the current *Children First: National Guidance*, but may offer further elaboration to ensure local relevance and applicability** (*see Appendix 8 for further guidance*). It is the responsibility of each organisation to ensure that such guidance and procedures are in place;

(iv) identify a designated person to act as a liaison with outside agencies and a resource person to any staff member or volunteer who has child protection concerns. The designated person is responsible for reporting allegations or suspicions of child abuse to the HSE Children and Family Services or to An Garda Síochána.

PART II: Definitions and Recognition of Child Abuse

Basis for reporting concerns and Standard Reporting Procedure

Interagency Cooperation

2. Definition and Recognition of Child Abuse

2.1 Types of child abuse

2.1.1 This chapter outlines the principal types of child abuse and offers guidance on how to recognise such abuse. Child abuse can be categorised into four different types: neglect, emotional abuse, physical abuse and sexual abuse. A child may be subjected to one or more forms of abuse at any given time. **More detail on each type of abuse is given in Appendix 1.**

2.1.2 In the *Children First: National Guidance*, 'a child' means a person under the age of 18 years, excluding a person who is or has been married.

2.2 Definition of 'neglect'

2.2.1 Neglect can be defined in terms of an *omission*, where the child suffers significant harm or impairment of development by being deprived of food, clothing, warmth, hygiene, intellectual stimulation, supervision and safety, attachment to and affection from adults, and/or medical care.

2.2.2 Harm can be defined as the ill-treatment or the impairment of the health or development of a child. Whether it is *significant* is determined by the child's health and development as compared to that which could reasonably be expected of a child of similar age.

2.2.3 Neglect generally becomes apparent in different ways *over* a *period of time* rather than at one specific point. For example, a child who suffers a series of minor injuries may not be having his or her needs met in terms of necessary supervision and safety. A child whose height or weight is significantly below average may be being deprived of adequate nutrition. A child who consistently misses school may be being deprived of intellectual stimulation.

2.2.4 The *threshold of significant harm* is reached when the child's needs are neglected to the extent that his or her well-being and/or development are severely affected.

2.3 Definition of 'emotional abuse'

2.3.1 Emotional abuse is normally to be found in the *relationship* between a parent/carer and a child rather than in a specific event or pattern of events. It occurs when a child's developmental need for affection, approval, consistency and security are not met. Unless other forms of abuse are present, it is rarely manifested in terms of physical signs or symptoms. Examples may include:

(i) the imposition of negative attributes on a child, expressed by persistent criticism, sarcasm, hostility or blaming;

(ii) conditional parenting in which the level of care shown to a child is made contingent on his or her behaviours or actions;

(iii) emotional unavailability of the child's parent/carer;

(iv) unresponsiveness of the parent/carer and/or inconsistent or inappropriate expectations of the child;

(v) premature imposition of responsibility on the child;

(vi) unrealistic or inappropriate expectations of the child's capacity to understand something or to behave and control himself or herself in a certain way;

(vii) under- or over-protection of the child;

(viii) failure to show interest in, or provide age-appropriate opportunities for, the child's cognitive and emotional development;

(ix) use of unreasonable or over-harsh disciplinary measures;

(x) exposure to domestic violence;

(xi) exposure to inappropriate or abusive material through new technology.

2.3.2 Emotional abuse can be manifested in terms of the child's behavioural, cognitive, affective or physical functioning. Examples of these include insecure attachment, unhappiness, low self-esteem, educational and developmental underachievement, and oppositional behaviour. The *threshold* of *significant harm* is reached when abusive interactions dominate and become *typical* of the relationship between the child and the parent/carer.

2.4 Definition of 'physical abuse'

2.4.1 Physical abuse of a child is that which results in actual or potential physical harm from an interaction, or lack of interaction, which is reasonably within the control of a parent or person in a position of responsibility, power or trust. There may be single or repeated incidents.

Physical abuse can involve:

(i) severe physical punishment;

(ii) beating, slapping, hitting or kicking;

(iii) pushing, shaking or throwing;

(iv) pinching, biting, choking or hair-pulling;

(v) terrorising with threats;

(vi) observing violence;

(vii) use of excessive force in handling;

(viii) deliberate poisoning;

(ix) suffocation;

(x) fabricated/induced illness (*see Appendix 1 for details*);

(xi) allowing or creating a substantial risk of significant harm to a child.

2.5 Definition of 'sexual abuse'

2.5.1 Sexual abuse occurs when a child is used by another person for his or her gratification or sexual arousal, or for that of others. Examples of child sexual abuse include:

(i) exposure of the sexual organs or any sexual act intentionally performed in the presence of the child;

(ii) intentional touching or molesting of the body of a child whether by a person or object for the purpose of sexual arousal or gratification;

(iii) masturbation in the presence of the child or the involvement of the child in an act of masturbation;

(iv) sexual intercourse with the child, whether oral, vaginal or anal;

(v) sexual exploitation of a child, which includes inciting, encouraging, propositioning, requiring or permitting a child to solicit for, or to engage in, prostitution or other sexual acts. Sexual exploitation also occurs when a child is involved in the exhibition, modeling or posing for the purpose of sexual arousal, gratification or sexual act, including its recording (on film, video tape or other media) or the manipulation, for those purposes, of the image by computer or other means. It may also include showing sexually explicit material to children, which is often a feature of the 'grooming' process by perpetrators of abuse;

(vi) consensual sexual activity involving an adult and an underage person. In relation to child sexual abuse, it should be noted that, for the purposes of the criminal law, the age of consent to sexual intercourse is 17 years for both boys and girls. An Garda Síochána will deal with the criminal aspects of the case under the relevant legislation.

2.5.2 It should be noted that the definition of child sexual abuse presented in this section is not a legal definition and is not intended to be a description of the criminal offence of sexual assault.

2.6 Recognising child neglect or abuse

2.6.1 Child neglect or abuse can often be difficult to identify and may present in many forms. A list of indicators of child abuse is contained in Appendix 1. No one indicator should be seen as conclusive in itself of abuse. It may indicate conditions other than child abuse. All signs and symptoms must be examined in the context of the child's situation and family circumstances.

2.7 Guidelines for recognition

2.7.1 The ability to recognise child abuse can depend as much on a person's willingness to accept the possibility of its existence as it does on their knowledge and information. There are commonly three stages in the identification of child neglect or abuse:

(i) considering the possibility;

(ii) looking out for signs of neglect or abuse;

(iii) recording of information.

Stage 1: Considering the possibility

2.7.2 The possibility of child abuse should be considered if a child appears to have suffered a suspicious injury for which no reasonable explanation can be offered. It should also be considered if the child seems distressed without obvious reason or displays persistent or new behavioural problems. The possibility of child abuse should also be considered if the child displays unusual or fearful responses to parents/carers or older children. A pattern of ongoing neglect should also be considered even when there are short periods of improvement.

Stage 2: Looking out for signs of neglect or abuse

2.7.3 Signs of neglect or abuse can be physical, behavioural or developmental. They can exist in the relationships between children and parents/carers or between children and other family members/other persons. A cluster or pattern of signs is more likely to be indicative of neglect or abuse. Children who are being abused may hint that they are being harmed and sometimes make direct disclosures. Disclosures should always be taken very seriously and should be acted upon, for example, by informing the HSE Children and Family Services. The child should not be interviewed in detail about the alleged abuse without first consulting with the HSE Children and Family Services. This may be more appropriately carried out by a social worker or An Garda Síochána. Less obvious signs could be gently explored with the child, *without direct questioning.* Play situations, such as drawing or story-telling, may reveal information.

2.7.4 Some signs are more indicative of abuse than others. These include:

(i) disclosure of abuse by a child or young person;

(ii) age-inappropriate or abnormal sexual play or knowledge;

(iii) specific injuries or patterns of injuries;

(iv) absconding from home or a care situation;

(v) attempted suicide;

(vi) underage pregnancy or sexually transmitted disease;

(vii) signs in one or more categories at the same time. For example, signs of developmental delay, physical injury and behavioural signs may together indicate a pattern of abuse.

2.7.5 Many signs of abuse are non-specific and must be considered in the child's social and family context. It is important to be open to alternative explanations for physical or behavioural signs of abuse.

Stage 3: Recording of information

2.7.6 If neglect or abuse is suspected and acted upon, for example, by informing the HSE Children and Family Services, it is important to establish the grounds for concern by obtaining as much information as possible. Observations should be accurately recorded and should include dates, times, names, locations, context and any other information that may be relevant. Care should be taken as to how such information is stored and to whom it is made available.

2.8 Children with additional vulnerabilities

2.8.1 Certain children are more vulnerable to abuse than others. Such children include those with disabilities, children who are homeless and those who, for one reason or another, are separated from their parents or other family members and who depend on others for their care and protection. The same categories of abuse – neglect, emotional abuse, physical abuse and sexual abuse – are applicable, but may take a slightly different form. For example, abuse may take the form of deprivation of basic rights, harsh disciplinary regimes or the inappropriate use of medications or physical restraints (*see also Chapter 8*).

2.9 Fatal child abuse

2.9.1 In the tragic circumstances where a child dies as a result of abuse or neglect, there are four important aspects to be considered: criminal, child protection, bereavement and notification.

2.9.2 **Criminal aspects:** This is the responsibility of An Garda Síochána and they must be notified immediately. The Coroner must also be notified and his or her instructions complied with in relation to post-mortems and other relevant matters.

2.9.3 **Child protection aspects:** These will be particularly relevant if there are other children in the family/ in the same situation, and will therefore require immediate intervention by the HSE Children and Family Services to assess risk.

2.9.4 **Bereavement aspects:** The bereavement needs of the family must be respected and provided for and all family members should be given an opportunity to grieve and say goodbye to the deceased child.

2.9.5 **Notification aspects:** The HSE should notify the death of a child to the National Review Panel and to the Health Information and Quality Authority in accordance with the HIQA's *Guidance for the Health Service Executive for the Review of Serious Incidents, including deaths of children in care* (HIQA, 2010):

- all deaths of children in care, including natural causes;
- all deaths of children known to the child protection system;
- serious incidents involving a child in care or known to the child protection services.

Managers and staff should cooperate fully with any review undertaken to establish the facts of the case and any actions that should be taken, to identify learning that will improve services in the future and to provide assurance to the public (*see Chapter 5, Section 5.20*).

LIBRARY
INSTITUTE OF TECHNOLOGY
CARLOW

2.10 Points to remember

2.10.1 **The severity of a sign does not necessarily equate with the severity of the abuse.** Severe and potentially fatal injuries are not always visible. Neglect and emotional and/or psychological abuse tend to be cumulative and effects may only be observable in the longer term. Explanations that are inconsistent with the signs should constitute a cause for concern.

2.10.2 **Neglect is as potentially fatal as physical abuse.** It can cause delayed physical, psychological and emotional development, chronic ill-health and significant long-term damage. It may place children at serious risk of harm. It may also precede, or co-exist with, other forms of abuse and must be acted upon.

2.10.3 **Experiencing recurring low-level abuse may cause serious and long-term harm.** Cumulative harm refers to the effects of multiple adverse circumstances and events in a child's life. The unremitting daily impact of these circumstances on the child can be profound and exponential, and diminish a child's sense of safety and well-being.

2.10.4 **Child abuse is not restricted to any socio-economic group, gender or culture.** All signs must be considered in the wider social and family context. Serious deficits in child safety and welfare transcend cultural, social and ethnic norms, and must elicit a response.

2.10.5 **Challenging behaviour by a child or young person should not render them liable to abuse**. Children in certain circumstances may present management problems. This should not leave them vulnerable to harsh disciplinary measures or neglect of care.

2.10.6 **Exposure to domestic violence is detrimental to children's physical, emotional and psychological well-being.** The adverse effects of domestic violence have been well established.

2.10.7 **While the impact of neglect is most profound on young children, it also adversely affects adolescents.** Neglect renders young people liable to risk-taking behaviors, such as running away, early school leaving, anti-social behavior, mental health and addiction problems, including the risk of suicide.

2.10.8 **It is sometimes difficult to distinguish between indicators of child abuse and other adversities suffered by children and families.** Deprivation, stress, addiction or mental health problems should not be used as a justification for omissions of care or commissions of harm by parents/carers. The child's welfare must be the primary consideration.

2.10.9 **Neglectful families may be difficult to engage.** Research shows that families may be reluctant to seek help in response to experiencing the factors associated with neglect.

2.10.10 **Families where neglect and abuse are prevalent may go to considerable lengths to deceive professionals.** It is important for professionals to approach cases with a wary trustfulness, seek evidence to substantiate claims of improvement and speak with the children concerned individually.

2.10.11 **Social workers need good observation and analytical skills** in order to be able to understand the nature of the relationship between a parent and child, to understand signs of non-compliance, to work alongside a family and to come to safe and evidence-based judgements about the best course of action.

2.10.12 **Working in the area of child abuse and neglect is dealing with uncertainty.** Social workers and other professionals should adopt a 'respectful uncertainty' on parental reporting of improvement until supported by clear evidence.

3. Basis for reporting concerns and Standard Reporting Procedure

3.1 Purpose

3.1.1 This chapter offers guidance to the general public and to all people, both professional and voluntary, working with or in direct contact with children who may be concerned or who suspect that children are being abused or neglected or at risk of abuse or neglect. It outlines the standard reporting procedure to be used in passing information to the statutory authorities about child protection concerns.

3.2 Responsibility to report child abuse or neglect

3.2.1 Everyone must be alert to the possibility that children with whom they are in contact may be suffering from abuse or neglect. This responsibility is particularly relevant for professionals such as teachers, child care workers, health professionals and those working with adults with serious parenting difficulties. It is also an important responsibility for staff and people involved in sports clubs, community activities, youth clubs, religious/faith sector and other organisations catering for children.

3.2.2 The HSE Children and Family Services should always be informed when a person has **reasonable grounds for concern** that a child may have been, is being or is at risk of being abused or neglected.

3.2.3 Child protection concerns should be supported by evidence that indicates the possibility of abuse or neglect.

3.2.4 A concern about *a potential risk* to children posed by a specific person, even if the children are unidentifiable, should also be communicated to the HSE Children and Family Services.

3.2.5 The guiding principles in regard to reporting child abuse or neglect may be summarised as follows:

(i) the safety and well-being of the child must take priority;

(ii) reports should be made without delay to the HSE Children and Family Services.

3.2.6 Any reasonable concern or suspicion of abuse or neglect must elicit a response. Ignoring the signals or failing to intervene may result in ongoing or further harm to the child.

3.2.7 Section 176 of the Criminal Justice Act 2006 introduced the criminal charge of **reckless endangerment of children**. It states:

> 'A person, having authority or control over a child or abuser, who intentionally or recklessly endangers a child by –
>
> (a) causing or permitting any child to be placed or left in a situation which creates a substantial risk to the child of being a victim of serious harm or sexual abuse, or
>
> (b) failing to take reasonable steps to protect a child from such a risk while knowing that the child is in such a situation,
>
> is guilty of an offence.'

The penalty for a person found guilty of this offence is a fine (no upper limit) and/or imprisonment for a term not exceeding 10 years.

3.2.8 The HSE has a statutory obligation to identify children who are not receiving adequate care and protection, to provide family support services and, where necessary, to take children into the care of the HSE. People who report concerns need to be assured that their information will be carefully considered with any other information available, and a child protection assessment will only proceed where sufficient risk is identified.

3.2.9 Any **professional** who suspects child abuse or neglect should inform the parents/carers if a report is to be submitted to the HSE Children and Family Services or to An Garda Síochána, unless doing so is likely to endanger the child.

3.2.10 The HSE will respect the wishes of non-professionals reporting concerns in good faith who ask to remain anonymous in as much as possible, but cannot give a guarantee that the information would not be sought and given within judicial proceedings. (The Data Protection Acts offer protection under privacy, but should the information be sought directly within legal proceedings, there is no guarantee.)

3.3 Designated Liaison Persons for reporting neglect or abuse

3.3.1 Every organisation, both public and private, that is providing services for children or that is in regular direct contact with children should:

(i) Identify a designated liaison person to act as a liaison with outside agencies and a resource person to any staff member or volunteer who has child protection concerns.

(ii) The designated liaison person is responsible for ensuring that the standard reporting procedure is followed, so that suspected cases of child neglect or abuse are referred promptly to the designated person in the HSE Children and Family Services or in the event of an emergency and the unavailability of the HSE, to An Garda Síochána.

(iii) The designated liaison person should ensure that they are knowledgeable about child protection and undertake any training considered necessary to keep themselves updated on new developments.

3.4 Standard Reporting Procedure

3.4.1 Any person reporting a child abuse or neglect concern should do so without delay to the HSE Children and Family Services. A report can be made in person, by telephone or in writing. **Contact numbers for all HSE offices nationwide are given in Appendix 2 of this national guidance and are also available on the HSE website (www.hse.ie) or through the HSE LoCall Tel. 1850 241850.**

3.4.2 Before deciding whether or not to make a formal report, you may wish to discuss your concerns with a health professional or directly with the HSE Children and Family Services (*see HSE contacts in Appendix 2*).

3.4.3 **Under no circumstances should a child be left in a situation that exposes him or her to harm or to risk of harm pending HSE intervention**. In the event of an emergency where you think a child is in immediate danger and you cannot get in contact with the HSE, you should contact the Gardaí. This may be done through any Garda station.

3.4.4 The **Standard Report Form for reporting child welfare and protection concerns to the HSE (*see Appendix* 3)** should be used by **professionals, staff and volunteers in organisations working with or in contact with children, or providing services to children** when reporting child protection and welfare concerns to the HSE Children and Family Services. If a report is made by telephone, this form should be completed and forwarded subsequently to the HSE.

3.4.5 The HSE will follow up on all referrals, even if the Standard Report Form has not been used.

3.5 Information to be included when making a report

3.5.1 The ability of the HSE Children and Family Services or An Garda Síochána to assess and investigate suspicions or allegations of child abuse or neglect will depend on the amount and quality of information conveyed to them by the people reporting concerns. As much as possible of the following detail should be provided:

(i) the name, address and age of the child (or children) for whom the report is being made;

(ii) the name of the child's school;

(iii) the name and contact details of the person reporting concerns;

(iv) whether the person reporting is a professional, a person working with children or a member of the public;

(v) the relationship to the child of the person making the report;

(vi) a full account of what constitutes the grounds for concern in relation to the protection and welfare of the child or children, e.g. details of the allegation, incident, dates, description of any injuries, etc;

(vii) the names and addresses of the parents/carers of the child or children;

(viii) the names of other children in the household;

(ix) the name, address and details of the person allegedly causing concern in relation to the child or children;

(x) the child's and/or parents/carers' own views, if known and relevant;

(xi) the names and addresses of other personnel or agencies involved with the child or children, e.g. GP, social worker, public health nurse, Gardaí, etc;

(xii) any other relevant information.

3.6 Retrospective disclosures by adults

3.6.1 An increasing number of adults are disclosing abuse that took place during their childhoods. Such disclosures often come to light when adults attend counselling. **It is essential to establish whether there is any current risk to any child who may be in contact with the alleged abuser revealed in such disclosures.**

3.6.2 If any risk is deemed to exist to a child who may be in contact with an alleged abuser, the counsellor/health professional should report the allegation to the HSE Children and Family Services without delay.

3.6.3 The HSE **National Counselling Service** is in place to listen to, value and understand those who have been abused in childhood. The service is a professional, confidential counselling and psychotherapy service and is available free of charge in all regions of the country (see www.hse-ncs.ie/en). The service can be accessed either through healthcare professionals or by way of self-referral (Freephone 1800 477477).

3.7 Deciding to share child protection concerns

3.7.1 The belief that parents/carers or other persons in charge of children would actually harm or neglect them is not easy to sustain. There may be a tendency, therefore, to deny, minimise or explain away any signs that a child is being harmed, even when evidence exists. At times, it is hard to distinguish between abusive situations and those where other problems are present, such as unemployment, poverty, poor housing, addiction, mental illness or isolation. Sympathy for families in difficult circumstances can sometimes dilute personal or professional concerns about the safety and welfare of children. However, the protection and welfare of the child must always be the paramount concern.

3.7.2 Reluctance to act on suspicions about child abuse or neglect can often stem from uncertainty and fear. Members of the public or professionals may be afraid of repercussions, afraid of being thought insensitive, afraid of breaking a confidence or afraid of being disloyal. Knowledge and information about child abuse will help to overcome reluctance to take action. So too will confidence in the child protection and welfare services.

3.7.3 It is the responsibility of all agencies working with children and for the public to recognise child protection concerns and share these with the agencies responsible for assessing or investigating them, not to determine whether the child protection concerns are evidenced or not.

3.8 Cases not reported to the HSE or An Garda Síochána

3.8.1 In those cases where an organisation decides not to report concerns to the HSE or An Garda Síochána, the individual employee or volunteer who raised the concern should be given a clear written statement of the reasons why the organisation is not taking such action. The employee or volunteer should be advised that if they remain concerned about the situation, they are free as individuals to consult with, or report to, the HSE or An Garda Síochána. The provisions of the Protections for Persons Reporting Child Abuse Act 1998 apply once they communicate 'reasonably and in good faith' (*see Paragraph 3.10.1*).

3.9 Confidentiality

3.9.1 The effective protection of a child often depends on the willingness of the staff in statutory and voluntary organisations involved with children to share and exchange relevant information. It is therefore critical that there is a clear understanding of professional and legal responsibilities with regard to confidentiality and the exchange of information.

3.9.2 All information regarding concern or assessment of child abuse or neglect should be shared on 'a need to know' basis in the interests of the child with the relevant statutory authorities.

3.9.3 No undertakings regarding secrecy can be given. Those working with a child and family should make this clear to all parties involved, although they can be assured that all information will be handled taking full account of legal requirements.

3.9.4 Ethical and statutory codes concerned with confidentiality and data protection provide general guidance. They are not intended to limit or prevent the exchange of information between different professional staff with a responsibility for ensuring the protection and welfare of children. **The provision of information to the statutory agencies for the protection of a child is not a breach of confidentiality or data protection.**

3.9.5 It must be clearly understood that information gathered for one purpose must not be used for another without consulting the person who provided that information.

3.9.6 The issue of confidentiality should be part of the training necessary for staff who work in the area of child protection and welfare and the general training of staff in organisations that work with children. Each organisation should have a written policy in this regard.

3.10 Legal protection

3.10.1 The **Protections for Persons Reporting Child Abuse Act 1998** makes provision for the protection from civil liability of persons who have communicated child abuse 'reasonably and in good faith' to designated officers of the HSE (*see Appendix 10*) or to any member of An Garda Síochána. This protection applies to organisations as well as to individuals. This means that even if a communicated suspicion of child abuse proves unfounded, a plaintiff who took an action would have to prove that the person who communicated the concern had not acted reasonably and in good faith in making the report.

3.10.2 A person who makes a report in good faith and in the child's best interests may also be protected under common law by the defence of qualified privilege.

3.11 Freedom of information

3.11.1 Notwithstanding the requirement of all professionals involved in child protection and welfare cases to share relevant information, records are nevertheless confidential. They do not belong to individuals (except for independent practitioners) and are the property of the organisations that keep them. Under the **Freedom of Information Acts 1997 and 2003**, members of the public have a right of access to records concerning them held by any public body and a right to have official information about themselves amended where it is incorrect, incomplete or misleading. Members of the public also have a right to be given reasons for decisions made concerning themselves. Requests to see records are processed in the first instance through the public body that holds the records. In the event of refusal of access, the decision may be appealed and the ultimate arbiter is the Information Commissioner. At present, these Acts apply to the HSE, but not to An Garda Síochána.

3.11.2 The **Data Protection Acts 1988 and 2003** afford similar rights to individuals to access personal data held about them by any entity whether in the public or private sector. The right to access applies to records held by the HSE and An Garda Síochána. However, the right to access does not apply in a range of circumstances that may be relevant in a child welfare context. Equally, the right of access does not extend to any information that identifies a third party where that third party had an expectation of confidence. Accordingly, it would not be necessary to provide any information that would identify a person making a child welfare report in response to a request under the Data Protection Acts.

3.11.3 A full list of the relevant legislation concerning child protection and welfare is provided in Appendix 7 of this national guidance.

4. Interagency Cooperation: Roles and responsibilities of organisations and personnel working with children

4.1 Purpose

4.1.1 No one professional has all the skills, knowledge or resources necessary to comprehensively meet all the requirements of an individual case. It is essential, therefore, that all professionals and organisations involved with a child and his or her parents/carers deliver a coordinated response. This chapter identifies the roles and responsibilities of Central Government, the HSE, An Garda Síochána and other organisations working with children. It also outlines the benefits of effective interagency cooperation.

4.2 Roles and responsibilities of Central Government

4.2.1 Central Government and its agencies, notably the HSE, share responsibility for promoting the welfare and safety of children, and should ensure that services reach the high standards that are required to protect and support children. Central Government, through the Department of Children and Youth Affairs, has responsibility for developing the legislative and policy framework through which the child protection and welfare services are delivered, monitored, inspected and measured. The Department of Children and Youth Affairs will keep under review the effectiveness of the *Children First: National Guidance*.

4.2.2 Every Government department or publicly funded body that delivers or funds services to children – whether directly or indirectly through bodies or agencies under its aegis – has a responsibility to ensure that there is an awareness within the relevant organisations of the *Children First: National Guidance* and that the standards in relation to child protection and welfare set out in the guidance are adhered to in the delivery of those services. This includes, in particular, the effective communication of roles and responsibilities under the national guidance.

4.3 Benefits of interagency cooperation and exchange of information in relation to child protection and welfare

4.3.1 Effective interagency cooperation has a number of benefits, including:

(i) ensuring provision of a comprehensive response to all concerns about children. This includes the pooling of resources and skills at all stages of intervention, from initial enquiry to assessment and case management, including early identification and prevention;

(ii) avoiding gaps in the service response, especially in cases where information might otherwise remain concealed or unknown;

(iii) providing mutual support for professionals in complex cases.

4.3.2 The effectiveness and usefulness of interagency and interprofessional cooperation and coordination is influenced by certain conditions that should be addressed specifically in training programmes. These conditions include:

(i) dissemination on a regular basis of procedures, guidelines and policies;

(ii) clear contractual arrangements between statutory and non-statutory bodies;

(iii) an understanding and acceptance by all professionals working with children of their responsibilities and roles in the promotion of child welfare;

(iv) mutual trust in the sharing of information;

(v) agreement on common goals with regard to a child's safety and welfare;

(vi) willingness of professionals to respect the contributions made by each other, irrespective of status and position within agencies and organisations;

(vii) awareness of the potential for interprofessional tensions, defensiveness, prejudices, rivalries and polarity of views, which may, from time to time, prevent the needs of children from taking precedence.

4.3.3 Training to promote interagency and interprofessional cooperation and coordination should include front-line personnel who meet or talk with the public (e.g. telephonists and receptionists), who are frequently the recipients of urgent information and have an essential role to play in communication (*see also Chapter 10, Paragraph 10.5.6*).

4.3.4 Interagency cooperation is as important in the later stages of child protection work as it is at the outset. All personnel involved in a case should consistently make efforts to remain in contact with the key worker (who is normally the HSE social worker) and to communicate any relevant information.

4.3.5 Interagency and interprofessional cooperation and coordination should never become an end in itself. The child's safety and protection must take precedence at all times. Collusion must be avoided.

Partnership working – Exchange of information

4.3.6 Arrangements for child protection and welfare can only be successful if staff in the statutory and non-statutory organisations concerned work in partnership and share relevant information, in particular with the HSE Children and Family Services and An Garda Síochána.

4.4 Roles and responsibilities of the HSE Children and Family Services

4.4.1 Under the Child Care Act 1991, the HSE has certain statutory obligations for the protection and welfare of children:

(i) the HSE must be open to receiving information from any source about a child who may not be receiving adequate care and protection;

(ii) having received such information, the HSE must seek to establish whether the child in question is receiving adequate care and protection. To this end, it must coordinate information from all relevant sources and make an assessment of the situation;

(iii) having identified a child who is not receiving adequate care and protection, the HSE is under a duty to take appropriate action to promote the welfare of the child.

4.4.2 The HSE has responsibility for operating a child protection and welfare service, putting in place and promoting written procedures and practice guidance, and providing leadership and commitment to interagency cooperation and training. The HSE also has responsibility for:

(i) regularly reviewing all policies and procedures for joint working;

(ii) resourcing child protection services in line with policies;

(iii) operating within clear management structures, providing training and supervision for all staff undertaking child protection and welfare work;

(iv) developing and maintaining effective information systems;

(v) developing and maintaining standards and operating a quality control system;

(vi) developing procedures that enable parents/carers, children and others to make representations, including complaints;

(vii) publishing advice for the general public, professionals and anyone caring for a child, clearly indicating who should be contacted if they have concerns about a child being harmed or at risk of being harmed;

(viii) developing procedures to safeguard information and ensure timely transfer of records when a child about whom there is a child protection concern or a family moves from one HSE area to another or from one jurisdiction to another. The procedure should state that, prior to the transfer of information to another jurisdiction, there is either consent, a legal basis or a serious child protection concern.

4.4.3 Every HSE Local Health Office area has a designated person within the HSE with responsibility for coordinating child protection services. These personnel are responsible for:

(i) receiving all notifications of child abuse (*see Chapter 5*);

(ii) taking decisions relating to the holding of child protection conferences;

(iii) promoting interagency cooperation on child protection and welfare;

(iv) promoting interprofessional and interprogramme cooperation on child protection and welfare;

(v) overseeing staff training programmes;

(vi) negotiating service agreements with non-statutory service providers.

4.4.4 An effective child protection and welfare environment requires close working relationships and interagency and interprofessional cooperation. This, in turn, requires cooperation at national, regional and local level by the key stakeholders.

4.4.5 In the interests of the continuous improvement of services, the HSE may redesign its structures and business processes in relation to the child protection and welfare system. This may include the redesign of procedures (such as standardised forms) and the revision of terminology. Any such changes must be consistent with national policy direction as articulated in the current *Children First: National Guidance*, must be implemented consistently across the HSE and must be clearly communicated to all relevant staff, service users and other agencies.

4.5 Roles and responsibilities of An Garda Síochána

4.5.1 The involvement of An Garda Síochána in cases of alleged child abuse and neglect stems from its primary responsibility to protect the community and to bring offenders to justice. Where it is suspected that a crime has been committed, An Garda Síochána has overall responsibility for the direction of any criminal investigation. It is the function of An Garda Síochána to interview and take any statements that will form part of the criminal investigation file.

4.5.2 The role of An Garda Síochána is to investigate and it is the responsibility of the Director of Public Prosecutions (DPP) to decide on, and to carry out, prosecution.

Garda Central Vetting Unit

4.5.3 The Garda Central Vetting Unit (GCVU) provides vetting on behalf of organisations employing personnel to work in a full-time, part-time, voluntary or student placement capacity with children and/or vulnerable adults. The GCVU provides its vetting service for each sector requiring vetting through a sectoral 'central point of contact', the task of which is to process vetting applications centrally for that sector. The Authorised Signatory is the point of contact appointed in each organisation to forward forms to the GCVU and any disclosures from Gardaí are returned to the Authorised Signatory confidentially, the implications of which can be assessed by prospective employers using a risk management approach. The GCVU does not deal with individual requests for vetting. An individual must make a written application through the organisation to which their area of work is affiliated.

4.5.4 Garda vetting is part of good recruitment practice. While Garda vetting is currently not statutory, it is intended to place it on a statutory basis. The GCVU does **not** decide on the suitability of any person to work with children and vulnerable adults. Rather, in response to a written request for vetting, the GCVU releases criminal history information on the person to be vetted to the prospective recruiting organisation. Decisions on suitability for recruitment rest at all times with the recruiting organisation and the results of vetting should form only one component of the recruitment decision.

4.5.5 Employers/heads of organisations where staff or volunteers have access to children should at all times implement safe recruitment practices, including vetting of applicants and staff, rigorous checking of references, interview procedures and monitoring of good professional practice.

4.6 Cooperation between An Garda Síochána and the HSE Children and Family Services

4.6.1 An Garda Síochána and the HSE Children and Family Services have different functions, powers and methods of working. The specific focus of the HSE is on the assessment of the welfare of the child and family. The specific focus of An Garda Síochána is on the investigation of alleged offences and whether a crime has been committed. Joint working between the HSE Children and Family Services and An Garda Síochána forms an integral part of the child protection and welfare service and is described in more detail in Chapter 7.

4.7 Roles and responsibilities of Other Statutory Agencies and Non-statutory Organisations

4.7.1 There are many organisations providing services to, working with and in direct contact with children. Some are statutory, some are non-statutory and/or not-for-profit organisations, while others are private for-profit organisations. All organisations involved with children have an obligation to provide them with the highest possible standard of care in order to promote their well-being and safeguard them from abuse. Organisations may also be legally responsible for their failure to provide adequate care and safeguards for children in their care.

4.7.2 All statutory, voluntary and community organisations working with and in direct contact with children should have procedures and guidelines **derived from and consistent with the current *Children First: National Guidance*** for their staff and volunteers. The content of such local guidelines should not be at variance with the national guidance, but there may be particular specificity or elaboration appropriate to local circumstances (*see Appendix 8 for guidance on developing local child protection procedures*). Voluntary and community organisations, for example, will need to outline specific procedures for personnel on how to respond to concerns or suspicions of child abuse. **Where these organisations have adapted the national guidance to local guidelines and wish to have them reviewed for their efficacy, the HSE Children and Family Services will facilitate this. Completed local guidelines should be forwarded to the HSE as a matter of good practice.**

4.7.3 *Our Duty to Care: The principles of good practice for the protection of children and young people,* published in 2002, offers specific guidance to the **community and voluntary sectors** on the promotion of child protection and welfare practices. The document includes information on the correct steps to be taken if child abuse is suspected, witnessed or disclosed. It also contains information on developing safe recruitment procedures and policies. It should be read in conjunction with the national guidance.

4.7.4 The HSE employs *Children First* Information and Advice Officers who are available to liaise with voluntary and community organisations and provide advice on child protection issues. Voluntary and community organisations should also be included in relevant training courses.

66891

4.7.5 All organisations in contact with or providing services to children have an overall corporate duty and responsibility to safeguard children by the following means:

(i) promoting the general welfare, health, development and safety of children;

(ii) adopting and consistently applying a safe and clearly defined method of recruiting and selecting staff and volunteers;

(iii) developing guidance and procedures for staff and volunteers who may have reasonable grounds for concern about the safety and welfare of children involved with the organisation. These procedures should not deviate from the current *Children First: National Guidance*, but could offer further elaboration to ensure local relevance and applicability. It is the responsibility of each organisation's Board of Directors or Management to ensure that such policies and procedures are in place and are operating effectively (*see Appendix 8 for guidance on developing local child protection procedures*);

(iv) identifying a designated liaison person to act as a liaison with outside agencies and a resource person to any staff member or volunteer who has child protection and welfare concerns. The designated liaison person is responsible for reporting allegations or concerns of child abuse to the HSE Children and Family Services or to An Garda Síochána;

(v) ensuring that the organisation has clear written procedures on the action to be taken if allegations of abuse against employees/volunteers are received (*see Appendix 9 on guidance for employers dealing with an allegation of abuse*);

(vi) raising awareness within the organisation about potential risks to children's safety and welfare;

(vii) developing effective procedures for responding to accidents and complaints;

(viii) ensuring that clear procedures in relation to record-keeping of child protection and welfare concerns are in place and are operating effectively, taking appropriate account of the need to ensure that such records are kept securely. Organisations that administer services through a number of individual units should standardise recording procedures in cases of children at risk. All agencies dealing with children must have a policy of cooperating with the HSE Children and Family Services on the sharing of their records where a child welfare or protection issue arises.

4.8 Roles and responsibilities of Schools

4.8.1 School authorities have primary responsibility for the care and welfare of their pupils. The Department of Education and Skills is responsible for developing and implementing child protection procedures for schools based on the *Children First: National Guidance*. The aim of such procedures is to give direction to school management and staff regarding the identification of and response to child protection concerns and the continued support of the child. It is the responsibility of the Department of Education and Skills to inspect and evaluate the implementation of these procedures for education staff.

Responsibilities of school management

4.8.2 It is the responsibility of the Board of Management of each school:

(i) to have clear procedures, which teachers and other school staff must follow where they suspect, or are alerted to, possible child abuse or neglect, including where a child discloses abuse or neglect;

(ii) to designate a senior member of staff to have specific responsibility for child protection (*see Chapter 3, Section 3.3 for role of designated liaison persons*). In larger schools, it may be necessary that the role be designated to other staff to ensure timely sharing of concerns, in which case organisational accountability must be kept;

(iii) to monitor the progress of children considered to be at risk;

(iv) to contribute to the prevention of child abuse or neglect through curricular provision;

(v) to provide or access in-service training for teachers and members of the Board of Management to ensure that they have a good working knowledge of child protection issues and procedures;

(vi) to have clear written procedures in place concerning action to be taken where allegations are received against school employees.

4.8.3 Teachers are particularly well placed to observe and monitor children for signs of abuse and neglect. They are the main care-givers to children outside the family context and have regular contact with children in the school setting.

4.8.4 Teachers have a general duty of care to ensure that arrangements are in place to protect children and young people from harm. In this regard, children need to be facilitated to develop their self-esteem, confidence, independence of thought and the necessary skills to cope with possible threats to their personal safety, both within and outside the school. Management arrangements within primary and post-primary schools should provide for the following:

(i) the planning, development and implementation of an effective child protection programme;

(ii) continuous monitoring and evaluation of the effectiveness of such a programme;

(iii) the effective implementation of agreed reporting procedures;

(iv) the planning and implementation of appropriate staff development and training programmes.

Responsibilities of school staff

4.8.5 If a child discloses to a teacher or to other school staff that he or she is being harmed by a parent/carer or any other person, including another child, the person who receives that information should listen carefully and supportively. This applies equally where the child implies that he or she is *at risk* of being harmed by a parent/carer or any other person. It also applies equally if a parent/carer or any other person discloses that he or she has harmed, or is at risk of harming, a child. The child should not be interviewed formally; the teacher or other staff member should obtain only necessary relevant facts if and when clarification is needed. **Confidentiality must never be promised to a person making a disclosure** subject to the provisions of the Data Protection Acts and the requirement to report to the HSE Children and Family Services must be explained in a supportive manner. The discussion should be recorded accurately and the record retained securely. The teacher or other staff member should then inform the designated liaison person who is responsible for reporting the matter to the HSE Children and Family Services, or in the event of an emergency and the unavailability of the HSE, to An Garda Síochána.

ROLES AND RESPONSIBILITIES OF THE HEALTH SECTOR

4.9 Roles and responsibilities of General Practitioners and Primary Care Teams

4.9.1 General practitioners (GPs) and Primary Care Teams are in a good position to identify indications of abuse and neglect or signs of family stress that may point, at an early stage, to a risk of child abuse. GPs may have certain knowledge of the family backgrounds of their patients, which may enable them to make a particular contribution to abuse prevention, child protection and the long-term support of the child and family.

4.9.2 Primary Care Teams and GP practice staff should receive appropriate training in the recognition of child abuse and in the operation of local procedures. They should have clearly defined professional support and clinical supervision.

4.9.3 While GPs have responsibilities to all their patients, their primary consideration should be the best interests of the child. Whenever a GP becomes concerned that a child may be at risk of, or the subject of, abuse of any kind, it is essential that these concerns are discussed with the HSE Children and Family Services without delay.

4.9.4 Where clinical uncertainty exists, GPs may need to discuss their concerns with other professionals who are experienced in working with child abuse cases. GPs should therefore be aware of how to contact the relevant personnel for expert medical advice. Where, following such discussion, a GP is satisfied that there are reasonable grounds for suspecting that a child is being, or has been, abused or neglected, he or she should immediately inform the HSE Children and Family Services in accordance with the standard reporting procedure (*see Chapter 3*).

4.10 Roles and responsibilities of Hospitals

4.10.1 Like GPs and Primary Care Teams, hospital staff are also in a pivotal position to identify cases where reasonable grounds for concern exist regarding the protection and welfare of children and to participate in the assessment of those concerns. Coordinated working arrangements should be established between hospitals and the HSE Children and Family Services for the identification of child abuse and for further interventions.

4.10.2 Concerns by hospital staff should be reported to line management. Hospital management should act in a protective and preventive manner by referring any concerns to the appropriate agencies in respect of children and families who are in need of support services.

4.10.3 All front-line staff, particularly in emergency departments, must be alert to indicators of actual or potential child abuse or neglect. Standardised record systems should be adopted by hospitals in order to highlight repeated visits by children presenting with injuries. Concerns noted by any staff member should be reported to line management. A multidisciplinary approach is essential. Medical and social histories should be obtained and accurately recorded, covering the following areas:

- (i) circumstances of the child's presentation to hospital;
- (ii) details of injuries or other signs of neglect;
- (iii) explanations offered by parents/carers and/or child;
- (iv) general demeanour of parents/carers and/or child;
- (v) family history;
- (vi) whereabouts and safety of other siblings or children in the same situation;
- (vii) whether or not the child should be admitted in order to guarantee safety.

4.10.4 It is essential that an open and honest approach is taken with parents/carers, who must be given full information about the concerns that exist, the need for any further medical or social assessments, and the intention of the hospital staff to report the concern to the HSE Children and Family Services.

4.10.5 The child must be kept appropriately informed of developments and should be allowed an opportunity to offer his or her view, taking into account level of maturity and stage of development. Contact between parents/carers and children should be facilitated, unless it is considered that the child would be endangered by so doing. The child's need for emotional support from parents/carers must be carefully balanced against concerns for his or her safety.

Medical examinations

4.10.6 The cooperation of parents/carers should be sought for any examinations and assessment considered necessary. If cooperation is not forthcoming, the possibility of legal action should be considered and conveyed to parents/carers (*see Chapter 5, Paragraph 5.18.3*).

Fatal child abuse

4.10.7 Where a child has died as a result of suspected or confirmed child abuse, the following actions must be taken by hospital authorities:

(i) An Garda Síochána and the HSE Children and Family Services must be notified immediately;

(ii) the Coroner must be notified;

(iii) the protection of other children in the family must be urgently considered;

(iv) the bereavement needs of the family must be addressed with sensitivity.

4.11 Roles and responsibilities of Mental Health and Addiction Services

4.11.1 Professionals who are treating a person with a mental health or addiction problem must consider the welfare and safety of any children in that person's family and/or children in regular contact with the person. Where there are concerns, these must be discussed and reported to the HSE Children and Family Services, as outlined in the standard reporting procedure (*see Chapter 3*).

4.11.2 Professionals in the adult mental health and addiction services may find themselves assessing people who have a history of abusing or neglecting children. In such cases, the potential risk to any child with whom this person may have contact must be considered and communicated to the HSE Children and Family Services and to any other service involved in providing treatment or other assistance to the family.

4.11.3 Where work with a family involves both the victim and the perpetrator of abuse, it is essential that efforts are coordinated and that information is shared between professionals. The child's needs must remain paramount. All decisions taken in relation to parents/carers with a mental health or addiction problem of relevance to the child's protection and welfare, such as a discharge back to their family or termination of treatment, must be communicated to the relevant HSE personnel.

4.12 Roles and responsibilities of Child and Adolescent Psychiatry Services

4.12.1 Child and adolescent psychiatric services often work with families over a long period and are particularly well placed to identify child protection concerns. It is the responsibility of staff in the child and adolescent psychiatric services to establish as far as possible the grounds for any child protection concern that may exist and to report this to the HSE Children and Family Services.

4.12.2 The HSE holds overall responsibility for the child protection aspects of a case. Non-HSE mental health services must operate child protection procedures in line with those of the HSE. It is essential that they coordinate their work with the HSE in a manner that facilitates joint working as far as possible between the two services in order to maximise the possibility of protecting any children involved. It is essential that information relevant to children's safety and protection is communicated between the two services at all stages of work.

4.13 Roles and responsibilities of Private Healthcare Providers and Non-statutory Providers of services to children

4.13.1 Professionals who see children and families on a private basis, or non-statutory providers of services to children, must also follow child protection guidance. It is the responsibility of the designated person within the HSE to ensure that, as far as possible, all private practitioners and non-statutory providers receive copies of procedures for communicating concerns to the HSE Children and Family Services.

4.14 Roles and responsibilities of Other Health Professionals

4.14.1 Other health professionals are major contributors to child protection and welfare. They promote the welfare of children through health promotion and health surveillance programmes. They are well placed to identify and refer child protection concerns, participate in assessment, attend child protection conferences and work with the HSE Children and Family Services in planning the ongoing support of the child and family.

4.15 Roles and responsibilities of Other Statutory Organisations

Health Information and Quality Authority and the Social Services Inspectorate

4.15.1 The Health Information and Quality Authority (HIQA) is an independent authority, established to drive continuous improvement in Ireland's health and social care services. The HIQA is responsible for the development of quality standards for child protection and welfare services, and in measuring performance against those standards. The Social Services Inspectorate (SSI) within the HIQA has responsibility for inspecting services for children in care and in detention schools.

National Educational Welfare Board

4.15.2 The National Educational Welfare Board (NEWB) has a statutory function to ensure that every child either attends a school or otherwise receives an education. The NEWB must also maintain a register of all children in receipt of an education in a place other than a recognised school, such as children who are educated at home. The NEWB has a responsibility to follow up on children who are out of school, have no school place or are not attending school regularly, and where there is a concern about the child's educational welfare. Educational Welfare Officers (EWOs) deliver a service directly to children, families and schools to ensure that each child attends and benefits from education. They focus on identifying the causes of the problems behind a child or young person not attending school and work with other services to overcome the barriers to school attendance. EWOs are well placed to identify children with additional needs and vulnerabilities. Any type of abuse will affect a child's educational welfare prospects and it is the duty of the NEWB to report when any abuse is suspected or evident. A protocol between the NEWB and the HSE Social Work Service will identify the main opportunities and obligations on staff in the two agencies to communicate and work together in relation to vulnerable children.

Ombudsman for Children

4.15.3 The Office of the Ombudsman for Children is an independent office, accountable to the Oireachtas, with statutory duties to promote and safeguard the rights and welfare of children. Its main functions are:

- to provide an independent complaints-handling service regarding public bodies;
- to initiate investigations under own motion to examine whether there are systemic problems that may give rise to difficulties for many children;
- to promote children's rights, including through participation and communications activities;
- to monitor and review legislation on matters relating to the rights and welfare of children;
- to advise any Government Minister on any matter relating to the rights and welfare of children;
- to ensure that law, policy and practice meet the highest standards and obligations in accordance with the UN Convention on the Rights of the Child.

The Probation Service

4.15.4 Probation officers may become involved in cases of child abuse and neglect as a result of their statutory responsibility for the supervision of offenders, including child offenders and those convicted of offences against children. Probation officers also undertake the preparation of reports on people charged with criminal offences and the provision of welfare services for prisoners and those recently released from prison.

4.15.5 In the course of these duties, probation officers may encounter cases of child abuse or the risk of abuse. The Probation Service should ensure that procedures are in place so that any potential, suspected or actual cases of child abuse are brought to the attention of the HSE Children and Family Services.

LIBRARY
INSTITUTE OF TECHNOLOGY
CARLOW

PART III:

Guidance for
HSE Children and Family Services
and Other Professionals

Protocol for
An Garda Síochána – HSE Liaison

5. Assessment and Management of child protection and welfare concerns

GENERAL GUIDELINES

5.1 Purpose

5.1.1 This chapter offers guidance on the steps to be taken by staff in the HSE Children and Family Services and other professionals in responding to reported child protection and welfare concerns. It describes the assessment process to be followed in order to establish whether reasonable grounds for concern exist. Guidance is offered on the effective use of child protection conferences, the development of a child protection plan and the aims and objectives of child protection review conferences.

5.2 Referral and Assessment

5.2.1 All child protection and welfare concerns reported to the HSE Children and Family Services must be acted upon immediately and formally recorded, and followed up as soon as possible.

5.2.2 Reported concerns about child protection and welfare are normally followed up by a HSE social worker. However, the HSE Social Work Manager may allocate this role to another professional or agency closely involved with the family. Alternatively, the work may be carried out jointly between the HSE and another agency. In these circumstances, the expectations held by the HSE or any non-HSE professionals or agency must be made clear. Any professional involved in following up child protection and welfare concerns must report the outcome of their enquiries without delay to the HSE Social Work Manager.

5.2.3 The HSE should operate standard assessment procedures for reported concerns about children. These procedures should cover notification to the designated person within the HSE, notification to An Garda Síochána, strategy meetings, child protection conferences, child protection review and assessment of risk to the child and any other child in the same situation (*see Chapter 7 for full details*).

5.2.4 Professional staff should adhere to HSE standard procedures for reported concerns about children.

5.2.5 The assessment of a child protection and welfare concern can often be complicated by factors outside the control of the professionals involved and does not always resemble the ordered process described in this national guidance. The safety and welfare of a child must remain the priority throughout and the remainder of the tasks dealt with in the most efficient and expeditious manner possible. Any difficulties in accessing information must be recorded and brought to the attention of the HSE Social Work Manager or designated person within the HSE.

5.2.6 Non-HSE agencies or professionals may have relevant information to contribute to the assessment of a child protection and welfare concern. These may include general practitioners, teachers, counsellors and other services with which the child and/or parents/carers have had contact. Information should normally only be sought from professionals working outside the HSE when the parents/carers concerned have been informed that such information will be sought. However, in circumstances where the perceived risk to the child is such that it is not deemed desirable to contact the parents/carers in the first instance, a HSE professional could justifiably request non-HSE professionals to release whatever information might enable clarification of the initial reported concern. The legal basis in the Child Care Act 1991 that allows non-HSE professionals to provide this information should be cited when making the request (*see Appendix 7*).

5.2.7 Assessment of child protection and welfare concerns is a continuous process and persists while the case is open to the HSE Children and Family Services.

5.3 Screening and Preliminary Enquiries

5.3.1 Reports and requests for services must be screened in order to establish their appropriateness to the HSE Children and Family Services.

5.3.2 HSE records must be checked at the earliest opportunity to establish whether a child or family is known to the HSE Children and Family Services and the nature of any information available. If internal records indicate that a case is already known within the HSE, the key professionals involved should be contacted as appropriate.

5.3.3 It may be necessary to contact the relevant public health nurse, area medical officer, social worker, child care worker or other HSE colleague for information or for clarification of existing information.

5.3.4 If, on the basis of the reported concern and/or any existing information, there is reason to believe that a child has been harmed or is at risk of further harm or ongoing neglect, or that their safety and welfare are at risk, the concern must be followed up immediately and any necessary interventions made. The available information should be reviewed with HSE management and formally recorded in order to establish an appropriate level of response.

5.4 Initial Assessment

5.4.1 The initial assessment of concerns is usually based on limited information with the emphasis being on the nature and degree of any harm and the immediate safety of the child. The assessment should also, insofar as possible, identify whether the child's needs are being adequately met and whether there is any other help the family may need in order to care adequately for the child. The assessment should include a review of the most critical areas of risk and need, should identify family strengths and protective factors and take account of available service resources.

5.4.2 A number of key tasks are involved when the HSE carries out an assessment of a child protection and welfare concern. These include:

(i) establishing with the child and his or her parents/carers whether grounds for concern exist;

(ii) if necessary, arranging for a medical examination, assessment for child sexual abuse and medical treatment (*see also Section 5.18*);

(iii) communicating with any professionals involved with the child and family, and eliciting their views on the report of abuse;

(iv) identifying the nature and severity of any risks;

(v) identifying any strengths and protective factors that appear to lessen the risk, such as protective care, support of extended family member or friend, or existing family support service;

(vi) when a decision is made to offer services to a child and his or her parents/carers, the case must be allocated to a key worker, if this has not already happened;

(vii) deciding on initial protective action pending, or prior to, further action, such as further assessment, strategy meeting, child protection conference or other developmental type assessments.

5.4.3 If a reported concern has been assessed as valid and there are unresolved child protection issues, a request for a child protection conference should be made to the designated person within the HSE. In other situations, where a child welfare concern is identified, the provision of support services must be considered. In such cases, where a high level of need is identified, the HSE Children and Family Services must ensure coordination and monitoring of services by means of a family support plan (*see Section 5.6*).

5.4.4 At any point during the initial assessment, it may be considered appropriate to hold a strategy meeting with all relevant professionals (*see Section 5.7*).

5.5 Unfounded concerns

5.5.1 When an assessment concludes that a concern or suspicion is unfounded, either initially or following any relevant appeals procedures, the files and records of the HSE Children and Family Services should reflect that fact.

5.5.2 Where a notification of suspected abuse has been made to An Garda Síochána, the HSE should also notify An Garda Síochána of this conclusion.

5.5.3 HSE staff may need to extend support to the family concerned and appropriate counselling services should be provided if required.

5.6 Provision of child welfare services

5.6.1 In many situations, preliminary enquiries/initial assessment may indicate there are child welfare concerns and that the parent(s) or carers may need support to adequately care for the child/children.

5.6.2 Intervention by way of family support services where child welfare concerns have been identified may help to prevent any deterioration of current difficulties being experienced by a family and assist the development of protective factors.

5.6.3 Family support services, by way of a family support plan, may be delivered formally through the direct services of statutory and voluntary organisations, and informally through the support of extended families, friends, neighbourhoods, communities, parishes and other local networks. Where support is being provided to a family where there are child welfare concerns, it needs to be coordinated and monitored by the HSE.

5.6.4 Local Health Office areas should have a plan, outlining the services available to provide support in child welfare cases. This family support service plan should take account of the views of all relevant service providers and representatives of community organisations.

5.6.5 Child welfare services by way of family support should aim to achieve the following:

- (i) respond in a supportive manner to families where children's welfare is under threat;
- (ii) reduce risk to children by enhancing their family life;
- (iii) prevent avoidable entry of children into the care system;
- (iv) address current problems being experienced by children and families;
- (v) connect families with supportive networks in the community;
- (vi) promote parental competence and confidence;
- (vii) provide direct services to children;
- (viii) where children have been in care, assist their re-integration with their families.

5.6.6 Parents/carers as well as children themselves may request a child welfare service directly or they may be referred by another source. A request for services should be responded to in a supportive and non-threatening manner. Families should be encouraged to identify their own solutions as much as possible.

5.6.7 Following the identification of child welfare needs, the aim of assessment for family support services is to gain sufficient understanding of the needs and strengths of the child and his/her parents/carers in order to identify, offer and agree appropriate services. The assessment should incorporate individual and family needs.

5.6.8 A child welfare plan should be based on an assessment and take the following factors into account:

(i) the level of agreement that either exists or is negotiable between parents/carers and others, such as family members, professionals and/or concerned other persons;

(ii) the concerns that require the most urgent attention;

(iii) short-term and long-term goals;

(iv) access to necessary resources;

(v) specified persons, disciplines or agencies that need to be involved;

(vi) the length of time that family support services may be required, bearing in mind that some families will need assistance only in times of crisis, others over a longer time;

(vii) a schedule for evaluation and review.

5.6.9 Where a review of the child welfare plan identifies an unresolved child protection issue or that the significant welfare needs of the child are not being met in a timely manner, the case must be referred for a child protection conference (*see Section 5.8*) in accordance with HSE procedures.

5.7 Strategy Meeting

5.7.1 The purpose of a strategy meeting is to facilitate the sharing and evaluation of information between professionals and to prepare a plan of action for the protection of a child, and the siblings if necessary. A strategy meeting may involve any or all of the professionals involved at either management or case assessment level, depending on the circumstances. It is important that the attendance of a Garda Síochána representative is secured at this meeting where appropriate, especially if a formal notification has been made.

5.7.2 It is the responsibility of the HSE Social Work Team Leader or Social Work Manager to hold a strategy meeting, if such a meeting is deemed necessary.

5.7.3 While, in the main, strategy meetings will be formally arranged, in certain circumstances, particularly where urgent, the strategy meeting may take the form of a less formal contact.

5.7.4 The objectives of the meeting are:

(i) to share available information;

(ii) to consider whether immediate action should be taken to protect the child and other children in the same situation;

(iii) to consider if Section 16(1)(b) of the Criminal Evidence Act 1992 interviews should take place;

(iv) to consider available legal options;

(v) to plan early intervention;

(vi) to identify possible sources of protection and support for the child;

(vii) to identify sources of further information;

(viii) to allocate responsibility;

(ix) to agree with An Garda Síochána how the remainder of the enquiry will be conducted;

(x) to identify if other children may be at risk and to take action.

5.8 Child Protection Conference

5.8.1 A child protection conference is an interagency and interprofessional meeting, convened by the designated person within the HSE.

5.8.2 The purpose of a child protection conference is:

(i) to facilitate the sharing and evaluation of information between professionals and parents/carers;

(ii) to formulate a child protection plan (*see Section 5.9*);

(iii) to identify tasks to be carried out as part of, or pending, a child protection plan;

(iv) to specify the appropriate service to carry out the tasks;

(v) to appoint a key worker for the purpose of coordinating the child protection plan.

5.8.3 An invitation to attend a child protection conference and the agenda to be covered should be sent in the first instance to the Garda Superintendent in order to facilitate the attendance of the designated Garda, if appropriate.

5.8.4 By their nature, child protection conferences are both critical and complex. Specialist training should be provided to anyone undertaking the role of chairperson.

5.8.5 The meeting normally occurs following assessment and, if relevant, emergency actions have taken place. The child's parents/carers and the child should be included at the meeting unless doing so would not be in the child's best interests. In cases where there is a language barrier, or a disability or sensory impairment, those with particular expertise (e.g. interpreters) should be included.

5.8.6 The child protection conference and notification to the Child Protection Notification System (CPNS) (*see Section 5.17*) should be carried out in accordance with standard HSE protocols.

5.9 Child Protection Plan

5.9.1 A child protection plan is an interagency plan formulated at a child protection conference (*see Section 5.8*). It outlines the actions that professionals and agencies directly involved with the family need to take in order to ensure the child's continued protection and well-being. The basic components of a child protection plan are:

(i) identification of current and potential sources of risk to the child;

(ii) identification of strategies to protect the child and reduce the risks over a specified period;

(iii) identification of protective aspects of the child's situation, which may need to be strengthened and developed;

(iv) identification of short-term and long-term goals to be achieved to secure the protection and welfare of the child;

(v) consultation and negotiation with the child and his or her parents/carers on the content and feasibility of the plan;

(vi) identification of a key worker, who will continue to coordinate the work of various personnel involved in carrying out the plan and who will be responsible for ensuring communication of information between all the parties involved;

(vii) clear allocation of specific roles and responsibilities to all professionals and agencies directly involved in implementing the plan;

(viii) clear allocation of the roles and responsibilities to the child's parents/carers and other relevant family members;

(ix) identification of resources necessary to carry out the plan, including family support and treatment services where required;

(x) consideration of the position of the abuser and need for treatment;

(xi) notification of the child's name to the Child Protection Notification System (CPNS) in accordance with standard HSE protocols *(see Section 5.17)*;

(xii) identification of and agreement to a review date.

5.9.2 When a child protection plan has been put in place, it is the responsibility of all identified professionals and agencies to implement those parts of the plan that relate to them and to communicate with the key worker. In order to ensure that the plan is implemented, the following conditions must be observed:

(i) each professional must be given a written copy of the child protection plan;

(ii) a written copy of the plan should be given to the child, depending on his or her age and stage of development, and to his or her parents/carers;

(iii) the key worker must ensure that the child and family understand the nature and objectives of the plan;

(iv) the specific expectations of all parties about the plan and its implementation must be clarified;

(v) in addition to consultation about the plan, the child and his or her parents/carers should be given the names of all personnel involved in implementing the plan, together with their specific roles;

(vi) any changes of personnel should be immediately notified to the child and his or her parents/carers.

5.9.3 The successful implementation of a child protection plan will depend on a number of functions: interagency and interprofessional cooperation; ongoing consultation with the child and with his or her parents/carers; ongoing monitoring of the implementation of short- and long-term goals; and supervision and support.

5.9.4 **Interagency and interprofessional cooperation:** Cooperation between disciplines and agencies is as crucial to the longer term management of a case as it is at the outset. Commitment and flexibility in relation to carrying out the work specified in the child protection plan, together with willingness to exchange information promptly, will be required from all professionals involved with the child (*see also Chapter 4, Section 4.3*).

5.9.5 **Ongoing consultation with the child:** The views of the child must be privately sought on an ongoing basis and taken into consideration if modifying the child protection plan.

5.9.6 **Ongoing consultation with the parents/carers:** The views of the parents/carers must also be sought on an ongoing basis and taken into consideration if modifying the child protection plan.

5.9.7 **Ongoing assessment:** The protection and welfare of the child should be assessed on a continual basis to take account of changes in circumstances.

5.9.8 **Supervision and support:** All front-line practitioners working with the child and family should have consistent and regular support and supervision.

5.10 Appointment of a key worker

5.10.1 Where there are welfare concerns and a decision is made to offer services to a child and his or her parents/carers, a key worker must be identified.

5.11 Child Protection Review Conference

5.11.1 Child protection review conferences are held initially 6 months after the child protection conference (*see Section 5.8*) or sooner if appropriate.

5.11.2 It is the responsibility of the designated person within the HSE to arrange child protection reviews conferences. Reviews should be attended by the core group of professionals involved with the case and each should submit a written report in advance. The child's parents/carers should attend, unless a specific reason for their exclusion is identified. The child may be involved depending on his or her age and level of understanding.

5.11.3 The child protection review conference has a number of purposes, including:

(i) to complete a full review of progress with evidence of positive or negative change in relation to the goals that were identified;

(ii) to coordinate the views and actions of professionals;

(iii) to consider the views of the child;

(iv) to consider the views of the parents/carers;

(v) to review the progress of any legal action or prosecution if relevant;

(vi) to review and amend the child protection plan and in particular to determine whether such a plan continues to be necessary;

(vii) to assess the availability of resources needed to carry out the child protection plan;

(viii) to recommend, where appropriate, the delisting of the child's name from the Child Protection Notification System in accordance with standard HSE protocols.

5.11.4 The child protection review should be documented as soon as possible and copies of the proceedings circulated to all professionals involved, as well as to the child and parents/carers. If the child and parents/carers have not attended the review, the key worker should give an explanation to them separately, or if appropriately together, of its contents, conclusions and implications.

5.12 Emergency action to protect a child

5.12.1 If a report made to the HSE Children and Family Services indicates the presence of immediate and serious risk, urgent action must be taken to protect any children in that situation who may be in danger.

5.12.2 This may be achieved by securing the cooperation of a protective carer, family member or other responsible adult in the child's home whose capacity to protect the child can be defined and agreed.

5.12.3 If it is not possible to make arrangements to have the child or children protected at home, they may need to be placed in the care of the HSE, preferably with the consent of the parents/carers, but if necessary using legal measures under the Child Care Act 1991. If emergency action has not already been agreed, consultation must take place between the practitioners involved and their line managers. Interventions involving the separation of children from their parents/carers can only be carried out by properly authorised officers with delegated powers from the Chief Executive Officer of the HSE. Legal advice must be sought at an early stage if Court action is planned.

5.12.4 It must be borne in mind that the removal of children from their parents/carers or their homes can be very stressful and requires sensitive handling. The likely effects of separation must be balanced against the danger of leaving the child at home.

5.12.5 If it is considered necessary to remove a child from his or her parents/carers or home, then the following must be considered:

(i) In the first instance, all possible efforts should be made to place the child in a situation that is familiar, preferably with family or friends (see *Child Care (Placement of Children with Relatives) Regulations 1995*, published by the Department of Health).

(ii) As far as possible, the timing of the move should be sensitively handled.

(iii) The child's parents/carers should be informed of the action proposed, unless doing so would endanger the child or jeopardise the placement process.

(iv) The child should be informed of the proposed action if he or she has not been involved in the decision.

(v) The child's parents/carers should be informed of the child's location, unless otherwise directed by the Court.

(vi) The child's parents/carers should be advised about and assisted in obtaining legal advice.

5.12.6 In the majority of cases, the perceived harm or risk does not warrant such emergency action and the concern should be followed up in a planned coordinated manner. This involves communicating with all professionals involved with the child and enlisting their assistance if appropriate.

5.12.7 **Under no circumstances should a child be left in a situation that exposes him or her to harm or risk of harm pending HSE intervention.** In cases of emergency, where a child appears to be at immediate and serious risk and a HSE duty social worker is not immediately available, An Garda Síochána should be contacted.

5.13 Closure of cases

5.13.1 Cases must only be closed when there are no longer concerns regarding a child's protection or welfare. When a case is closed, all professionals involved and the child and family must be informed. Ideally, closure would ensue following a review, but if not, the designated person within the HSE must endorse the decision.

5.13.2 Where a child has been listed on the Child Protection Notification System, the name will be delisted in accordance with standard HSE protocols.

5.14 Responsibility of the HSE Children and Family Services

5.14.1 The HSE Children and Family Services are obliged to treat seriously all child protection and welfare concerns, whatever their source, and to consider carefully and fairly the nature of the information reported. In determining the most appropriate response, a balance needs to be struck between protecting the child and avoiding unnecessary and distressing intervention. The HSE response must:

(i) consider the protection and welfare of the child as the priority;

(ii) avoid actions that cause the child or family undue distress;

(iii) respect the rights of parents/carers to have their views heard and to be fully informed of any steps taken;

(iv) respect the rights of children to have their views heard.

Joint working with other professionals

5.14.2 It is normally the role of social workers in the HSE Children and Family Services to carry out enquiries into reported concerns. However, other disciplines, such as public health nurses or clinical psychologists, may be allocated this task in certain cases where, for example, they have a close relationship with the family concerned. If a child protection concern has been notified to An Garda Síochána, it may conduct a parallel investigation in coordination with the HSE Children and Family Services (*see Chapter 7*).

5.14.3 Any professional making enquiries into a reported concern about child protection must first consider the issue of cooperation of the parents/carers. This is especially true if the professional is making enquiries of agencies external to the HSE. Professionals who work in the HSE may consult with their colleagues and check internal records at a preliminary stage. However, the parents/carers must be informed if the professional wishes to make enquiries of external agencies, except in exceptional circumstances. If a parent or carer refuses, the protection and welfare of the child must be the overriding consideration.

5.14.4 Professionals in voluntary agencies, schools, clinics or other settings are in a good position to observe a child and his or her relationship with parents/carers. It may be appropriate for a professional from one of these organisations to pursue the enquiry jointly with, or on behalf of, the HSE Children and Family Services. This should be discussed with the HSE Children and Family Services.

5.14.5 When suspicions of child abuse exist but cannot be ascertained, HSE social workers may encourage other professionals who are in contact with the child to substantiate or eliminate concerns in a sensitive manner. For example, a teacher may observe a child's behaviour, interactions with peers, school work or informal conversations. A therapist, child care worker or anyone working with a child might gently explore the reasons for particular actions or statements, or use a play situation to enable the child to express him or herself. Any strategies used in this manner should be agreed with the HSE social worker.

5.14.6 Professionals who contact or who are contacted by the HSE for information about a child in the course of an assessment should be informed in due course of the outcome where this is relevant to their professional care/treatment of the child.

5.14.7 Under Data Protection legislation, the HSE may not provide specific information on the outcome or status of a child protection assessment to the person who reported the concern except in the professional context outlined above. The HSE should contact such a person to let them know that their information has been of assistance, but not divulge further information.

5.14.8 It is the responsibility of the HSE social worker, or other key worker assigned, to collate all the information available and to make an initial assessment of risk to the child and any other children in the same situation. Such an assessment should be carried out within a standardised framework developed by the HSE.

5.15 Confidentiality and anonymity

5.15.1 All information regarding a concern or an assessment of child abuse should be shared on a 'need to know' basis in the interests of the child.

5.15.2 No undertakings regarding secrecy can be given. Those working with a child and family should make this clear to all parties involved.

5.15.3 Concerns about a child that are reported anonymously should be followed up fully in accordance with HSE standard procedures. If the report has been made through a third party, the person mediating should be requested to facilitate contact between the original person who reported the concern and the HSE Children and Family Services. If, however, contact is not facilitated, for whatever reason, the concerns reported via the third party must be fully investigated.

5.15.4 It is preferable for the management of cases if those reporting concerns are encouraged to provide contact details.

5.15.5 Further details on confidentiality are given in Chapter 3, Section 3.9.

5.16 Response to persons reporting concerns

5.16.1 People who report or discuss their concerns about the care and protection of children with HSE staff should be informed of the likely general steps to be taken by the professionals involved.

5.16.2 Other professionals involved should be kept updated and informed about the outcomes of any enquiry or investigation into the reported concern, where this is appropriate to their professional care/treatment of the child or the performance of their own duties and within the normal limits of confidentiality.

5.17 Child Protection Notification System

5.17.1 The Child Protection Notification System (CPNS) is a HSE record of every child about whom the HSE is satisfied that there are unresolved child protection issues, including neglect.

5.17.2 A child's name is placed on the CPNS by the designated person within the HSE in accordance with the HSE child protection procedures.

5.17.3 The parent, guardian or carer, other relevant agencies and, where appropriate, the child should be informed when his or her name is listed on the CPNS.

5.17.4 The CPNS is the specific responsibility of the designated person within the HSE. It should be held securely and separately from other records. Information about how to access the CPNS should be available to all agencies concerned and held in a secure manner.

5.17.5 The system should record all enquiries, whether the child is on the list or not. If a CPNS enquiry is repeated, a report should be made to the HSE Children and Family Services.

5.17.6 Any changes in information relating to a child whose name is recorded on the CPNS should be referred to the child's allocated social worker, who, in turn, will inform the designated officer with responsibility for the CPNS, i.e. the designated person within the HSE.

5.17.7 It is the responsibility of the designated person within the HSE to ensure that the CPNS is managed and maintained in such a way as:

(i) to provide adequate information to appropriate professionals who have a need to access relevant information about a child;

(ii) to facilitate the provision of statistical information to appropriate sources.

5.17.8 The HSE should agree which professional groups require access and formulate procedures for confirming the identities of persons making enquiries. The HSE may amend this list in the light of changing circumstances and experience.

5.17.9 The name of the allocated social worker only should be given to the enquirer. The relevant social worker should be informed when an enquiry is made.

5.17.10 The CPNS should allow for 24-hour access. The HSE should keep relevant agencies and services up to date on how to access the system.

5.17.11 The CPNS should record case transfers when a child and/or his or her parents/carers move between jurisdictions or within the HSE to another area.

5.17.12 Cases must only be closed and the child's name removed or delisted from the CPNS when the child (or children) is no longer considered at risk. When a case is closed and the name delisted, all professionals involved and the child and family must be informed. Ideally, closure would ensue following a child protection review, but if not, the designated person within the HSE must endorse the decision.

5.18 Medical/Specialist examinations

5.18.1 If there is reason to believe that a medical examination will indicate more clearly whether or not a child has been *physically abused*, or seriously deprived or neglected, or if a child appears to require medical treatment, then appropriate arrangements should be made immediately in consultation with An Garda Síochána. Wherever possible, a doctor with appropriate experience should carry out the examination.

5.18.2 If there is reason to believe that a specialist assessment will indicate more clearly whether a child has been *sexually abused*, a referral should be made to the appropriate service. If any doubt exists as to whether referral to a specialist unit is required, the child sexual abuse assessment service for the area should be consulted for an opinion. Only a doctor with appropriate training and experience should carry out a physical examination for sexual abuse.

5.18.3 In all cases where medical examinations or assessments for child sexual abuse are carried out, permission must be gained from the child's parents/carers, who should also be given the opportunity to attend. If permission is refused by the parents/carers, they should be advised of the HSE's option to apply for an Emergency Care Order or, if and where appropriate, a Supervision Order as provided for in the Child Care Act 1991. Such action should be considered if cooperation is still withheld.

5.18.4 The medical or specialist practitioner who carries out the examination or assessment must give a written report of the findings and must be made aware that he or she may be required to give evidence in Court.

5.19 Case transfer

5.19.1 The HSE Children and Family Services should have in place a Case Transfer Protocol. This should provide direction on the steps to be taken when a child about whom there are child protection or welfare concerns and/or his or her parents/carers move to another jurisdiction or to another area within the HSE. The protocol should state that, prior to the transfer of information to another jurisdiction, there is either consent, a legal basis or a child protection or welfare concern. It should also include the arrangements made for the transfer of relevant records relating to the child protection or welfare case.

5.20 Serious Incident Reviews

5.20.1 The HSE may instigate a Serious Incident Review in discharging its statutory role with regard to the protection and welfare of children having regard to the Health Information and Quality Authority's *Guidance for the Health Service Executive for the Review of Serious Incidents, including deaths of children in care* (HIQA, 2010).

5.20.2 A serious incident review is a review of the response, manner and quality of services provided to children and families. The purpose of the review is to learn lessons from the handling of specific cases so that deficits in the system can be addressed.

5.20.3 The National Review Panel is a functionally independent group, contracted by the HSE, that carries responsibility for reviewing serious incidents, including the deaths of children in care and those known to the child protection services. The Panel consists of an independent chair and deputy chair, and a number of independent professionals with expertise in relevant areas. It operates under the HIQA's (2010) *Guidance for the Health Service Executive for the Review of Serious Incidents, including deaths of children in care*. Deaths or serious incidents are notified by the HSE to the HIQA and to the National Review Panel; if they fall within the criteria laid down in the *Guidance*, they will be reviewed by the National Review Panel.

All deaths and serious incidents conforming to the following criteria are notifiable:

- all deaths of children in care;
- all deaths of children known to the HSE child protection system;
- all deaths of young adults (up to 21 years) who were in the care of the HSE in the period immediately prior to their 18th birthday or were in receipt of aftercare services;
- when a case of suspected or confirmed abuse involves the death of a child known to the HSE or a HSE-funded service;
- a death or potentially life-threatening injury, or serious and permanent impairment of health, well-being or development.

5.20.4 There may be cases where the National Review Panel, in consultation with the HSE, considers that it would be more appropriate for a death or serious incident review to be conducted at local level. In such cases, the review should be conducted by a HSE senior staff member who is not involved with the case, using the methodology prescribed in the HIQA's *Guidance*.

When a review is conducted locally, the report must be forwarded to the National Review Panel. If questions arise concerning either the quality or independence of the review, the National Review Panel will then conduct the most appropriate type of review. The review will ultimately be forwarded to the HIQA.

5.20.5 The HIQA's *Guidance* states that the purpose of these reviews is as follows:

'Reviews are completed for the following reasons:

- to determine the specific circumstances leading to the death or serious incident, and ascertain whether abuse, or whether an act or failure to act, was a contributing factor to the child's death or serious incident. The review may also identify whether other separate actions, such as disciplinary action or a referral to any regulatory body, need to be undertaken;
- to determine whether compliance with *Children First* and other set down procedures and the relevant standards of governance (leadership, organisation and management, business planning, risk management and meeting the legal requirements) and accountability among the professionals and service providers were satisfactory within the context of the information available at the time;
- to make recommendations and develop an action plan;
- to provide reassurance to the public on the standards of care and protection provided to children, that reviews are carried out to an appropriate standard and are independently monitored and published as appropriate;
- a review or a number of reviews viewed together may identify system-wide strengths and weaknesses, and the findings used to provide high-quality and safe care to people using health and social care services.'

5.20.6 In addition to the above, the HIQA may undertake a separate investigation as set out in Section 9 of the Health Act 2007.

5.21 Record-keeping

5.21.1 Record-keeping is of critical importance in this area of work. Unless accurate records are maintained, the ability to adequately protect vulnerable children may be severely curtailed. It is essential that professionals keep contemporaneous records of all reported concerns in a safe place. These should include details of contacts, consultations and any actions taken.

5.21.2 Case notes must be kept for the following reasons:

(i) to record details of referral, investigation and assessments of child care concerns;

(ii) to record essential details concerning the child and his or her parents/carers;

(iii) to record the nature and level of services offered, as well as those that are required;

(iv) to establish a record that may be accessed by a number of professionals and agencies where this arises in the assessment of the child care concern;

(v) to record and review developments in a case;

(vi) to provide a tool for use in the supervision of professional work;

(vii) to establish a measure of accountability between practitioners and their line managers;

(viii) to facilitate case transfers or the transfer of information between key professionals from different areas in line with the *Children First: National Guidance*.

5.21.3 Comprehensive, standardised case notes, consistent with *Children First* principles (*see Chapter 1*), must be kept in accordance with best practice and in a manner to be prescribed by the HSE. The management of child protection records within the HSE is to be strengthened through the development of a National Child Care Information System.

5.21.4 The management of records held by the HSE social worker or other designated key worker should be standardised throughout the HSE. Each child should have an individual file containing the following:

(i) a summary sheet containing family details;

(ii) a record of all enquiries made about the case and the response obtained;

(iii) a record of all contacts between the worker and the child and his or her parents/carers;

(iv) a record of all contacts between the worker and other professionals, including working arrangements and agreements;

(v) a summary, to be updated regularly, on recent events and their significance;

(vi) a report of all Court proceedings, child protection conferences, reviews and any other meetings, as well as any other relevant documentation in the worker's possession;

(vii) details of assessment and outcomes;

(viii) a record of any decisions made;

(ix) a copy of any child protection plans;

(x) a copy of all correspondence about the case.

5.21.5 Records should be factual, accurate and legible; should be dated and signed after each entry; and should be recorded on the day that the action took place or, at the latest, the following day. If an assessment or evaluation is made, an explanation for its basis must be offered.

5.21.6 Records should be signed off by the line manager.

5.21.7 Records should be accessible at all times during a key worker's absence from the office, but must be stored in a secure manner that ensures they are only available on a strictly 'need to know' basis. It is the responsibility of line managers to ensure that files are kept up to date and good recording practices are maintained.

6. Supervision, Support and Additional Guidance for HSE child protection and welfare work

6.1 Corporate risk strategy and staff supervision and support policy in the HSE

6.1.1 Given the nature of child protection and welfare work, the HSE as an employer should have the risks involved in child protection and welfare work included in its Corporate Risk Strategy and should implement risk assessment procedures accordingly.

6.1.2 The HSE should ensure that there is a Staff Supervision and Support Policy in place that supports the staff involved in the delivery of child protection and welfare services.

6.1.3 It is essential that managers of all disciplines involved in child protection and welfare work acknowledge the levels of actual or potential stress that may affect their staff, including when clients may exhibit aggressive behaviours, and take steps to address any problems. These steps may include:

(i) adequate and regular supervision of staff;

(ii) regular review of caseloads;

(iii) acknowledgement of positive achievement;

(iv) provision of opportunities for professional development, such as training, staff rotation, special assignments;

(v) development of interagency links;

(vi) putting in place the necessary arrangements and procedures to ensure the safety and security of child protection and welfare staff.

6.2 Guidance on allegations against employees and volunteers

6.2.1 The HSE Children and Family Services receive allegations of abuse against people who have contact with children in their workplace or in a recreational setting. If the HSE considers that children are, or may be, at immediate risk from the alleged abuser, contact should be made with the institution or employer immediately. In this situation, it is not necessary to notify the alleged abuser in advance of the allegations against him or her.

6.2.2 Where the HSE proposes to notify an alleged abuser's employer or person-in-charge where he or she attends, and where there is no immediate danger to children, the alleged abuser must be notified in advance of the allegations against him or her. The approach to an employer or person-in-charge in such cases may take place at any stage in a wider investigation and it may be practical that such an approach does not occur until any criminal investigation or HSE assessment has concluded.

6.2.3 The HSE Children and Family Services should provide feedback to the employer or person-in-charge on the progress of a child abuse assessment/investigation involving an employee. The HSE should seek to complete its assessment as quickly as possible, bearing in mind the serious implications for innocent employees. Employers or persons-in-charge should be notified of the outcome of the HSE assessment and/or the Garda investigation. This will assist them in reaching a decision about the action to be taken in the longer term concerning the employee.

6.3 Guidance on interviewing parents/carers

6.3.1 When a concern about a child's care or protection is reported to the HSE Children and Family Services, the child's parents/carers should be contacted by a HSE social worker or other professional who has agreed to carry out this assessment task. It must be borne in mind that the experience of being contacted by the HSE Children and Family Services about the care and protection of one's children can be both traumatic and intimidating for parents/carers; thus a degree of sensitivity must be used in conducting the interviews. The quality of any relationship that may later exist between the family and professionals will be influenced by the manner in which this initial meeting is handled.

6.3.2 If An Garda Síochána has already been notified and is likely to be carrying out a parallel investigation, it is essential that the activities of the two organisations are agreed and coordinated (*see Chapter 7*).

6.3.3 All professionals, whether in the HSE Children and Family Services or other services, should observe the following procedures when interviewing parents/carers:

- (i) inform parents/carers in an open and honest way of existing concerns and reports about their child or children;
- (ii) explain how information about the case has been, and will be, obtained;
- (iii) identify the professionals who have been contacted so far;
- (iv) invite the parents/carers to give an explanation of their view of the concern;
- (v) show a willingness to consider different interpretations of the concern;
- (vi) ensure that the parents/carers are fully aware of the way that information is going to be assessed and evaluated, and what expectations are held of them about the way they care for and protect their children;
- (vii) if relevant, explain the legal context in which the concern is being investigated;
- (viii) if the concern arose from an incident perpetrated by one of the child's parents/carers, the worker should try to gain the support and cooperation of the other parent/carer to facilitate ongoing protection of the child.

6.3.4 Where the interests of the parents/carers and the child appear to conflict, the child's interests must be considered paramount. It may be necessary to provide a separate worker for each of the parents/carers if, for example, one of them is the alleged abuser.

6.4 Guidance on interviewing children

6.4.1 In the course of child protection work, different types of interview may be carried out with children. In most instances, depending on the nature of the concern, the child should be seen by the professional conducting the enquiry or assessment and spoken to personally, in a manner appropriate to his or her age and stage of development. **The child should not usually be interviewed in the first instance in detail about sexual or serious physical abuse. This may be done more appropriately at a later stage by specially trained social workers or An Garda Síochána, or both.**

6.4.2 The interview should take place in a location that is comfortable for the child and, if the child desires it, in the presence of a support person, such as a protective parent/carer, another professional or an adult friend. If the child has a learning disability or sensory impairment, it may be necessary to employ expert assistance to facilitate communication. **It is important that the child is not interviewed in the company of any person who may have a vested interest in the child's version of events or who might influence what the child may say.**

6.4.3 Section 16(1)(b) of the Criminal Evidence Act 1992 states that the video recording of statements by children under 14 years during an interview with a member of An Garda Síochána or other competent person shall be admissible as evidence in Court. Special facilities for the holding of such interviews have been developed, together with training for social workers and Gardaí undertaking such interviews.

6.4.4 Interviews with children should normally be carried out with the permission of their parents/carers and the child must be able to give his or her own consent.

6.4.5 In some circumstances, children may present themselves to a HSE social worker without either the knowledge or presence of their parents/carers. Depending on the perceived maturity of the child, the social worker should give them the opportunity to discuss whatever concerns have prompted them to make contact.

6.4.6 No avoidable action should be taken that will cause a child to feel intimidated or distressed. The worker must use language that the child can understand and explain who they are and why they are there. It is essential to conduct the interview at the child's pace and communicate with him or her in a warm and responsive manner.

6.4.7 The reasons for interviewing the child include:

(i) to get a picture of the child's physical and emotional state;

(ii) to establish whether the child needs urgent medical attention;

(iii) to hear the child's version of the circumstances leading to the concern;

(iv) to get a picture of the child's relationship with their parents/carers;

(v) to support the child to participate in decisions affecting them according to their age and maturity;

(vi) to find out who the child trusts;

(vii) to inform the child of any further steps to be taken in the enquiry.

6.4.8 It is the responsibility of the HSE to ensure that staff carrying out child protection and welfare enquiries have sufficient training and experience in interviewing children. If the child is not present and the parents/carers are not willing to cooperate in allowing him or her to be seen, the matter should be brought to the attention of the key worker's line manager and a decision made regarding any further action.

6.5 Conflict between parents/carers and children

6.5.1 Where the interests of the parents/carers and child appear to conflict, the child's interests should be paramount. It may be necessary in such circumstances for professionals to provide a separate worker specifically for the parents/carers, in particular where one of the parents/carers is the alleged abuser.

7. Protocol for An Garda Síochána – HSE Liaison

7.1 Introduction

7.1.1 The HSE and An Garda Síochána are the key agencies empowered by law to carry out assessments and investigations, respectively, of suspected child abuse and neglect. Each agency manages the responsibility within its brief and their joint efforts are designed to ensure that the protection of vulnerable children receives priority attention. Their separate and complementary roles require careful understanding if the shared objectives of child protection are to be realised. An Garda Síochána has the additional responsibility of preparing an investigation file for the directions of the Director of Public Prosecutions (DPP), who decides on and carries out prosecutions.

7.1.2 An Garda Síochána is vested with the power to remove a child to safety under Section 12 of the Child Care Act 1991 where a member of the Gardaí has reasonable grounds for believing that there is an immediate and serious risk to the health or welfare of a child and it would not be sufficient for the protection of that child to await the making of an application for an Emergency Care Order by the HSE under Section 13 of the Child Care Act 1991. Where a child has been removed by An Garda Síochána under Section 12, the child shall be delivered into the custody of the HSE as soon as possible.

7.1.3 Note that where 'the HSE' is referred to in this chapter, it refers to the staff working in the HSE Children and Family Services.

7.2 Designated personnel

7.2.1 It is essential that the HSE and An Garda Síochána designate personnel at assessment/investigation and management levels who will remain involved with the case until the assessment/investigation is completed.

7.2.2 A Social Work Team Leader from the HSE and a designated Inspector/Sergeant from within An Garda Síochána should constitute a **Liaison Management Team**, the functions of which are:

(i) to consider the notification to An Garda Síochána of suspected child abuse or neglect;

(ii) to assign additional personnel, where necessary, and supervise investigations;

(iii) to review progress in the case.

7.3 Tracking systems

7.3.1 It is important for both the HSE and An Garda Síochána to chart the progress of an assessment/investigation into a notified suspicion of child abuse or neglect. A standardised **Record of Garda – HSE Liaison Form** should be used to assist managers and other personnel in this task (*see Appendix 6*). The adoption of this procedure should ensure accountability in all cases.

7.4 Cases to be formally notified by the HSE to An Garda Síochána

7.4.1 Where the HSE suspects that a child has been or is being physically or sexually abused or wilfully neglected, An Garda Síochána must be formally notified in accordance with the procedure set out in Paragraph 7.4.5 below. The process of establishing whether grounds exist for suspecting such abuse may involve consulting relevant professional personnel within the HSE and, where appropriate, in outside agencies. However, the HSE must not await confirmation of such abuse, whether from a child abuse assessment unit or otherwise, before notifying An Garda Síochána.

7.4.2 In all such cases, the HSE must inform the person reporting a suspicion of child abuse that their information will be shared with An Garda Síochána.

7.4.3 The HSE is not expected to routinely notify suspected cases of emotional abuse or unintentional neglect to An Garda Síochána since the circumstances of such cases may not involve law enforcement issues. In cases of doubt, however, An Garda Síochána should be consulted as to whether a notification may be necessary.

7.4.4 On occasion, the HSE may become aware of abuse to unknown children involving being photographed, videotaped or filmed for pornographic purposes without their knowledge. This information should be conveyed to An Garda Síochána.

Procedure for the HSE to notify An Garda Síochána

7.4.5 The procedure for the HSE to notify An Garda Síochána of a suspected case of physical or sexual abuse, or wilful neglect of a child is as follows:

(i) The designated person within the HSE sends the **Standard Notification Form** to the local Garda Superintendent (*see Appendix 4*). Where more than one child is involved, a separate Standard Notification Form should be sent in respect of each child. A copy is retained in the file on each child. The social worker handling the case (or other designated person) is named on the form.

(ii) On receipt of the Standard Notification Form, the Garda Superintendent arranges to have a designated Garda assigned to the case and immediately informs the designated person within the HSE of the Garda's name and station.

(iii) The designated Garda makes direct contact without delay with the HSE social worker (or other designated person) dealing with the case in order to obtain details.

(iv) When contact is established, both the designated Garda and the social worker commence completion of the Record of Garda – HSE Liaison Form (*see Appendix 6*).

(v) At the same time, the Garda Superintendent will assign a designated Inspector/Sergeant to manage the investigation, monitor its progress and consult with the appointed HSE designated person of the case.

(vi) Where contact cannot be established between the designated Garda and the social worker, the matter will revert immediately to the HSE Social Work Team Leader of the case and the designated Garda Inspector/Sergeant for resolution.

7.5 Informal consultation

7.5.1 In cases where the HSE is aware of concerns about a child but is unable to establish sufficient grounds for formal notification, the HSE should consult with An Garda Síochána on an informal basis. Such contact is to be actively encouraged in order to protect the welfare of the child concerned.

7.6 Emergency intervention

7.6.1 In circumstances where a child's immediate safety is deemed to be at risk, the HSE is obliged to take immediate protective action. It is essential that the HSE informs An Garda Síochána as soon as possible of any actions taken or planned, by sending the Standard Notification Form as soon as circumstances permit (*see Appendix 4*).

7.7 Cases to be formally notified by An Garda Síochána to the HSE

7.7.1 Where An Garda Síochána suspects that a child has been or is being the victim of emotional, physical or sexual abuse or neglect (whether wilful or unintentional), the HSE must be formally notified in accordance with the procedure set out in Paragraph 7.7.4 below. It is not necessary for An Garda Síochána to have sufficient evidence to support a criminal prosecution before notifying the HSE.

7.7.2 An Garda Síochána should notify the HSE of cases if they give rise to child protection issues, such as when the suspected abuser has ongoing contact with other children. In cases involving law enforcement only, An Garda Síochána should contact the HSE where there is need for appropriate counselling and other support services for the victims of assaults.

7.7.3 An Garda Síochána may be involved in investigating a case of child abuse, or a retrospective disclosure of abuse, where the HSE is not involved. Where appropriate, An Garda Síochána should seek the advice of the HSE regarding counselling and other support services for victims.

Procedure for An Garda Síochána to notify the HSE

7.7.4 The procedure for An Garda Síochána to notify the HSE of a suspected case of emotional, physical or sexual abuse or neglect of a child is as follows:

(i) The Garda Superintendent sends the **Standard Notification Form** to the designated person within the HSE (*see Appendix 5*). A copy is held by the designated Garda dealing with the case and by the designated Garda Inspector/Sergeant. Where more than one child is involved, a separate Standard Notification Form should be sent in respect of each child.

(ii) On receipt of the notification form, the designated person within the HSE arranges, through the HSE Social Work Team Leader, to have a social worker (or other designated person) assigned to the case and immediately notifies the Garda Superintendent of the name and location of the designated social worker.

(iii) The social worker assigned to the case makes direct contact without delay with the designated Garda in charge of the case in order to obtain details.

(iv) When contact is established, both the designated Garda and the social worker commence completion of the Record of Garda – HSE Liaison Form (*see Appendix 6*).

(v) At the same time, the Garda Superintendent will assign a designated Inspector/Sergeant to manage the investigation, monitor its progress and consult with the appointed HSE manager of the case.

(vi) Where contact cannot be established between the designated Garda and HSE social worker, the matter will revert immediately to the HSE Social Work Team Leader and the designated Garda Inspector/Sergeant for resolution.

7.7.5 The **Liaison Management Team** – comprising the HSE Social Work Team Leader and the Garda Inspector/Sergeant – will be responsible for ensuring that interagency liaison occurs and that each Standard Notification Form is appropriately processed, as follows:

- Within An Garda Síochána, the notification process requires that the Standard Notification Form from the HSE (*see Appendix 4*) must be received by the designated Garda, the designated Garda Inspector/ Sergeant and the Garda Superintendent.
- Within the HSE, the notification process requires that the Standard Notification Form from An Garda Síochána (*see Appendix 5*) must be received by the designated social worker, the designated Social Work Team Leader and designated person within the HSE.

7.8 Informal consultation

7.8.1 In cases where An Garda Síochána is aware of concerns about a child but is unable to establish sufficient grounds for formal notification to the HSE, An Garda Síochána should consult with the HSE on an informal basis. Such contact is to be actively encouraged in order to protect the welfare of the child concerned.

7.9 Emergency intervention

7.9.1 There may be occasions when An Garda Síochána has to take immediate action to protect a child without first notifying the HSE. It is essential that An Garda Síochána informs the HSE as soon as possible of any actions taken, by sending the Standard Notification Form as soon as circumstances permit (*see Appendix 5*).

7.10 Assessment and Investigation of cases

7.10.1 It is essential that enquiries by the HSE and An Garda Síochána should be coordinated to ensure that:

(i) the welfare of the child is protected;

(ii) everything possible is done to assist the criminal investigation and protect the available evidence;

(iii) there is an effective flow of relevant information between both agencies;

(iv) decisions and actions follow consultation within and between both agencies.

7.11 Matters to be considered by the HSE and An Garda Síochána during the assessment, investigation and management of suspected child abuse cases

7.11.1 **Interviewing:** In cases where a specialist assessment of child sexual abuse is underway, the early interviewing of the child by An Garda Síochána should be facilitated to ensure that statements may be obtained in a manner least likely to cause stress to the child (*see Chapter 6, Section 6.4*). It is important to note that the person who initially reported the allegation of child sexual abuse, or to whom the allegation was made, may be a vital witness and should be interviewed by An Garda Síochána at an early stage. Section 16(1)(b) of the Criminal Evidence Act 1992 states that the video recording of statements by children under 14 years during an interview with a member of An Garda Síochána or other competent person shall be admissible as evidence in Court. Special facilities for the holding of such interviews have been developed, together with training for social workers and Gardaí undertaking such interviews.

7.11.2 **Record-keeping:** The HSE and An Garda Síochána should keep a written record of decisions taken in relation to the case (*see Chapter 5, Section 5.21*). This record should be accessible in the absence of the specific personnel allocated to the case. All contacts between the HSE and An Garda Síochána should be recorded. A decision that is made by either the HSE or An Garda Síochána not to proceed must be recorded in detail.

7.11.3 **Child Protection Plan:** All persons involved should agree a child protection plan. Plans will be reviewed on an ongoing basis (*see Chapter 5, Section 5.9*).

7.11.4 **Strategy Meetings and Child Protection Conferences:** An invitation to attend and the agenda to be covered should be sent in the first instance to the Garda Superintendent in order to facilitate the attendance of the designated Garda, if appropriate.

7.11.5 **Liaison with parents/carers:** Every possible effort should be made to keep the child's parents/carers informed of developments in the case, except where this might place the child at further risk or impede the criminal investigation. It is common practice to invite parents/carers to attend child protection conferences. If this conflicts with the investigative process, the matter should be resolved between the relevant case managers, namely the Social Work Team Leader and the designated Garda Inspector/Sergeant. The views of parents/carers should be sought on the issues to be raised at a child protection conference, so that they can get advice and prepare their representations. All actions in response to concerns about child abuse should be taken in a manner that supports the possibility of families providing safe and nurturing care for their children, now or in the future. For parents/carers, being asked to participate in, or cooperate with, an investigation into suspected child abuse can provoke powerful emotions, such as anger, fear, shame, guilt or powerlessness. Moreover, parents/carers are usually unaware of the complexity of what is likely to be involved and are unsure of the appropriate rules of behaviour.

Professionals need to try to build trust with families when involved in child abuse assessments/investigations in so far as is possible. It may be unrealistic to expect the HSE/Garda and families to trust each other in such difficult circumstances. Nevertheless, in many cases a relationship of trust can be established if the professionals involved create the right conditions for its development.

If the child or parent/carer has a communication difficulty, arrangements must be made to help them during any interviews. This may involve a sign language interpreter, large print, tape or braille. For those whose first language is not English, the services of an interpreter should be made available.

7.11.6 **Extra familial abuse:** Where a concern is made known to the HSE or An Garda Síochána that a child is at risk or has been abused by a person outside the family, the HSE shall:

(i) undertake an assessment of need on the child and provide support as required;

(ii) endeavour to undertake a risk assessment of the alleged perpetrator, where known, in accordance with HSE policy.

7.11.7 **Investigation of organised abuse:** The investigation of organised abuse requires particularly sensitive cooperation between the HSE and An Garda Síochána. It may involve surveillance work and a higher degree of secrecy than would normally be expected in child protection work. It may be undesirable to share information fully with families in the early stages of investigation since breaches of confidentiality may seriously impede detection (*see Paragraphs 7.16.9-12*).

7.12 Confidentiality

7.12.1 It is essential that all information exchanged between the HSE and An Garda Síochána is treated with the utmost confidentiality in order to safeguard the privacy of the children and families concerned and to avoid prejudicing any subsequent legal proceedings.

7.12.2 Regard must be taken of the Freedom of Information Acts 1997 and 2003 when considering a request for confidentiality (*see Appendix 7*). At present, these Acts apply to the HSE, but not to An Garda Síochána. HSE records containing references to communications with An Garda Síochána, including records of meetings where Gardaí are in attendance, will be considered 'third party' records and, as such, will be referred to the Garda Commissioner when any request for information release under the Freedom of Information Acts is being considered.

7.12.3 Similar considerations will apply to requests received under the provisions of the Data Protection Acts 1988 and 2003 (*see Appendix 7*).

7.13 Ongoing liaison

7.13.1 The HSE social worker and the designated Garda should stay in regular contact and inform each other of developments in the case as they take place and record these on the Record of Garda – HSE Liaison Form (*see Appendix 6*). The link between both agencies should be maintained until the criminal investigation and the prosecution (where applicable) is completed.

7.13.2 Certain aspects of the investigation should be considered by both agencies, including:

(i) impact of a prosecution on the child (victim);

(ii) impact of the alleged abuse on the child;

(iii) support for child and adult witnesses;

(iv) victim support services.

7.14 Strategy Meeting

7.14.1 The purpose of a strategy meeting is to facilitate the sharing and evaluation of information between professionals and to prepare a plan of action for the protection of a child, and their siblings if necessary. A strategy meeting may involve any or all of the professionals involved at either management or case assessment level, depending on the circumstances. It is important that the attendance of a designated Garda is secured at this meeting where appropriate, especially if formal notification procedures are, or have been, invoked.

7.14.2 It is the responsibility of the HSE Social Work Team Leader or Social Work Manager to hold a strategy meeting.

7.14.3 While, in the main, strategy meetings will be formally convened, in certain circumstances, particularly where urgent, the strategy meeting may take the form of a less formal contact.

7.14.4 The objectives of the meeting are outlined in detail in Chapter 5, Paragraph 5.7.4.

7.15 Child Protection Conference

7.15.1 A child protection conference is an interagency and interprofessional meeting, convened by the designated person within the HSE (*see Chapter 5, Section 5.8*).

7.15.2 The purpose of a child protection conference is to facilitate the sharing and evaluation of information between professionals and parents/carers, and to formulate a child protection plan (*see Chapter 5, Section 5.9*).

7.15.3 An invitation to attend a child protection conference and the agenda to be covered should be sent in the first instance to the Garda Superintendent in order to facilitate the attendance of the designated Garda, if appropriate.

7.16 Special considerations

7.16.1 Certain child protection concerns that come to the attention of the HSE are of particular relevance to An Garda Síochána.

Age of consent

7.16.2 For the purposes of criminal law, the age of consent to sexual activity is 17 years. This means, for example, that a sexual relationship between two 16-year-olds who are boyfriend and girlfriend is illegal, although it might not be regarded as constituting 'child sexual abuse'. In any event, investigations should be sensitive to the needs of the child.

7.16.3 In cases where abuse is not suspected or alleged but the boy or girl is underage, consultation must be held between the HSE and An Garda Síochána, and all aspects of the case will be examined. Both agencies must acknowledge the sensitivity required in order to facilitate vulnerable young people in availing of all necessary services, while at the same time satisfying relevant legal requirements.

Underage pregnancy

7.16.4 When a pregnant girl under 17 years presents to a health service, a health professional will attempt to establish whether there is any cause for concern regarding child sexual abuse. Where concerns exist, the health professional will refer the case to the HSE Children and Family Services.

7.16.5 Where such abuse is suspected or alleged and the designated person within the HSE has been so informed, then An Garda Síochána must be notified by the designated person within the HSE using the Standard Notification Form (*see Appendix 4*).

7.16.6 In cases where abuse is not suspected or alleged, HSE procedures should be in place to provide guidance on consultation with An Garda Síochána to examine all aspects of such cases. Both agencies must acknowledge the sensitivity required in order to facilitate vulnerable young girls to avail of medical or therapeutic services, while at the same time satisfying relevant legal requirements.

Retrospective disclosure by adults

7.16.7 When a disclosure is made by an adult of abuse suffered during their childhood and it comes to the attention of either the HSE or An Garda Síochána or other service, it is essential to establish whether there is any current risk to any child who may be in contact with the alleged abuser revealed in the adult's disclosure. If any risk is deemed to exist, this information must be shared between both agencies, following the notification procedures (*see Paragraphs 7.4.5 and 7.7.4*). It is essential that all relevant information in relation to any of the above eventualities is carefully collated and that each agency informs the other of any such concerns during an investigation.

7.16.8 The need to refer an adult for counselling, treatment and/or other support services for victims of assaults should also be considered.

Organised abuse

7.16.9 Cases of organised abuse comprise only a very small proportion of the child protection concerns that come to the attention of the HSE. Nevertheless, they are complex and require particularly careful handling. Essentially, organised abuse occurs either when one adult moves into an area or institution and systematically entraps children for abusive purposes (mainly sexually) or when two or more adults conspire to similarly abuse children, using inducements.

7.16.10 Organised abuse can occur in different settings, such as the community, clubs, the family or extended family, or an institution.

7.16.11 The following factors are particularly associated with organised abuse:

(i) Detection can take several years.

(ii) Calculating the number of victims involved can be difficult since many will have moved away from the area. Particular efforts, such as helplines and advertisements, may be required in order to contact victims.

(iii) Victims who grew up in care are often more powerless and vulnerable than those in other abuse cases.

(iv) Victims may be under particular pressure not to disclose because of threats or feelings of shame and responsibility.

(v) Some victims may have helped abusers to entrap other children and may have gone on to become abusers themselves.

(vi) Families may have unwittingly colluded with the abuse by accepting gifts and friendship from the abuser and encouraging their children to associate with the abuser.

7.16.12 The investigation of organised abuse requires particularly sensitive cooperation between the HSE and An Garda Síochána. It may involve surveillance work and a higher degree of secrecy than would normally be expected in child protection work. It may be undesirable to share information fully with families in the early stages of investigation since breaches of confidentiality may seriously impede detection.

7.17 Arrangements for the protection of children at risk in other areas or jurisdictions

7.17.1 When a family with children who are considered by the HSE or An Garda Síochána to be at risk are believed to have moved from one area to another within the State, the relevant information will be furnished to the appropriate Local Health Office. The HSE will develop a protocol for the exchange of information in these circumstances, taking account of data protection considerations.

7.17.2 When a family with children who are considered by the HSE or An Garda Síochána to be at risk are believed to have moved to another jurisdiction, the relevant information should be sent to the appropriate authority in that State. The HSE will develop a protocol for the exchange of information in these circumstances, as well as in circumstances where a person whom the HSE considers poses a risk to children moves to another jurisdiction, taking account of data protection considerations.

7.17.3 Information on children who are in need of care and protection who move to countries other than the United Kingdom must be sent through the Irish correspondent for International Social Service (ISS), who will forward it to the appropriate ISS contact in the relevant country. To avail of the ISS network, the relevant information should be sent to the Irish ISS correspondent at:

International Social Service
HSE West
South East Wing
St. Joseph's Hospital
Mulgrave Street
Limerick, Co. Limerick, Ireland
Tel: 00353 61 461380
Fax: 00353 61 412355
E-mail: ISS@hse.ie

7.18 Arrangements for the protection of children at risk who migrate to Ireland from another jurisdiction

7.18.1 Information received from the International Social Service (ISS) on children who are in need of care and protection who come to Ireland from abroad is channelled through the Irish ISS correspondent at the address given in Paragraph 7.17.3 above.

7.18.2 When the HSE or An Garda Síochána is informed that children who are considered to be at risk have moved into their area, immediate notification procedures must be followed. If required, a strategy meeting must be arranged between the HSE and An Garda Síochána to review relevant information.

PART IV:
Special Considerations

8. Especially vulnerable children

8.1 Purpose

8.1.1 This chapter provides additional guidance on children who may be especially vulnerable and who may have been abused or neglected, or who are at risk of abuse or neglect. These include:

- children in residential settings;
- children in the care of the State under the Child Care Act 1991:
  - foster care;
  - relative care;
  - residential care.
- children who are homeless;
- children with disabilities;
- separated children seeking asylum;
- children being trafficked.

8.2 Role of the HSE

8.2.1 Under the Child Care Act 1991, the HSE is required to assume primary responsibility for an assessment and to take appropriate steps to protect the welfare of the child or children in question. In practice, this means that the designated person within the HSE coordinates the services necessary to identify whether a particular child, or children, needs care or protection, and if so to initiate appropriate action. In doing this, the designated person will liaise closely with the referring service and, where required, enlist its assistance.

8.3 Role of the HIQA and SSI

8.3.1 The Health Information and Quality Authority (HIQA) has statutory responsibility for developing Standards for Health and Social Services, including Standards for Children's Services. The national standards developed for children's services include good practice guidance on keeping children and young people safe and protected.

8.3.2 The Social Services Inspectorate (SSI) of the HIQA has responsibility for inspecting HSE children's residential centres, special care, hostels, relative/foster care and Children Detention Schools, including how child protection is practised. (The HSE registers and inspects children's residential centres and hostels run in the private and voluntary sectors.) When fully commenced under the Health Act 2007, the SSI will register and inspect all residential accommodation for children in care and residential care for adults and children with disabilities.

8.4 Children in residential, educational and recreational settings

8.4.1 All those involved in caring for children in residential settings, including those for educational and recreational purposes, outside of the home must be alert to the possibility of abuse by other children, visitors and members of staff. Policies and procedures aimed at preventing abuse must be in place. There must be clear written procedures on how to deal with suspected abuse. These must be accessible to children and staff.

8.4.2 When a child has been abused by another child in a residential setting, child protection procedures should be applied to both the abuser and the victim.

8.5 Safeguarding children in residential settings

8.5.1 Children in residential settings should have contact outside the residence. These children may be particularly vulnerable and may find it very difficult to make their problems known. The following measures should be in place in all residential settings for children:

(i) a complaints system should be in place and children should be told about it and how to use it if they need to;

(ii) children should have easy access to a telephone where they can speak privately;

(iii) children should be made aware of telephone helpline numbers;

(iv) approved visitors from outside the residence should be available to see the children.

8.6 Abuse of children in residential settings by visitors

8.6.1 The possibility of abuse by visitors must be recognised and protected against. If such abuse occurs, it should normally be dealt with in the same way as other incidents of suspected abuse.

8.7 Abuse or neglect of children in residential settings by staff

8.7.1 Children and staff must be able to report their concerns. There should be clear written guidance on reporting suspected abuse or neglect. The need to be vigilant and to report concerns should be reinforced through training and supervision.

8.7.2 Children and staff need to be reassured that raising concerns is important. Management should respond to all reports of a concern quickly and appropriately, and ensure that effective action is taken. A written record of the report should be confirmed with the person who reported the concern.

8.7.3 Throughout the investigation, all interviews with children should be pre-arranged and the children should be provided with the following:

(i) support;

(ii) information about the investigation and its outcome;

(iii) privacy during interviews and in access to the telephone and correspondence;

(iv) access to independent advice if required;

(v) alternative accommodation if required.

8.7.4 There should be clear procedures on what the child or member of staff should do if they feel that inappropriate or insufficient action has been taken.

8.7.5 Where abuse or neglect by a member of staff is suspected, normal child protection procedures should be instigated. Staff and management should cooperate fully with the investigation. The possibility of involvement and collusion of other members of staff must be recognised. Where such abuse is suspected, it will be necessary for An Garda Síochána and the HSE, when agreeing their strategy for investigation, to weigh the need for evidence carefully against the rights of the individual children concerned.

LIBRARY
INSTITUTE OF TECHNOLOGY
CARLOW

8.8 Children in the care of the State under the Child Care Act 1991

8.8.1 Additional guidance is set out below in respect of children who are in the care of the State and who may be vulnerable to abuse.

Foster/Relative care and Residential care

8.8.2 The HSE Children and Family Services have responsibilities for children whom they place with relatives or with foster carers or in residential placements, as provided for in the Child Care Act 1991 and the Child Care Regulations 1995. In arranging, providing or supervising placements with foster/relative carers or in residential centres, the welfare of the child must be paramount. The wishes and feelings of the child and his or her parents should be taken into account.

8.8.3 The national standards developed for children in foster/relative care and for children in residential care should be readily available to children, foster/relative carers and their families, and to all HSE staff involved in the provision of these services *(see Paragraph 8.3.1)*.

8.8.4 Children entering the care of the State under the Child Care Act 1991 may have previously been abused or neglected. Any allegation of abuse or neglect, past or present, must be dealt with sensitively and support provided to the child and others who have developed close relationships with that child, e.g. the foster carers and their family, other children in the residence.

8.8.5 When the HSE Children and Family Services are assessing the allegation of alleged abuse or neglect of children in foster care or in a residential centre, the safety of any other children in the house/centre should be considered.

8.9 Other vulnerable children

8.9.1 Research has shown that abuse of children with disabilities is a significant problem. The abuser is most likely to be known to the victim.

8.9.2 Parents, teachers and all staff in services for children with disabilities need to be familiar with the indicators of abuse and to be alert for signs of abuse.

8.9.3 All agencies/organisations working with children with disabilities should have clear guidelines for preventing, identifying and reporting child abuse or neglect and should ensure that staff and volunteers are trained in the use of the *Children First: National Guidance*.

8.9.4 Particular attention should be paid to the welfare and protection of children who are living apart from their birth parents and whose first language is not English.

8.9.5 An area of growing concern is where children and young people may be trafficked into this country for purposes of exploitation, either employment or sexual. These children may resist offers of assistance from the HSE due to fears for their own safety or that of their families. They are frequently hidden within communities since they do not attend educational, religious or social events.

8.10 Children who are homeless

8.10.1 Occasionally, children will come to the attention of the HSE whose circumstances are unclear and who, because of what may be temporary difficulties, are without accommodation. In such circumstances, the following actions should be taken by the HSE Children and Family Services in line with the Youth Homeless Strategy 2001:

(i) Establish with the child, in a manner appropriate to his or her age and stage of development, the circumstances in which he or she became homeless.

(ii) Assess the potential for the child to return to his or her family home, including whether family support is needed to achieve this.

(iii) Assess the child's physical, social and psychological well-being, including the need for medical treatment or treatment for drug/alcohol problems.

(iv) Assess the short and longer term accommodation/care arrangements for the child if he or she is unable to return home.

8.10.2 If a return to the child's parents/carers is not considered the most appropriate action, an alternative temporary placement should be identified, with a family member or friend, which is acceptable to the parents/carers and the child, and agreed by them.

8.10.3 Where it is not possible to return a child who is not at home to his or her parents/carers or to find a temporary placement with relatives or friends, then the HSE Children and Family Services have three options:

(i) If circumstances warrant, the HSE may pursue an Emergency Care Order under the Child Care Act 1991.

(ii) There may be a voluntary reception of the child into the care of the HSE.

(iii) If grounds for receiving the child into care are not clear or do not exist and there appears to be no suitable accommodation for the child, then the HSE has an obligation to provide him or her with a place to stay which is suitable to his or her needs. This placement should be on an emergency or short-term basis, pending a full assessment.

8.10.4 Any concern about the care and protection of children who are homeless should be assessed in the same way as any other child protection concern.

9. Peer abuse

9.1 Purpose

9.1.1 In some cases of child abuse, the alleged perpetrator will be another child. In such situations, it is particularly important to consider how the HSE Children and Family Services and other agencies can provide care for both the child victim *and* the child abuser. The purpose of this chapter is to provide guidance on the identification of and response to such cases.

9.2 General guidelines

9.2.1 In a situation where child abuse is alleged to have been carried out by another child, the child protection procedures should be adhered to for both the victim *and* the alleged abuser – i.e. it should be considered a child care and protection issue for *both* children.

9.2.2 Abusive behaviour that is perpetrated by children must be acted upon. If there is any conflict of interest between the welfare of the alleged abuser and the victim, the victim's welfare is of paramount importance.

9.2.3 As in all cases of child abuse, it is essential to respond to the needs of children who are abused by their peers. Each individual case will require its own unique intervention. Appropriate support and services should be provided to the child and his or her parents/carers as quickly as possible. In the case of child sexual abuse by peers, treatment approaches may include individual treatment and/or group therapy for the child or adolescent.

9.2.4 Children who are abusive towards other children also require comprehensive assessment and therapeutic intervention by skilled child care professionals. Treatment is more likely to be effective if begun early in the child's life.

It is known that some adult abusers begin abusing during childhood and adolescence, that significant numbers will have suffered abuse themselves and that the abuse is likely to become progressively more serious. Early referral and intervention is therefore essential.

9.2.5 Future abuse can be prevented if intervention takes place early in the child's life. Therefore, it is essential to refer concerns about peer abuse immediately to the HSE Children and Family Services. The HSE should establish appropriate treatment programmes to cater for children who engage in abusive behaviour with other children.

9.2.6 It should be anticipated that an allegation of peer abuse will have a detrimental impact on relationships between the alleged abuser, his or her parents/carers and other family members. A negative impact on other social relationships, such as with peers and neighbours, should also be anticipated. As a result, the child and family may experience isolation, and in some situations victimisation, following an allegation of abuse. The child's parents/carers will need support and advice to help them understand the abusive behaviour and to deal with the situation. Active participation and commitment by parents/carers can be an important factor in the success of treatment and may be crucial in influencing the general outcome of the case. It is therefore essential to provide adequate support services to the child and family throughout the assessment and treatment processes.

9.3 Sexual abuse by children and young people

9.3.1 Research shows that teenagers perpetrate a considerable proportion of child sexual abuse. Such cases should be referred to the HSE Children and Family Services. It is important that the different types of behaviour are clearly identified and that no young person is wrongly labelled 'a child abuser' without a clear analysis of the particular behaviour. Four categories of behaviour warrant attention: normal sexual exploration; abuse reactive behaviour; sexually obsessive behaviour; and abusive behaviour by adolescents and young people.

9.3.2 **Normal sexual exploration:** This could consist of naive play between two children that involves the exploration of their sexuality. This type of behaviour may be prompted by exchanges between children, such as 'You show me yours and I'll show you mine'. One of the key aspects of this behaviour is its tone: there should not be any coercive or dominating aspects to this behaviour. Usually, there is no need for child protection intervention of any kind in this type of situation.

9.3.3 **Abuse reactive behaviour:** In this situation, one child who has been abused already acts out the same behaviour on another child. This is serious behaviour and needs to be treated as such. In addition to responding to the needs of the abused child, the needs of the child perpetrator in this situation must also be addressed.

9.3.4 **Sexually obsessive behaviour:** In this type of situation, the children may engage in sexually compulsive behaviour. An example of this would be excessive masturbation, which may well be meeting some other emotional need. Most children masturbate at some point in their lives. However, in families where care and attention is missing, they may have extreme comfort needs that are not being met and may move from masturbation to excessive interest or curiosity in sex, which takes on excessive or compulsive aspects. These children may not have been sexually abused, but they may be extremely needy and may require very specific help in addressing those needs.

9.3.5 **Abusive behaviour by adolescents and young people:** Behaviour that is abusive will have elements of domination, coercion or bribery, and certainly secrecy. The fact that the behaviour is carried out by an adolescent, for example, does not, in itself, make it 'experimentation'. However, if there is no age difference between the two children or no difference in status, power or intellect, then one could argue that this is indeed experimentation. On the other hand, if, for example, the adolescent is aged 13 and the child is aged 3, this gap in itself creates an abusive quality that should be taken seriously.

9.4 Bullying

9.4.1 Bullying can be defined as repeated aggression – whether it be verbal, psychological or physical – that is conducted by an individual or group against others. It is behaviour that is intentionally aggravating and intimidating, and occurs mainly among children in social environments such as schools. It includes behaviours such as teasing, taunting, threatening, hitting or extortion by one or more persons against a victim. Bullying can also take the form of racial abuse. With developments in modern technology, children can also be the victims of non-contact bullying, via mobile phones, the Internet and other personal devices.

9.4.2 Bullying of children can also be perpetrated by adults, including adults who are not related to the child. Bullying behaviour when perpetrated by adults, rather than children, could be regarded as physical or emotional abuse. However, other major forms of child abuse, such as neglect and sexual abuse, are not normally comprehended by the term 'bullying'.

Bullying in schools

9.4.3 It is recognised that bullying in schools is a particular problem. It is imperative that school management boards should have a policy in place to deal with bullying and that teachers are aware of this policy and of procedural guidelines to deal with it. In situations where the incident is serious and where the behaviour is regarded as potentially abusive, the school should consult the HSE Children and Family Services with a view to drawing up an appropriate response, such as a management plan.

9.4.4 In the first instance, it is the school authorities that are responsible for dealing with bullying in school. School authorities should exercise this responsibility by having regard to the existing advice and to the *Guidelines on countering bullying behaviour in primary and post-primary schools* from the Department of Education (1993).

9.4.5 **Serious instances** of bullying behaviour should be referred to the HSE Children and Family Services.

10. Training in child protection and welfare

10.1 Purpose

10.1.1 The purpose of this chapter is to outline the role of training for effective child protection and the levels of training required for different types of staff in all organisations working with children. One of the core issues identified in child abuse enquiries is the breakdown in communication between disciplines and agencies. Accordingly, it is essential that training is provided on a multidisciplinary and interagency basis.

10.1.2 Training aims to promote effective interventions in the care and protection of children. Effective child protection depends on the skills, knowledge and values of personnel working with children and families, as well as cooperation *between* agencies (interagency) and *within* agencies (intra-agency). Relevant training and education is an essential prerequisite for achieving this. All agencies involved with children have a responsibility to ensure that such training is available on an ongoing basis.

10.1.3 For voluntary and community providers of services, regard should be had to *Our Duty to Care: The principles of good practice for the protection of children and young people* (Department of Health and Children, 2002) in the provision of child protection training for staff and volunteers.

10.2 Objectives of child protection and welfare training

10.2.1 Training in child protection and welfare has a number of objectives:

(i) to ensure that personnel are equipped with appropriate skills, knowledge and values to deliver an effective service to children;

(ii) to ensure that personnel are aware of relevant legislation, national guidelines and local child protection procedures and protocols;

(iii) to translate learning into a better service for children and families in collaboration with other service providers;

(iv) to strengthen relationships through interagency training.

10.3 Approach to child protection and welfare training

10.3.1 The level and type of training required depends on the degree of involvement that the staff of particular agencies have in child protection and welfare work. All relevant staff should be trained in the recognition of signs of abuse (*see Chapter 2 and Appendix 1*) and what immediate action to take (*see Chapter 3*).

10.3.2 A strategy for training in child protection and welfare must be developed in the HSE. This strategy will set out the training aims involved, learning outcomes, target groups, proposed initiatives, performance indicators and evaluation processes.

10.3.3 Training in child protection and welfare is required at two levels – basic and advanced – in order to meet the diversity of needs within the HSE and other organisations that provide services to children and families.

10.3.4 **Basic-level training** in child protection and welfare should aim to equip personnel with knowledge of the relevant child care legislation, national and local agency policies, procedures and protocols (as well as a knowledge of the local network within which they work) and skills in the use of these. Such basic training must be delivered on a multidisciplinary interagency basis so that the key learning that takes place results from discussion and the sharing of knowledge, experience and perspectives across disciplines and services. The target group for basic-level training in child protection and welfare should be personnel whose roles involve regular direct or indirect contact with children and families.

10.3.5 **Advanced-level training** in child protection and welfare should aim to equip personnel with knowledge, skills and critical perspectives in specific areas of policy and practice, for example, risk assessment and working in partnership with parents/carers. Training should be appropriate to the person's professional role and, again, should be delivered on a multidisciplinary interagency basis. The target group for advanced-level training in child protection and welfare should be personnel whose core duties involve the supervision or practice of child protection and the provision of support services to children and families.

10.3.6 **Training for managers:** Training should be in place for managers of child protection services who have no direct professional expertise or experience in the area. The training should include an overview of child protection activity and interventions, the statutory responsibilities delegated within the HSE, the management functions of *Children First* and the information requirements of the manager in order to monitor and support good quality practice within the area. This training should assist with decisions relating to planning, resourcing, staffing, budgeting and management oversight.

10.4 Target groups

10.4.1 There are a number of key target groups for training in child protection and welfare. The first are staff in the HSE Children and Family Services and An Garda Síochána, by virtue of their statutory responsibility for child protection. The second are staff in a wide range of agencies, both statutory and non-statutory, who provide services to children and families and who have a social responsibility to safeguard the welfare of children. These include, among others, disability organisations, schools, GPs, pre-school services, sports clubs, faith-based institutions and other voluntary organisations.

10.4.2 Training is essential for professionals involved in front-line child protection work, such as social workers, public health nurses, medical doctors (especially GPs and staff in emergency departments) and Gardaí. Professionals also have a responsibility to see that they keep up to date with current developments in this area.

10.4.3 Child protection and welfare is a corporate responsibility of all employees of the HSE. The development of training strategies at HSE level must reflect this premise, with appropriate training at a multidisciplinary level.

10.5 Interagency training

10.5.1 Interdisciplinary and interagency cooperation is essential in order to promote the welfare of children. This is an essential element in the professional task of protecting children from abuse. All agencies involved with children should participate in interagency training programmes.

10.5.2 Training in child protection and welfare is also needed for residential care staff, foster carers and family support workers. Social work teams in the HSE are encouraged to support the development of interagency and multidisciplinary training for all staff engaged in child protection work and to provide places on their training courses for non-HSE staff.

10.5.3 All agencies should establish joint training programmes on child abuse issues, with access for all professional groups in direct contact with children and families. These programmes, preferably involving trainers from a variety of relevant agencies, should help to promote understanding of the respective roles of staff in each agency and thus promote effective working relationships.

10.5.4 A designated senior staff member in each agency or organisation should play a central role in developing, monitoring and evaluating training in child protection and welfare. Staff in all relevant agencies should be made aware of any training opportunities that exist and be encouraged to participate.

10.5.5 The management of schools, pre-school services and voluntary organisations must also ensure that personnel are trained in the recognition of signs of abuse (*see Chapter 2 and Appendix 1*) and on the standard reporting procedure (*see Chapter 3*).

10.5.6 Front-line personnel in such services who meet the public, like telephonists and receptionists, should be given clear instructions on what action to take if contacted by anyone wishing to report suspected child abuse.

10.5.7 Training needs will change continuously and training in child protection and welfare must be an integral part of the plans in all agencies. A percentage of the annual budget in each agency should be explicitly committed to child protection training. An annual review of the training strategy for child protection and welfare should be undertaken.

10.5.8 Specialist training is required for selected HSE staff and members of An Garda Síochána who will be involved in the parallel investigation of cases and subsequent intervention (*see Chapter 7*). The aim of this training is to enable members of each service to understand fully each other's role, to learn how to work together on a joint basis and to learn how to interview children who may have been abused by adults (i.e. Specialist Interviewer Training under Section 16(1)(b) of the Criminal Evidence Act 1992).

References and Official Websites

References

Colbourn Faller, K. (1989) *Child Sexual Abuse. An Interdisciplinary Manual for Diagnosis Case Management and Treatment*. Basingstoke: Macmillan.

Commission to Inquire into Child Abuse (2009) *Report of the Commission to Inquire into Child Abuse, Volumes I-V.* Available at: www.childabusecommission.ie

Department of Education (1993) *Guidelines on countering bullying behaviour in primary and post-primary schools.* Dublin: Government Publications.

Department of Education and Science (2001) *Child Protection – Guidelines and Procedures.* Dublin: Department of Education and Science.

Department of Education and Department of Health (1993) *Child Abuse Prevention Programme*. Dublin: Government Publications.

Department of Health (1987) *Child Abuse Guidelines*. Dublin: Government Publications.

Department of Health (1995) *Garda Síochána – Health Board Guidelines.* Dublin: Government Publications.

Department of Health (1995) *Child Care (Placement of Children in Foster Care) Regulations, 1995.* Dublin: Government Publications.

Department of Health (1995) *Child Care (Placement of Children in Residential Care) Regulations, 1995.* Dublin: Government Publications.

Department of Health (1995) *Child Care (Placement of Children with Relatives) Regulations, 1995.* Dublin: Government Publications.

Department of Health (1997) *Putting Children First – Promoting and Protecting the Rights of Children*. Dublin: Government Publications.

Department of Health and Children (1999) *Children First: National Guidelines for the Protection and Welfare of Children* (1st edition). Dublin: Government Publications.

Department of Health and Children (2000) *The National Children's Strategy: Our Children – Their Lives.* Dublin: Government Publications.

Department of Health and Children (2002) *Our Duty to Care: The principles of good practice for the protection of children and young people.* Dublin: Government Publications.

Department of the Taoiseach (1997) *An Action Programme for the Millennium: A Programme for Government*. Dublin: Government Publications. Available at: www.taoiseach.ie

Department of the Taoiseach (2002) *Programme for Government.* Dublin: Government Publications. Available at: www.taoiseach.ie

Department of the Taoiseach (2006) *Towards 2016: Ten-Year Framework Social Partnership Agreement 2006-2015.* Dublin: Government Publications. Available at: www.taoiseach.ie

Department of the Taoiseach (2007) *Programme for Government*. Dublin: Government Publications. Available at: www.taoiseach.ie

Dubowitz, Howard (1999) *Neglected Children: Research, Practice and Policy.* London: SAGE Publications.

Government of Ireland (1988) *Data Protection Act*. Dublin: Government Publications.

Government of Ireland (1991) *Child Care Act.* Dublin: Government Publications.

Government of Ireland (1996) *Domestic Violence Act.* Dublin: Government Publications.

Government of Ireland (1997) *Freedom of Information Act.* Dublin: Government Publications.

Government of Ireland (1997) *Non-Fatal Offences against the Person Act.* Dublin: Government Publications.

Government of Ireland (1998) *Education Act.* Dublin: Government Publications.

Government of Ireland (1998) *Protections for Persons Reporting Child Abuse Act 1998.* Dublin: Government Publications.

Government of Ireland (2001) *Children Act.* Dublin: Government Publications.

Government of Ireland (2007) *Child Care (Amendment) Act.* Dublin: Government Publications.

HIQA (2010) *Guidance for the Health Service Executive for the Review of Serious Incidents, including deaths of children in care.* Dublin: Health Information and Quality Authority.

HSEA (2005) *Trust in Care: Guidelines for Health Service Employers on preventing patient/client abuse and dealing with allegations of abuse against employees*. Dublin: Health Service Executive.

National Board for Safeguarding Children in the Catholic Church (2009) *Safeguarding Children: Standards and Guidance Document for the Catholic Church in Ireland.* Maynooth: National Board for Safeguarding Children in the Catholic Church in Ireland. Available at: www.safeguarding.ie

Ombudsman for Children's Office (2010) *A report based on an investigation into the implementation of Children First, National Guidelines for the Protection and Welfare of Children.* Dublin: Ombudsman for Children's Office. Available at: www.oco.ie

OMC (2007) *The Agenda for Children's Services: A Policy Handbook,* Office of the Minister for Children. Dublin: Government Publications. Available at: www.dcya.ie

OMCYA (2008) *National Review of Compliance with Children First: National Guidelines for the Protection and Welfare of Children,* Office of the Minister for Children and Youth Affairs. Dublin: Government Publications. Available at: www.dcya.ie

OMCYA (2009) *Report of the Commission to Inquire into Child Abuse, 2009: Implementation Plan,* Office of the Minister for Children and Youth Affairs. Dublin: Government Publications. Available at: www.dcya.ie

Skuse, D. (1989) 'Emotional Abuse and Neglect'. In: R. Meadow (ed.), *ABC of Child Abuse*. London: British Medical Journal Publications.

Skuse, D. and Bentovim, A. (1994) 'Physical and Emotional Maltreatment'. In: M. Rutter, E. Taylor and L. Hersor (eds.), *Child and Adolescent Psychiatry* (3rd edition). Oxford: Blackwell Scientific Publications.

UN (1989) *United Nations Convention on the Rights of the Child.* Geneva: United Nations Office of the High Commissioner for Human Rights. Available at: www2.ohchr.org/english/law/crc.htm

Official websites

An Garda Síochána	www.garda.ie
Department of Children and Youth Affairs	www.dcya.ie
Department of Education and Skills	www.education.ie
Department of Health	www.dohc.ie
Department of Justice and Law Reform	www.justice.ie
Health Information and Quality Authority	www.hiqa.ie
Health Service Executive	www.hse.ie
Office of the Attorney General	www.attorneygeneral.ie
Oireachtas of Ireland	www.oireachtas.ie
Ombudsman for Children's Office	www.oco.ie
UN Office of the High Commissioner for Human Rights	www.ohchr.org

Appendices

Appendix 1: Signs and symptoms of child abuse

1. Signs and symptoms of neglect

Child neglect is the most common category of abuse. A distinction can be made between 'wilful' neglect and 'circumstantial' neglect. 'Wilful' neglect would generally incorporate a direct and deliberate deprivation by a parent/carer of a child's most basic needs, e.g. withdrawal of food, shelter, warmth, clothing, contact with others. 'Circumstantial' neglect more often may be due to stress/inability to cope by parents or carers.

Neglect is closely correlated with low socio-economic factors and corresponding physical deprivations. It is also related to parental incapacity due to learning disability, addictions or psychological disturbance.

The neglect of children is 'usually a passive form of abuse involving omission rather than acts of commission' (Skuse and Bentovim, 1994). It comprises 'both a lack of physical caretaking and supervision and a failure to fulfil the developmental needs of the child in terms of cognitive stimulation'.

Child neglect should be suspected in cases of:

- abandonment or desertion;
- children persistently being left alone without adequate care and supervision;
- malnourishment, lacking food, inappropriate food or erratic feeding;
- lack of warmth;
- lack of adequate clothing;
- inattention to basic hygiene;
- lack of protection and exposure to danger, including moral danger or lack of supervision appropriate to the child's age;
- persistent failure to attend school;
- non-organic failure to thrive, i.e. child not gaining weight due not only to malnutrition but also to emotional deprivation;
- failure to provide adequate care for the child's medical and developmental problems;
- exploited, overworked.

2. Characteristics of neglect

Child neglect is the most frequent category of abuse, both in Ireland and internationally. In addition to being the most frequently reported type of abuse; neglect is also recognised as being the most harmful. Not only does neglect generally last throughout a childhood, it also has long-term consequences into adult life. Children are more likely to die from chronic neglect than from one instance of physical abuse. It is well established that severe neglect in infancy has a serious negative impact on brain development.

Neglect is associated with, but not necessarily caused by, poverty. It is strongly correlated with parental substance misuse, domestic violence and parental mental illness and disability.

Neglect may be categorised into different types (adapted from Dubowitz, 1999):

- **Disorganised/chaotic neglect:** This is typically where parenting is inconsistent and is often found in disorganised and crises-prone families. The quality of parenting is inconsistent, with a lack of certainty and routine, often resulting in emergencies regarding accommodation, finances and food. This type of neglect results in attachment disorders, promotes anxiety in children and leads to disruptive and attention-seeking behaviour, with older children proving more difficult to control and discipline. The home may be unsafe from accidental harm, with a high incident of accidents occurring.
- **Depressed or passive neglect:** This type of neglect fits the common stereotype and is often characterised by bleak and bare accommodation, without material comfort, and with poor hygiene and little if any social and psychological stimulation. The household will have few toys and those that are there may be broken, dirty or inappropriate for age. Young children will spend long periods in cots, playpens or pushchairs. There is often a lack of food, inadequate bedding and no clean clothes. There can be a sense of hopelessness, coupled with ambivalence about improving the household situation. In such environments, children frequently are absent from school and have poor homework routines. Children subject to these circumstances are at risk of major developmental delay.
- **Chronic deprivation:** This is most likely to occur where there is the absence of a key attachment figure. It is most often found in large institutions where infants and children may be physically well cared for, but where there is no opportunity to form an attachment with an individual carer. In these situations, children are dealt with by a range of adults and their needs are seen as part of the demands of a group of children. This form of deprivation will also be associated with poor stimulation and can result in serious developmental delays.

The following points illustrate the consequences of different types of neglect for children:

- inadequate food – failure to develop;
- household hazards – accidents;
- lack of hygiene – health and social problems;
- lack of attention to health – disease;
- inadequate mental health care – suicide or delinquency;
- inadequate emotional care – behaviour and educational;
- inadequate supervision – risk-taking behaviour;
- unstable relationship – attachment problems;
- unstable living conditions – behaviour and anxiety, risk of accidents;
- exposure to domestic violence – behaviour, physical and mental health;
- community violence – anti social behaviour.

3. Signs and symptoms of emotional neglect and abuse

Emotional neglect and abuse is found typically in a home lacking in emotional warmth. It is not necessarily associated with physical deprivation. The emotional needs of the children are not met; the parent's relationship to the child may be without empathy and devoid of emotional responsiveness.

Emotional neglect and abuse occurs when adults responsible for taking care of children are unaware of and unable (for a range of reasons) to meet their children's emotional and developmental needs. Emotional neglect and abuse is not easy to recognise because the effects are not easily observable. Skuse (1989) states that 'emotional abuse refers to the habitual verbal harassment of a child by disparagement, criticism, threat and ridicule, and the inversion of love, whereby verbal and non-verbal means of rejection and withdrawal are substituted'.

Emotional neglect and abuse can be identified with reference to the indices listed below. However, it should be noted that no one indicator is conclusive of emotional abuse. In the case of emotional abuse and neglect, it is more likely to impact negatively on a child where there is a cluster of indices, where these are persistent over time and where there is a lack of other protective factors.

- rejection;
- lack of comfort and love;
- lack of attachment;
- lack of proper stimulation (e.g. fun and play);
- lack of continuity of care (e.g. frequent moves, particularly unplanned);
- continuous lack of praise and encouragement;
- serious over-protectiveness;
- inappropriate non-physical punishment (e.g. locking in bedrooms);
- family conflicts and/or violence;
- every child who is abused sexually, physically or neglected is also emotionally abused;
- inappropriate expectations of a child relative to his/her age and stage of development.

Children who are physically and sexually abused and neglected also suffer from emotional abuse.

4. Signs and symptoms of physical abuse

Unsatisfactory explanations, varying explanations, frequency and clustering for the following events are high indices for concern regarding physical abuse:

- bruises (*see below for more detail*);
- fractures;
- swollen joints;
- burns/scalds (*see below for more detail*);
- abrasions/lacerations;
- haemorrhages (retinal, subdural);
- damage to body organs;
- poisonings – repeated (prescribed drugs, alcohol);
- failure to thrive;
- coma/unconsciousness;
- death.

There are many different forms of physical abuse, but skin, mouth and bone injuries are the most common.

Bruises

Accidental

Accidental bruises are common at places on the body where bone is fairly close to the skin. Bruises can also be found towards the front of the body, as the child usually will fall forwards.

Accidental bruises are common on the chin, nose, forehead, elbow, knees and shins. An accident-prone child can have frequent bruises in these areas. Such bruises will be diffuse, with no definite edges. Any bruising on a child before the age of mobility must be treated with concern.

Non-accidental

Bruises caused by physical abuse are more likely to occur on soft tissues, e.g. cheek, buttocks, lower back, back, thighs, calves, neck, genitalia and mouth.

Marks from slapping or grabbing may form a distinctive pattern. Slap marks might occur on buttocks/cheeks and the outlining of fingers may be seen on any part of the body. Bruises caused by direct blows with a fist have no definite pattern, but may occur in parts of the body that do not usually receive injuries by accident. A punch over the eye (black eye syndrome) or ear would be of concern. Black eyes cannot be caused by a fall on to a flat surface. Two black eyes require two injuries and must always be suspect. Other distinctive patterns of bruising may be left by the use of straps, belts, sticks and feet. The outline of the object may be left on the child in a bruise on areas such as the back or thighs (areas covered by clothing).

Bruises may be associated with shaking, which can cause serious hidden bleeding and bruising inside the skull. Any bruising around the neck is suspicious since it is very unlikely to be accidentally acquired.. Other injuries may feature – ruptured eardrum/fractured skull. Mouth injury may be a cause of concern, e.g. torn mouth (frenulum) from forced bottle-feeding.

Bone injuries

Children regularly have accidents that result in fractures. However, children's bones are more flexible than those of adults and the children themselves are lighter, so a fracture, particularly of the skull, usually signifies that considerable force has been applied.

Non-accidental

A fracture of any sort should be regarded as suspicious in a child under 8 months of age. A fracture of the skull must be regarded as particularly suspicious in a child under 3 years. Either case requires careful investigation as to the circumstances in which the fracture occurred. Swelling in the head or drowsiness may also indicate injury.

Burns

Children who have accidental burns usually have a hot liquid splashed on them by spilling or have come into contact with a hot object. The history that parents give is usually in keeping with the pattern of injury observed. However, repeated episodes may suggest inadequate care and attention to safety within the house.

Non-accidental

Children who have received non-accidental burns may exhibit a pattern that is not adequately explained by parents. The child may have been immersed in a hot liquid. The burn may show a definite line, unlike the type seen in accidental splashing. The child may also have been held against a hot object, like a radiator or a ring of a cooker, leaving distinctive marks. Cigarette burns may result in multiple small lesions in places on the skin that would not generally be exposed to danger. There may be other skin conditions that can cause similar patterns and expert paediatric advice should be sought.

Bites

Children can get bitten either by animals or humans. Animal bites (e.g. dogs) commonly puncture and tear the skin, and usually the history is definite. Small children can also bite other children.

Non-accidental

It is sometimes hard to differentiate between the bites of adults and children since measurements can be inaccurate. Any suspected adult bite mark must be taken very seriously. Consultant paediatricians may liaise with dental colleagues in order to identify marks correctly.

Poisoning

Children may commonly take medicines or chemicals that are dangerous and potentially life-threatening. Aspects of care and safety within the home need to be considered with each event.

Non-accidental

Non-accidental poisoning can occur and may be difficult to identify, but should be suspected in bizarre or recurrent episodes and when more than one child is involved. Drowsiness or hyperventilation may be a symptom.

Shaking violently

Shaking is a frequent cause of brain damage in very young children.

Fabricated/induced illness

This occurs where parents, usually the mother (according to current research and case experience), fabricate stories of illness about their child or cause physical signs of illness. This can occur where the parent secretly administers dangerous drugs or other poisonous substances to the child or by smothering. The symptoms that alert to the possibility of fabricated/induced illness include:

(i) symptoms that cannot be explained by any medical tests; symptoms never observed by anyone other than the parent/carer; symptoms reported to occur only at home or when a parent/carer visits a child in hospital;
(ii) high level of demand for investigation of symptoms without any documented physical signs;
(iii) unexplained problems with medical treatment, such as drips coming out or lines being interfered with; presence of unprescribed medication or poisons in the blood or urine.

5. Signs and symptoms of sexual abuse

Child sexual abuse often covers a wide spectrum of abusive activities. It rarely involves just a single incident and usually occurs over a number of years. Child sexual abuse most commonly happens within the family.

Cases of sexual abuse principally come to light through:

(a) disclosure by the child or his or her siblings/friends;
(b) the suspicions of an adult;
(c) physical symptoms.

Colburn Faller (1989) provides a description of the wide spectrum of activities by adults which can constitute child sexual abuse. These include:

Non-contact sexual abuse

- 'Offensive sexual remarks', including statements the offender makes to the child regarding the child's sexual attributes, what he or she would like to do to the child and other sexual comments.
- Obscene phone calls.
- Independent 'exposure' involving the offender showing the victim his/her private parts and/or masturbating in front of the victim.
- 'Voyeurism' involving instances when the offender observes the victim in a state of undress or in activities that provide the offender with sexual gratification. These may include activities that others do not regard as even remotely sexually stimulating.

Sexual contact

- Involving any touching of the intimate body parts. The offender may fondle or masturbate the victim, and/or get the victim to fondle and/or masturbate them. Fondling can be either outside or inside clothes. Also includes 'frottage', i.e. where offender gains sexual gratification from rubbing his/her genitals against the victim's body or clothing.

Oral-genital sexual abuse

- Involving the offender licking, kissing, sucking or biting the child's genitals or inducing the child to do the same to them.

Interfemoral sexual abuse

- Sometimes referred to as 'dry sex' or 'vulvar intercourse', involving the offender placing his penis between the child's thighs.

Penetrative sexual abuse, of which there are four types:

- 'Digital penetration', involving putting fingers in the vagina or anus, or both. Usually the victim is penetrated by the offender, but sometimes the offender gets the child to penetrate them.
- 'Penetration with objects', involving penetration of the vagina, anus or occasionally mouth with an object.
- 'Genital penetration', involving the penis entering the vagina, sometimes partially.
- 'Anal penetration' involving the penis penetrating the anus.

Sexual exploitation

- Involves situations of sexual victimisation where the person who is responsible for the exploitation may not have direct sexual contact with the child. Two types of this abuse are child pornography and child prostitution.
- 'Child pornography' includes still photography, videos and movies, and, more recently, computer-generated pornography.
- 'Child prostitution' for the most part involves children of latency age or in adolescence. However, children as young as 4 and 5 are known to be abused in this way.

The sexual abuses described above may be found in combination with other abuses, such as physical abuse and urination and defecation on the victim. In some cases, physical abuse is an integral part of the sexual abuse; in others, drugs and alcohol may be given to the victim.

It is important to note that physical signs may not be evident in cases of sexual abuse due to the nature of the abuse and/or the fact that the disclosure was made some time after the abuse took place.

Carers and professionals should be alert to the following physical and behavioural signs:

- bleeding from the vagina/anus;
- difficulty/pain in passing urine/faeces;
- an infection may occur secondary to sexual abuse, which may or may not be a definitive sexually transmitted disease. Professionals should be informed if a child has a persistent vaginal discharge or has warts/rash in genital area;
- noticeable and uncharacteristic change of behaviour;
- hints about sexual activity;
- age-inappropriate understanding of sexual behaviour;
- inappropriate seductive behaviour;
- sexually aggressive behaviour with others;
- uncharacteristic sexual play with peers/toys;
- unusual reluctance to join in normal activities that involve undressing, e.g. games/swimming.

Particular behavioural signs and emotional problems suggestive of child abuse in **young children (aged 0-10 years)** include:

- mood change where the child becomes withdrawn, fearful, acting out;
- lack of concentration, especially in an educational setting;
- bed wetting, soiling;
- pains, tummy aches, headaches with no evident physical cause;
- skin disorders;
- reluctance to go to bed, nightmares, changes in sleep patterns;
- school refusal;
- separation anxiety;
- loss of appetite, overeating, hiding food.

Particular behavioural signs and emotional problems suggestive of child abuse in **older children (aged 10+ years)** include:

- depression, isolation, anger;
- running away;
- drug, alcohol, solvent abuse;
- self-harm;
- suicide attempts;
- missing school or early school leaving;
- eating disorders.

All signs/indicators need careful assessment relative to the child's circumstances.

Appendix 2: National contacts for HSE Children and Family Services

Also listed on HSE website (www.hse.ie/go/socialworkers) and from HSE LoCall Tel. 1850 241850. These contact numbers may be updated from time to time. Please check HSE website for latest information.

HSE Area	Address	Telephone No.
DUBLIN NORTH	Health Centre, Cromcastle, Coolock, Dublin 5	(01) 816 4200 (01) 816 4244
DUBLIN NORTH CENTRAL	Social Work Office, 22 Mountjoy Square, Dublin 1	(01) 877 2300
	Social Work Office, Ballymun Health Centre, Dublin 11	(01) 846 7236
DUBLIN NORTH WEST	Health Centre, Wellmount Park, Finglas, Dublin 11	(01) 856 7704
	Social Work Department, Rathdown Road, Dublin 7	(01) 882 5000
DUBLIN SOUTH EAST	Social Work Department, Vergemount Hall, Clonskeagh, Dublin 6	(01) 268 0320 (01) 2680333
DUBLIN SOUTH CITY	Duty Social Work Carnegie Centre, 21-25 Lord Edward Street, Dublin 2	(01) 648 6555
	Public Health Nursing, 21-25 Lord Edward Street, Dublin 2	(01) 648 6730
	Family Support Service, 78B Church House, Donore Avenue, Dublin 8	(01) 416 4441
DUBLIN SOUTH WEST	Milbrook Lawn, Tallaght, Dublin 24	(01) 452 0666 (01) 427 5000
DUBLIN WEST	Social Work Department, Bridge House, Cherry Orchard Hospital, Ballyfermot, Dublin 10	(01) 620 6387
DUBLIN SOUTH	Social Work Department, Our Lady's Clinic, Patrick Street, Dun Laoghaire, Co. Dublin	(01) 663 7300
CARLOW	Carlow Social Work Office, Ground Floor, St. Dympna's Hospital, Athy Road, Co. Carlow	(059) 913 6587
CAVAN	HSE Community Child and Family Services, Drumalee Cross, Co. Cavan	(049) 437 7305 (049) 437 7306
CLARE	Clare Duty Social Worker, River House, Gort Road, Ennis, Co. Clare	(065) 686 3935 (Mon – Fri, 2pm - 5pm)
	Social Work Department, Shannon Health Centre, Shannon, Co. Clare	(061) 718 400
	Social Work Department, Kilrush Health Centre, Kilrush, Co. Clare	(065) 905 4200
CORK	North Cork Social Work Department, 134 Bank Place, Mallow, Co. Cork	(022) 54100
	North Lee Child Lee Social Work Department, (adjacent to Shopping Centre), Blackpool, Co. Cork	(021) 492 7000
	South Lee Social Work Department, St. Finbarr's Hospital, Douglas Road, Cork	(021) 492 3001
	West Cork Social Work Department, Coolnagarrane, Skibbereen, Co. Cork	(028) 40447
DONEGAL	Links Business Centre, Lisfannon, Buncrana, Co. Donegal (East Team)	(074) 932 0420
	Euro House, Killybegs Road, Donegal, Co. Donegal (West Team)	(074) 972 3540
	Social Work Department, Millennium Court, Pearse Road, Letterkenny, Co. Donegal (East Central Team and West Central Team)	(074) 912 3672 (074) 912 3770
GALWAY	Galway City, Social Work Department, Local Health Office, 25 Newcastle Road, Galway, Co. Galway	(091) 546366
	Galway County, Tuam Social Work Department, Health Centre, Vicar Street, Tuam, Co. Galway	(093) 37200
	Loughrea Social Work Department, Health Centre, Loughrea, Co. Galway	(091) 847820
	Ballinasloe Social Work Department, Health Centre, Brackernagh, Ballinasloe, Co. Galway	(090) 964 6200
	Oughterard Social Work Department, Health Centre, Oughterard, Co. Galway	(091) 552200

KERRY	Social Work Department, HSE Community Services, Rathass, Tralee, Co. Kerry Killarney Social Work Department, St. Margaret's Road, Killarney, Co. Kerry	(066) 712 1566 (064) 663 6030
KILDARE	Social Work Department, St Mary's Craddockstown Road, Naas, Co. Kildare	(045) 873200 (045) 882 400
KILKENNY	Social Work Office – Child Care Department, Child Youth and Families, Carlow/Kilkenny, HSE South, St. Canice's Hospital, Dublin Road, Kilkenny, Co. Kilkenny	(056) 778 4057 (056) 778 4532
LIMERICK	Social Work Department, Ballynanty Health Centre, Ballynanty, Limerick (East Team), Co. Limerick Social Work Department Roxtown Health Centre, Roxtown Terrace, Old Clare Street, Limerick (East Team) , Co. Limerick Parkbeg Social Work Department, Parkbeg House, 2 Elm Drive, Caherdavin Lawns, Ennis Road, Limerick, Co. Limerick Social Work Department, Southill Health Centre, O'Malley Park, Southill, Limerick, Co. Limerick Newcastlewest Social Work Department, Newcastlewest Health Centre, Newcastle West, Co. Limerick.	(061) 457 100 (061) 417 622 (061) 483 091 (061) 206 820 (061) 209 985 (069) 62155
LAOIS	Social Work Department, Child and Family Centre, Portlaoise, Co. Laois	(057) 869 2567 (057) 869 2568
LEITRIM	Social Work Department, Community Care Office, Leitrim Road, Carrick on Shannon, Co. Leitrim	(071) 965 0324
LONGFORD	Social Work Department, Tivoli House, Dublin Road, Co. Longford	(043) 335 0584
LOUTH	Social Work Department, Local Health Care Unit, Wilton House, Stapleton Place, Dundalk, Co. Louth Ballsgrove Health Centre, Ballsgrove, Drogheda, Co. Louth	(042) 939 2200 (041) 983 8574 (041) 983 3163
MAYO	Ballina Social Work Team, Ballina Health Centre, Mercy Road, Ballina, Co. Mayo Castlebar Social Work Team, St. Mary's Headquarters, Castlebar, Co. Mayo Swinford Social Work Team, Swinford Health Centre, Aras Attracta, Swinford, Co. Mayo	(096) 21511 (096) 248 41 (094) 902 2283 (094) 905 0133
MEATH	Community Social Work Services, Enterprise Centre, Navan, Co. Meath Community Social Work Services, Child and Family Centre, Navan, Co. Meath Community Social Work Services, Dunshaughlin Health Care Unit, Dunshaughlin, Co. Meath	(046) 909 7817 (046) 907 8830 (01) 802 4102
MONAGHAN	Social Work Department, Local Health Care Unit, Rooskey, Co. Monaghan	(047) 30426 (047) 30427
OFFALY	Social Work Department, Derry Suite, Castlebuildings, Tara Street, Tullamore, Co. Offaly	(057) 937 0700
ROSCOMMON	Social Work Team, Abbeytown House, Abbey Street, Roscommon, Co. Roscommon Social Work Team, Roscommon PCCC, Lanesboro' Road, Roscommon, Co. Roscommon (Roscommon Area) Social Work Team, Health Centre, Elphin Street, Boyle, Co. Roscommon (Boyle Area) Social Work Team, New HSE Offices, Knockroe, Castlerea, Co. Roscommon (Castlerea Area)	(090) 662 6732 (090) 663 7528 (090) 663 7529 (071) 966 2087 (090) 663 7851 (090) 663 7842

SLIGO	Sligo Town and surrounding areas: Markievicz House, Barrack Street, Sligo, Co. Sligo	(071) 915 5133
	South County Sligo: One Stop Shop, Teach Laighne, Humbert Street, Tubercurry, Co. Sligo	(071) 912 0062
NORTH TIPPERARY	North Tipperary Duty Social Work Team, Civic Offices, Limerick Road, Nenagh, Co. Tipperary	(067) 46 636
	North Tipperary Child Protection Services: Social Work Department, Annbrook, Nenagh, Co. Tipperary	(067) 41 934
	St. Mary's Health Centre, Parnell Street, Thurles, Co. Tipperary	(0504) 24 609
SOUTH TIPPERARY	South Tipperary Child Protection Services: Social Work Team, South Tipperary Community Care Services, Western Road, Clonmel, Co. Tipperary	(052) 617 7302 (052) 617 7303
WATERFORD	Waterford: Social Work Service, Waterford Community Services, Cork Road, Co. Waterford	(051) 842827
	Dungarvan and surrounding areas: Social Work Department, Dungarvan Community Services, St. Joseph's Hospital, Dungarvan, Co. Waterford	(058) 20906
WESTMEATH	Social Work Department, Athlone Health Centre, Coosan Road, Athlone, Co. Westmeath	(090) 648 3106
	Social Work Department, Child and Family Centre, St. Loman's, Springfield, Mullingar, Co. Westmeath	(044) 934 4877
WEXFORD	Gorey Health Centre, Hospital Grounds, Gorey, Co. Wexford	(053) 943 0100
	Enniscorthy Health Centre, Millpark Road, Enniscorthy, Co. Wexford	(053) 923 3465
	New Ross Health Centre, Hospital Grounds, New Ross, Co. Wexford	Contact through Ely House below
	Social Work Department, Ely House, Ferrybank, Co. Wexford	(053) 912 3522 Ext. 201
WICKLOW	Social Work Department, HSE Glenside Road, Wicklow Town, Co. Wicklow	(0404) 60800
	Bray: Social Work Department, The Civic Centre, Main Street, Bray, Co. Wicklow	(01) 274 4180 (01) 274 4100
	Delgany: Social Work Department, Delgany Health Centre, Delgany, Co. Wicklow	(01) 287 1482

Appendix 3: STANDARD REPORT FORM
for reporting child protection and/or welfare concerns to the HSE

FORM NUMBER: CC01:01:00

Feidhmeannacht na Seirbhíse Sláinte
Health Service Executive

STANDARD REPORT FORM

(For reporting CP&W Concerns to HSE)

A. To Principal Social Worker/Designate: ______________________

1. Date of Report	

2. Details of Child

Name:		Male	☐	Female	☐	
Address:		DOB		Age		
		School				
Alias		Correspondence address (if different)				

3. Details of Persons Reporting Concern(s)

Name:		Telephone No.	
Address:		Occupation:	
		Relationship to client:	
Reporter wishes to remain anonymous ☐		Reporter discussed with parents/guardians ☐	

4. Parents Aware of Report

	Yes	No
Are the child's parents/carers aware that this concern is being reported to the HSE?	☐	☐

5. Details of Report

(Details of concern(s), allegation(s) or incident(s) dates, times, who was present, description of any observed injuries, parent's view(s), child's view(s) if known.)

National Child Care Information System Project – Phase 3

FORM NUMBER: CC01:01:00

STANDARD REPORT FORM

(For reporting CP&W Concerns to HSE)

Feidhmeannacht na Seirbhíse Sláinte
Health Service Executive

6. Relationships

Details of Mother		**Details of Father**	
Name:		Name:	
Address: (if different to child)		Address: (if different to child)	
Telephone Nos.		Telephone Nos.	

7. Household composition

Name	**Relationship**	**DOB**	**Additional information, e.g. school/occupation/other**

8. Name and Address of other personnel or agencies involved with this child:

	Name	**Address**
Social Worker		
PHN		
GP		
Hospital		
School		
Gardaí		
Pre-School/Crèche/YG		
Other (*specify*):		

9. Details of person(s) allegedly causing concern in relation to the child

Relationship to child:		Age		Male	☐	Female	☐
Name:		Occupation:					
Address:							

10. Details of person completing form

Name:		Occupation:	
Signed		Date:	

Guidance Notes

The HSE has a statutory responsibility under the Child Care Act 1991 to promote the protection and welfare of children. The HSE therefore has an obligation to receive information about any child who is not receiving adequate care and/or protection.

This Report Form is for use by:

- Any professional, individual or group involved in services to children, including HSE personnel, who becomes aware of a child protection or welfare concern, or to whom a child protection or child welfare concern is reported.
- Professionals and individuals in the provision of child care services in the community who have service contracts with the HSE.
- Designated persons in a voluntary or community agency.

Please fill in as much information and detail as is known to you. This will assist the Social Work Department in assessing the level of risk to the child or the support services required. If the information requested is not known to you, please indicate this by putting a line through the question. It is likely that a social worker will contact you to discuss your report.

The HSE aims to work in partnership with parents. If you are making this report in confidence, you should note that the HSE cannot guarantee absolute confidentiality for the following reasons:

- A Court could order that information be disclosed.
- Under the Freedom of Information Act 1997, the Freedom of Information Commissioner may order that information be disclosed.

You should also note that in making a 'bona fide report', you are protected under the Protections for Persons Reporting Child Abuse Act 1998.

If you are unsure if you should report your concerns, please telephone the HSE duty social worker and discuss your concerns with them (*see Appendix 2 for a full list of HSE offices nationwide*).

Appendix 4:
STANDARD NOTIFICATION FORM for use by the HSE in notifying cases to An Garda Síochána

CONFIDENTIAL

____________________ HSE Local Health Office Area

____________________ Address

To: Superintendent
Garda Síochána
Address ____________________ Ref. No. ____________

NOTIFICATION OF SUSPECTED CHILD ABUSE

Child's Name ____________________

D.O.B. ____________________ Sex ____________________

Address ____________________

Father's Name ____________________ Mother's Name ____________________

1. The above named child has come to notice as a possible victim of child abuse.
2. Form(s) of abuse suspected:
   ☐ Neglect ☐ Physical Abuse ☐ Emotional Abuse* ☐ Sexual Abuse

   * All abuse involves an element of emotional ill-treatment; this category should be used where it is the main or sole form of abuse suspected.
3. Additional information ____________________

   ____

The Designated Social Worker dealing with this matter is:

Name ____________________ Tel. No. ____________________

Address ____________________

Signed ____________________ Date ____________________
Designated Officer

RETURN SLIP (to be returned to relevant HSE Local Health Office Area)

Garda ____________________ Garda Ref. No. ____________________

Address ____________________ Child's Name ____________________

I acknowledge receipt of your notification.

The Designated Garda assigned to this case is:

Name ____________________ Tel. No. ____________________

Address ____________________ Signed ____________________

Appendix 5:
STANDARD NOTIFICATION FORM for use by An Garda Síochána in notifying cases to the HSE

CONFIDENTIAL

Garda Síochána ______________________________ Ref. No. ____________

Address ____

To: Designated Officer

______________________________ HSE Local Health Office Area

______________________________ Address

NOTIFICATION OF SUSPECTED CHILD ABUSE

Child's Name ____

D.O.B. ______________________________ Sex ______________________________

Address ____

Father's Name ______________________________ Mother's Name ______________________________

1. The above named child has come to notice as a possible victim of child abuse.
2. Form(s) of abuse suspected:
   ☐ Neglect ☐ Physical Abuse ☐ Emotional Abuse* ☐ Sexual Abuse

   * All abuse involves an element of emotional ill-treatment; this category should be used where it is the main or sole form of abuse suspected.
3. Additional information ____

   ____

The Designated Garda dealing with this matter is:

Name ______________________________ Tel. No. ______________________________

Address ____

Signed ______________________________ Date ______________________________
Designated Officer

RETURN SLIP (to be returned to relevant Garda Station)

HSE Local Health Office Area ____

HSE Local Health Office Area Ref. No. ____

Address ______________________________ Child's Name ______________________________

I acknowledge receipt of your notification.

The Designated Social Worker allocated to this case is:

Name ______________________________ Tel. No. ______________________________

Address ______________________________ Signed ______________________________

Appendix 6:
RECORD OF GARDA – HSE LIAISON FORM

Feidhmeannacht na Seirbhíse Sláinte
Health Service Executive

Part 1

Record of Garda – HSE Liaison

Children First: National Guidance for Protection and Welfare of Children

HSE Notification No. ______________________

Date of receipt of Formal Notification (*Children First* – Appendix 4/Appendix 5) __________

Date of Informal Notification __________________

Child's Name ______________________________ D.O.B. ____________

Child's Address ____

____

____

Category of Abuse ____

____

Joint Action Team (*Children First* – Sections 7.2/7.3)

Designated Garda ________________ Garda Station ________________

Designated Social Worker ________________ HSE Office ________________

Liaison Management Team:

Garda Sergeant/Inspector ______________________________

Social Work Team Leader ______________________________

1

Part 2

Strategy Discussion on receipt of Notification

Day ____________ Date ______________ Time __________ Place ____________

Garda ______________________________

Social Worker _______________________

Date for Strategy meeting ______________________________________

Responsibility undertaken by ____________________________________ for seeing child.

Emergency Intervention Yes □ No □

Section 12 Child Care Act, 1991: Yes □ No □

If Yes, by whom exercised ________________________ Date exercised _____________

Reason for decision: ____

Emergency Care Order: Yes □ No □

Application made by _______________________ Date application made _____________

Reason for decision: ____

Forensic Evidence to be obtained: Yes □ No □

Scene
Who preserved scene ______________________ Date preserved ____________________

Reason for decision: ____

Person
Who took the evidence _____________________ Date evidence taken _______________

Reason for decision: ____

Change of clothing provided by: ____

Medical Examination required: * Yes □ No □

Garda contacted __________________________ Date and Time contacted ___________

Reason ____

** If Yes – Garda Forensic Evidence Sexual Offences Kit may be required.*

2

Part 3

Strategy Meeting (*Children First* – Section 5.7)

Convened by ______________________ HSE (*Children First* – Paragraph 5.7.2)

Who present ______________________ ______________________

______________________ ______________________

______________________ ______________________

______________________ ______________________

Location ____

Day/Date/Time ____

DECISIONS – (*Children First* – Paragraph 7.14.3). Complete as appropriate.

***Children First* Guidelines – Paragraph 5.7.4**	**Action**	**By whom action carried out**	**Reason for action**	**Date completion of action**	**Review by Liaison Management Team**
Information shared					
Immediate action to protect child or children					
Section 16(1)(b) Criminal Evidence Act, 1992 Interview					
Legal options					
Early interventions					

Part 3 *continued*

***Children First* Guidelines – Paragraph 5.7.4**	**Action**	**By whom action carried out**	**Reason for action**	**Date completion of action**	**Review by Liaison Management Team**
Protection/Supports for child					
Sources of information					
Further enquiries					
Agreed plan for remainder of enquiry					

Signed ______________________________ **Designated Garda**

Signed ______________________________ **Designated Social Worker**

If more than one strategy meeting, a new form at Part 3 to be completed in each case.

4

Part 4

Child Protection Conference

Convened by ______________________ HSE (*Children First* – Paragraph 5.8.3)

Who present ______________________ ______________________

______________________ ______________________

______________________ ______________________

______________________ ______________________

Location ____

Day/Date/Time ____

Key Worker ____

Child Protection Plan in place ____

Date for Review ____

Part 5

Liaison Management Meeting

Day/Date/ Time/Place	Progress review	Matters arising/ Decisions	Reasons for decisions	Signatures

Part 6

Closure of Record of Garda – HSE Liaison

DPP Decision: ______________________________

Court Date: ______________________________

Court Outcome: ______________________________

Reason for closure of Record of Garda – HSE Liaison:

____

____

____

Signed: ____________________ **Designated Garda**

Date: ____________________

Signed: ____________________ **Designated Social Worker**

Date: ____________________

Signed: ____________________ **Inspector/Sergeant – Liaison Management Team**

Date: ____________________

Signed: ____________________ **Team Leader – Liaison Management Team**

Date: ____________________

7

Appendix 7: Relevant Legislation

Children Act 2001

The Children Act 2001 replaced provisions of the Children Act 1908 and associated legislation with a modern comprehensive statute. The 2001 Act covers three main areas of the law. Firstly, and predominantly, it provides a framework for the development of the juvenile justice system. Secondly, it re-enacts and updates provisions in the 1908 Act protecting children against persons who have the custody, charge or care of them. Thirdly, it provides for family welfare conferences and other new provisions for dealing with children where there is a real and substantial risk to their life, health, safety, welfare and development.

Child Care Act 1991

The purpose of the Child Care Act 1991 is to 'update the law in relation to the care of children who have been assaulted, ill-treated, neglected or sexually abused, or who are at risk'. The main provisions of the Act are:

- (i) the placing of a statutory duty on the HSE to promote the welfare of children who are not receiving adequate care and protection up to the age of 18;
- (ii) the strengthening of the powers of the HSE to provide child care and family support services;
- (iii) the improvement of the procedures to facilitate immediate intervention by the HSE and An Garda Síochána where children are in danger;
- (iv) the revision of provisions to enable the Courts to place children who have been assaulted, ill-treated, neglected or sexually abused, or who are at risk, in the care of or under the supervision of the HSE;
- (v) the introduction of arrangements for the supervision and inspection of pre-school services;
- (vi) the revision of provisions in relation to the registration and inspection of residential centres for children.

Criminal Justice Act 2006

Section 176 of the Criminal Justice Act 2006 introduced the criminal charge of 'reckless endangerment of children'. It states:

'A person, having authority or control over a child or abuser, who intentionally or recklessly endangers a child by –

- (a) causing or permitting any child to be placed or left in a situation which creates a substantial risk to the child of being a victim of serious harm or sexual abuse, or
- (b) failing to take reasonable steps to protect a child from such a risk while knowing that the child is in such a situation, is guilty of an offence.'

The penalty for a person found guilty of this offence is a fine (no upper limit) and/or imprisonment for a term not exceeding 10 years.

Domestic Violence Act 1996

The Domestic Violence Act 1996 introduced major changes in the legal remedies for domestic violence. There are two main types of remedies available:

- (i) **Safety Order:** This Order prohibits a person from further violence or threats of violence. It does not oblige that person to leave the family home. If the parties live apart, the Order prohibits the violent person from watching or being in the vicinity of the home.
- (ii) **Barring Order:** This Order requires the violent person to leave the family home.

The legislation gives the HSE the power to intervene to protect individuals and their children from violence. Section 6 of the Act empowers the HSE to apply for Orders for which a person could apply on his or her own behalf but is deterred from doing so through fear or trauma. The consent of the victim is not a prerequisite for such an application, although he or she must be consulted. Under Section 7 of the Act, the Court may, where it considers it appropriate, adjourn proceedings and direct the HSE to undertake an investigation of the dependent person's circumstances with a view to:

- (i) applying for a Care Order or a Supervision Order under the Child Care Act 1991;
- (ii) providing services or assistance for the dependent person's family; or
- (iii) taking any other action in respect of the dependent person.

Protections for Persons Reporting Child Abuse Act 1998

This Act came into operation on 23 January 1999. The main provisions of the Act are:

- (i) the provision of immunity from civil liability to any person who reports child abuse 'reasonably and in good faith' to designated officers of the HSE or to any member of An Garda Síochána;
- (ii) the provision of significant protections for employees who report child abuse. These protections cover all employees and all forms of discrimination up to, and including, dismissal;
- (iii) the creation of a new offence of false reporting of child abuse, where a person makes a report of child abuse to the appropriate authorities 'knowing that statement to be false'. This is a new criminal offence, designed to protect innocent persons from malicious reports.

A wide range of nursing, medical, paramedical and other staff has been appointed as designated officers for the purposes of this Act (*see Appendix 10 of the Children First: National Guidance*). Section 6 of the Act is a saving provision, which specifies that the statutory immunity provided under the Act for persons reporting child abuse is additional to any defences already available under any other enactment or rule of law in force immediately before the passing of the Act.

Data Protection Acts 1988 and 2003

The Data Protection Act 1988 applies to the processing of personal data. It gives a right to every individual, irrespective of nationality or residence, to establish the existence of personal data, to have access to any such data relating to him or her, and to have inaccurate data rectified or erased. It requires data controllers to make sure that the data they keep are collected fairly, are accurate and up-to-date, are kept for lawful purposes and are not used or disclosed in any manner incompatible with those purposes. It also requires both data controllers and data processors to protect the data they keep, and imposes on them a special duty of care in relation to the individuals about whom they keep such data.

Education Act 1998

The Education Act 1998 places an obligation on those concerned with its implementation to give practical effect to the constitutional rights of children as they relate to education and, as far as practicable and having regard to the resources available, to make available to pupils a level and quality of education appropriate to meeting their individual needs and abilities.

Education (Welfare) Act 2000

The Education (Welfare) Act 2000, which was fully commenced in July 2002, replaced previous school attendance legislation and provided for the creation of a single national agency, the National Educational Welfare Board (NEWB), which has statutory responsibility to ensure that every child either attends school or otherwise receives an education or participates in training. The NEWB also assists in the formulation and implementation of Government education policy.

Non-Fatal Offences against the Person Act 1997

The two relevant provisions of this Act are:

- (i) it abolishes the rule of law under which teachers were immune from criminal liability in respect of physical chastisement of pupils;
- (ii) it describes circumstances in which the use of reasonable force may be justifiable.

Freedom of Information Acts 1997 and 2003

The Freedom of Information Acts 1997 and 2003 enable members of the public to obtain access, to the greatest extent possible consistent with the public interest and the right to privacy, to information in the possession of public bodies. The specific provisions of the Acts include:

- (i) to provide for a right of access to records held by such public bodies, for necessary exceptions to that right and for assistance to persons to enable them to exercise it;
- (ii) to enable persons to have corrected any personal information relating to them in the possession of such bodies;
- (iii) to provide for independent review by an Information Commissioner both of decisions of such bodies relating to that right and of the operation of the Acts generally;
- (iv) to provide for the publication by public bodies of guides to their functions and national guidelines, such as these, for the public.

Under the Acts, a person about whom a public body holds personal information has:

- (i) right of access to this information, subject to certain conditions;
- (ii) the right to correct this information if it is inaccurate.

Where a public body makes a decision that affects an individual, that individual has a right to relevant reasons and findings on the part of the body reaching that decision.

The Acts are also designed to protect the privacy of individuals and, in general, requires the prior consent of an individual before releasing personal information about them. Where the release of social work or medical records contains information that would be harmful to a person's well-being, the release may be made to a health professional who acts on the person's behalf. Under the Acts, there are regulations and guidelines relating to access by parents to their children's records; these emphasize that the overriding concern is the best interests of the child.

The exemptions and exclusions that are relevant to child protection include the following:

- (i) protecting records covered by legal professional privilege;
- (ii) protecting records that would facilitate the commission of a crime;
- (iii) protecting records that would reveal a confidential source of information.

Appendix 8: Guidance for developing local child protection and welfare procedures

In developing local guidelines, the **definitions, reporting procedure** and **guidance on confidentiality** (*as provided in Chapters 2 and 3 of the Children First: National Guidance*) **SHOULD NOT BE CHANGED OR ADAPTED IN ANY WAY**. This is because it is essential that there is **consistency** on definitions, the basis for reporting and the standard reporting procedure.

All organisations providing services to children when developing local procedures should ensure the following elements are included:

(i) clear descriptions of responsibility at local level, both individual and corporate;

(ii) organisation and management arrangements, as well as procedures for child protection, including arrangements for interagency cooperation;

(iii) expectations of best professional practice;

(iv) arrangements for training and support of staff;

(v) approach to family support and the involvement of the child.

Appendix 9: Guidance for employers dealing with an allegation of abuse

When an allegation of abuse is received, it should be assessed promptly and carefully by the employer. Action taken in reporting an allegation of child abuse against an employee should be based on an opinion formed 'reasonably and in good faith'. It will be necessary to decide whether a formal report should be made to the HSE Children and Family Services. This decision should be based on reasonable grounds for concern, as outlined in Chapter 3 of this national guidance.

The first priority is to ensure that no child is exposed to unnecessary risk. The employer should as a matter of urgency take any necessary protective measures. These measures should be proportionate to the level of risk and should not unreasonably penalise the employee, financially or otherwise, unless necessary to protect children. Where protective measures penalise the employee, it is important that early consideration be given to the case.

Any action taken should be guided by agreed procedures, the applicable employment contract and the rules of natural justice.

The head of the organisation should be informed about the allegation as soon as possible.

When an employer becomes aware of an allegation of abuse of a child or children by an employee during the execution of that employee's duties, the employer should privately inform the employee of the following:

(i) the fact that an allegation has been made against him or her;
(ii) the nature of the allegation.

The employee should be afforded an opportunity to respond. The employer should note the response and pass on this information if making a formal report to the HSE Children and Family Services.

Employers or persons-in-charge should take care to ensure that actions taken by them do not undermine or frustrate any investigations/assessments conducted by the HSE Children and Family Services or An Garda Síochána. It is strongly recommended that employers maintain a close liaison with the statutory authorities to achieve this.

Employers or persons-in-charge should be notified of the outcome of an investigation and/or assessment. This will assist them in reaching a decision about the action to be taken in the longer term concerning the employee.

The **Protections for Persons Reporting Child Abuse Act 1998** makes provision for the protection from civil liability of persons who have communicated child abuse 'reasonably and in good faith' to designated officers within the HSE (*see Appendix 10*) or to any member of An Garda Síochána. This protection applies to organisations as well as to individuals. This means that even if a communicated suspicion of child abuse proves unfounded, a plaintiff who took an action would have to prove that the person who communicated the concern had not acted reasonably and in good faith in making the report.

A person who makes a report in good faith and in the child's best interests may also be protected under common law by the defence of qualified privilege.

Appendix 10: List of HSE Designated Officers – Protections for Persons Reporting Child Abuse Act 1998

Please see Chapter 3, Paragraph 3.10.1 of the *Children First: National Guidance*

The Protections for Persons Reporting Child Abuse Act 1998 makes provision for the protection from civil liability of persons who have communicated child abuse 'reasonably and in good faith' to designated officers of the HSE or to any member of An Garda Síochána. The Chief Executive Officer of the HSE will appoint as designated officers each person falling within the following categories of officer of the HSE (details also available on HSE website, www.hse.ie):

Social Workers	Designated person within the HSE
Child Care Workers	Family Support Coordinators
Public Health Nurses	Family Support Workers
Hospital Consultants	Environmental Health Officers
Psychiatrists	Pre-school Services Inspectors
Non-Consultant Hospital Doctors	Childminder Coordinators
All other HSE Medical and Dental Personnel	Managers of Disability Services
Community Welfare Officers	Residential Care Managers/Residential Child Care Workers
Speech and Language Therapists	HIV and AIDS Services
All HSE Nursing Personnel	Counsellors in Services for AVPA
Psychologists	*Children First* Information and Advice Persons
Radiographers	*Children First* Implementation Officers
Physiotherapists	Quality Assurance Officers
Occupational Therapists	Advocacy Officers
Health Education/Health Promotion Personnel	Access Workers
Substance Abuse Counsellors	Project Workers
Care Assistants	Training and Development Officers

N-552-503

The Development of a National Set of Child Well-Being Indicators

EXECUTIVE SUMMARY

June 2005

The National Children's Office,
1st Floor, St. Martin's House, Waterloo Road, Dublin 4
Tel: 353 1 2420000 Fax: 353 1 6641929
Email: nco@health.gov.ie Website: www.nco.ie

68968

Design: Penhouse Design www.penhouse.ie
Printed by: New Oceans

LIBRARY I.T. CARLOW
ACC. NO. 68468 DATE 31/5/12
CLASS NO. 305.23109417 PRICE €10.00
VENDOR DAW

CONTENTS

01

ACKNOWLEDGEMENTS

DR. SINÉAD HANAFIN AND MS. ANNE-MARIE BROOKS, CO-DIRECTORS OF THE DEVELOPMENT OF THIS NATIONAL SET OF CHILD WELL-BEING INDICATORS, ARE GRATEFUL TO ALL THE PEOPLE WHO ASSISTED IN THE PROJECT. WE WERE FORTUNATE TO HAVE HAD AN ADVISORY GROUP WHO HELD CONSIDERABLE EXPERTISE IN DIFFERENT AREAS. THEIR WILLINGNESS TO SHARE THEIR EXPERIENCES AND KNOWLEDGE WITH US AND TO PROVIDE INSIGHTFUL GUIDANCE AT ALL TIMES WAS OF ENORMOUS BENEFIT IN UNDERTAKING THIS STUDY. THE MEMBERS OF THE ADVISORY GROUP WERE:

- DR. ED. CARROLL, INDEPENDENT RESEARCHER
- MS. DEIRDRE CULLEN, CENTRAL STATISTICS OFFICE
- MS. EITHNE FITZGERALD, NATIONAL DISABILITY AUTHORITY
- DR. MAEVE HENCHION, TEAGASC

WE WOULD ALSO LIKE TO THANK:

- MS. EITHNE FITZGERALD FOR HER WORK ON DATA SOURCES ON CHILDREN'S LIVES;
- DR. SAOIRSE NICGABHAINN AND MS. JANE SIXSMITH FOR THEIR CONTRIBUTION ON CHILDREN'S UNDERSTANDINGS OF WELL-BEING;
- MEMBERS OF THE PANEL OF EXPERTISE WHO GAVE FREELY OF THEIR TIME AND KNOWLEDGE;
- INDIVIDUALS AND ORGANISATIONS WHO PROVIDED SPECIFIC DETAILS ABOUT INDIVIDUAL INDICATOR AREAS; AND
- PEOPLE WHO PROVIDED TECHNICAL AND OTHER SUPPORT FOR THE STUDY.

03

1. INTRODUCTION

The identification of a national set of child well-being indicators to form the basis for the State of the Nation's Children report was identified as a key objective in the National Children's Strategy[1]. This objective reflects a growing national and international awareness of the need to understand and represent the complexity and multi-dimensional nature of children's lives in a way that is easily understood by different stakeholders[2].

A child well-being indicator is a measure that assesses well-being at 'a point in time, over time and across geographic areas and population groups'[3] (p.6). Ben-Arieh et al., drawing on the work of Adamson and Morrison, note that when used to their greatest potential, child well-being indicators *'enable societies to inform their policies, galvanise and reward effort, mark their achievement, introduce accountability and be a means by which sustained pressure can be brought to bear for the fulfilment of political promises'* (p.7)[2].

Although there was no overall policy focus on measuring child well-being in Ireland prior to National Children's Strategy[4], several important developments by individuals[5, 6, 7], agencies[8 - 11] and Government Departments [12 - 15] had already taken place. Their work, coupled with Ireland's participation in a number of international initiatives [16 - 20] and surveys[21, 22] to advance the measurement of child well-being has provided a basis on which a national set of child well-being indicators can now be developed.

The multi-dimensional nature of the work already undertaken highlights the complexity of the challenge in developing a national set of well-being indicators and supports the observation made by the National Statistics Board[23] that there is an increasing proliferation of indicators and a need for stakeholders to come to agreement about the most appropriate ones. Such a task however, is greatly complicated by the many different understandings of children and their lives and also by the many different understandings of well-being itself.

Well-being is not the preserve of any single discipline, professional group or sector and developments and understandings of well-being have been reported on in many different literatures, including, among others, economics, health, psychology and sociology[24, 25]. The various literatures have addressed different aspects of well-being and consequently different concerns have emerged[24-28]. Other difficulties have also arisen because of the ways in which different terms are used. Some authors use terms such as 'life satisfaction' and 'quality of life' interchangeably with 'well-being'[5, 6, 29-35], while others stress differences between them[36-39]. All of these issues combine to increase the levels of conceptual confusion that exist around this area[26].

This is also true of the literature and practice around children's lives where various groups, organisations and Government Departments, among others, have different foci, roles and responsibilities. Within the National Children's Strategy[1] however, a common conceptualisation of children's lives was presented and this 'whole child perspective' provides a unifying lens for understanding children's lives. The perspective recognises the child as an active participant in shaping their own lives and, takes as its starting point, a domain of the child's own capacity, which includes nine dimensions of children's development:

- physical and mental well-being;
- emotional and behavioural well-being;
- intellectual capacity;

- spiritual and moral well-being;
- identity;
- self care;
- family relationships;
- social and peer relationships; and
- social presentation.

These dimensions are manifested in different ways as children grow, develop and express themselves. Two other domains are also identified as important and these are 'formal and informal supports' and 'children's relationships'. The use of the 'whole child perspective' to underpin the development of a national set of child well-being indicators facilitated a broad and holistic understanding of children's lives and ensured that key principles, such as 'respect for the voice of the child', permeated every part of the process.

The definition of well-being used to guide this Study was that of Andrews et al.[40] who note that well-being is:

> **'healthy and successful individual functioning (involving physiological, psychological and behavioural levels of organisation), positive social relationships (with family members, peers, adult caregivers, and community and societal institutions, for instance, school and faith and civic organisations), and a social ecology that provides safety (e.g. freedom from interpersonal violence, war and crime), human and civil rights, social justice and participation in civil society.' (p.103)[40]**

This definition was used because the inclusion of many different dimensions of children's lives along with children's relationships and formal and informal supports meant it was coherent with the conceptualisation of the child as described in the 'whole child perspective'.

Recent developments in the field of child well-being measurement also provided some direction in this Study. Specifically, the need to recognise that:

- well-being goes beyond survival and it is important, therefore, to include indicators other than, for example, basic indicators on mortality or school enrolment[2, 41];
- well-being indicators that examine current well-being, such as play and recreation, in addition to 'well-becoming' indicators that examine future well-being, such as school completion rates, are important[2,42]; and
- well-being focuses on both positive as well as negative aspects of a child's life and refers to both objective conditions for well-being and to the subjective perceptions and experiences of the individual and indicators chosen should reflect this[43, 44].

An indicator set should have a manageable number of indicators, which adequately cover the wide range of issues associated with the topic[10, 45]. According to National Economic and Social Council[46], a small number of indicators are important for three reasons:

1. A SMALL NUMBER OF INDICATORS KEEPS THE PROJECT MANAGEABLE AND FOCUSED;
2. A SMALL NUMBER OF INDICATORS HAVE A GREATER CHANCE OF ACCEPTANCE IN THE POLICY ARENA AND AMONG THE POTENTIAL AUDIENCE OF POLICY MAKERS AND POLITICIANS; AND

3. A SMALL NUMBER OF INDICATORS, WHICH ARE READILY UNDERSTOOD, ARE MORE LIKELY TO BECOME PART OF A GENERALISED UNDERSTANDING (OF CHILD WELL-BEING) THAN A MORE EXHAUSTIVE LIST.

They suggest that the number of indicators within an indicator set should range between fifteen and twenty. Maryland Partnership for Children, Youth and Families in the United States[47] in developing their indicator set, noted that three to five indicators was usually accepted as a manageable number of indicators per domain of interest while the New Policy Institute[10] suggested that the total number of indicators should range between fifty to one hundred, with one hundred indicators reaching the absolute limits of manageability. Given the multiplicity of potential indicators to be included in the national set, a key challenge in this development was to identify the smallest number of indicators that would yield the most comprehensive representation of children's lives in Ireland.

07

2. METHODOLOGY

A multi-stage incremental approach was taken for the development of the national set of child well-being indicators and there were four main components. These were:

1. A BACKGROUND REVIEW OF INDICATOR SETS IN USE ELSEWHERE AND THE COMPILATION OF AN INVENTORY OF KEY INDICATORS, DOMAINS AND INDICATOR SELECTION CRITERIA[48];
2. A FEASIBILITY STUDY OF THE AVAILABILITY OF NATIONAL STATISTICS TO CONSTRUCT THE INDICATORS IDENTIFIED IN THE PREVIOUS STEP[4];
3. A STUDY ON CHILDREN'S UNDERSTANDINGS OF WELL-BEING[49]; AND
4. A CONSENSUS PROCESS REFERRED TO AS A DELPHI TECHNIQUE, WHERE PARTICIPANTS ON 'A PANEL OF EXPERTISE' AGREED INDICATORS FOR USE IN THE IRISH CONTEXT[50, 51].

A small Advisory Group (N = 4) was convened at the outset of the Delphi Study and each member was chosen for their capacity to provide expertise in a specific area.

A short synopsis of each component is now presented. A report on each, however, is available elsewhere and can be accessed through the National Children's Office website at www.nco.ie.

INVENTORY OF KEY INDICATORS, DOMAINS AND INDICATOR SELECTION CRITERIA

A systematic examination of eighty international, national and regional indicator sets resulted in the identification of more than 2,500 indicators for potential inclusion in the indicator set. An analysis of these indicator sets allowed for commonly used, and previously validated, indicators and domains of child well-being to be identified as well as key indicator selection critiera.

The analysis also highlighted a number of challenges in respect of identifying indicators capable of drawing international comparisons (due to different situations and different circumstances, references to country-specific systems and/or policies and variations in indicator definitions used across countries).

In some indicator sets, for example, local circumstance meant that 'the incidence of malaria' or 'the percentage of young people carrying guns to school' was important. These indicators however, clearly have less relevance to the Irish context.

In other indicator sets, wide variations in indicator definitions emerged. The threshold for poverty for example, was set by some at 50% of the median household income while for others it was set at 60%.

Other challenges also emerged particularly around the different age groupings used and because of the imbalance in the availability of data for all periods of childhood from infancy to adolescence, where a notable paucity of data for the middle childhood period emerged.

FEASIBILITY STUDY ON DATA SOURCES[4]

A Feasibility Study of the availability of national statistics to construct the indicators identified in the Inventory was commissioned and findings from this Study are included in a larger report published in 2004[4].

The aim of this Study was to identify indicators that could be readily compiled from data currently available in Ireland.

The results of this Study demonstrated that Ireland has good data, compiled to international standards, on population, employment status of parents, household living standards, and maternal and infant health. These can all be examined by the main social and demographic variables such as social group, family size, marital status and geographic area.

The results of this Study also showed the absence of qualitative data on childhood, on children's relationships, parenting styles and children's use of time. The absence is most acute in respect of younger children. In addition there are gaps in our information on children at risk, such as children in homes where there is domestic violence and children showing behavioural problems.

STUDY ON CHILDREN'S UNDERSTANDINGS OF WELL-BEING[49]

This Study was commissioned and explicitly designed to reflect Goal One of the National Children's Strategy, that of giving children a voice in matters that affect them.

The design of this Study, which used photography as a core method, incorporated individual level data collection, group level data analysis and feedback with a final group level integration process with children aged 8-19 years.

The findings of this Study demonstrated the breadth of perspective that children have on well-being; the centrality of inter-personal relationships with family and friends (including school friends); the importance of pets and animals in their lives; and the value of activities or things to do. A full description of the integration of the findings from this Study into the overall development is available elsewhere[50].

DELPHI STUDY[51]

The Delphi technique provided an over-arching mechanism for integrating data from the three previously described studies as well as enabling consensus to be achieved around the final set of child well-being indicators. The Delphi technique has been defined as a research approach used to gain consensus through a series of rounds of questionnaire surveys, usually two or three, where information and results are fed back to panel members between each round[52].

The main purpose of adopting a Delphi technique to decision-making is to provide a structured approach to collecting data in situations where the only available alternative may be an anecdotal or an entirely subjective approach[52]. A systematic review of empirical studies (N = 25) comparing the Delphi technique with standard interacting groups concluded, with some caution, that Delphi groups outperform groups in decision-making and forecasting[53].

A panel of expertise (Appendix 1) comprising policy-makers, service providers, researchers and parents (N = 87) were drawn together and we are grateful to the members of the Research Development Advisory Group (N = 18) at the National Children's Office who provided a starting point for this panel.

Three questionnaire rounds were undertaken and response rates varied between 70% and 87%. Additional consultation took place between the second and third questionnaire rounds with Government Departments, Agencies and other stakeholders in order to identify specific indicators for each key area prioritised by the panel of expertise (Appendix 2).

Almost 98% of participants in the Delphi Study indicated that they were satisfied (48%) or very satisfied (50%) with the approach used and this, coupled with the high response rates, is a reflection of the suitability of this approach to indicator set development.

Findings from each support Study were integrated into the Delphi Study as appropriate. Data from the Study of 'Children's Understandings of Well-Being', for example, were integrated at each questionnaire round and this Study was particularly useful for identifying the importance of pets and animals to child well-being. Findings from the scientific review of literature and Inventory were used to develop each questionnaire and to identify the selection criteria. Individual indicators for inclusion in the indicator set were also identified using the Inventory and this facilitated a focused consultation with Government Departments, Agencies and other stakeholders between rounds two and three. The Feasibility Study on data sources ensured the best possible data source was identified in the course of indicator selection.

11

3. NATIONAL SET OF CHILD WELL-BEING INDICATORS

The agreed indicator set comprises forty-two child well-being indicators and seven socio-demographic indicators, which will be used to contextualise children's lives in Ireland. Some key areas have more than one indicator and this reflects the advice given from relevant stakeholders. More than 90% of participants in the Delphi Study indicated they were satisfied with the overall indicator set.

Specific indicators were chosen using the following guiding selection criteria:

- rigorous methods;
- geographically detailed;
- cost efficient; and
- international comparability.

Other selection criteria were applied to the overall indicator set and participants were asked to indicate whether they agreed that these selection criteria had been met. These criteria included:

- comprehensiveness;
- children of all ages;
- clear;
- positive and negative;
- reflective of social goals;
- objective and subjective; and
- well-being and well-becoming.

There was agreement by more than 80% of participants that the indicator set met all the selection criteria and this level of agreement was above 90% for all but two criteria. These criteria were 'children of all ages' and 'well-being and well-becoming'.

In respect of the selection criteria 'children of all ages', 15% (N = 8) of participants in the third round questionnaire felt there were insufficient measures for the middle childhood period. While this is a problem that besets indicator sets in many other countries, we are committed to further development in this area in order to address this gap. Issues raised in respect of 'well-being and well-becoming' primarily related to the key areas around which indicators remain to be developed. These are:

- pets and animals;
- the quality of early childhood care and education;
- values and respect; and
- nutritional outcomes.

Work is already underway in this regard. Other indicators in the indicator set require further development including, for example, the measure of 'public expenditure on services for children and young people', which currently takes account of expenditure on education only and the measure of 'breastfeeding', which currently takes account of breastfeeding initiation rates only.

We recognise therefore, that despite the comprehensiveness of this approach, the systematic nature of the development and the integration of children's voices within the process, the developed indicator set is but the first step in the process of ensuring that the lives of children living in Ireland are measured in a comprehensive and multi-dimensional way. This indicator set will be reviewed periodically to ensure it reflects changing policy interests, scientific views and advances in our national statistical systems.

The agreed national set of child well-being indicators along with the data sources used to compile and construct the indicators is now presented. The indicators requiring further development are also highlighted. These indicators require significant work, either to formulate an appropriate definition or create an appropriate data source, before they can be measured.

CHILD WELL-BEING INDICATORS

Abuse and Maltreatment

Definition: The number of children referred to the Child Protection Notification System, expressed as a proportion of all children. This can be sub-divided by the most serious types of harm: a) physical; b) emotional; c) sexual; and d) neglect

Source: Child Care Interim Data Set, Department of Health and Children

Definition: The number of children subject to substantiated notification, expressed as a proportion of all children. This can be sub-divided by the most serious types of harm: a) physical; b) emotional; c) sexual; and d) neglect

Source: Child Care Interim Data Set, Department of Health and Children

Accessibility of Basic Health Services for Children and Young People

Definition: The number of children on hospital waiting lists for in-patient admission, expressed as a proportion of all children

Source: Health Services National Performance Indicators, Department of Health and Children

Attendance at School

Definition: The number of children who are absent from school for 20 days or more in the school year, expressed as a proportion of all children

Source: Education Welfare Board Database, National Education Welfare Board

Availability of Housing for Families with Children

Definition: The number of children in families on a local authority housing waiting list, expressed as a proportion of all children

Source: Housing Needs Assessments published in the Quarterly Bulletin on Housing Statistics, Department of the Environment, Heritage and Local Government

Children and Young People in Care

Definition: The number of children who are in the care of the Health Services Executive (HSE), expressed as a proportion of all children. This can be sub-divided by the types of care arrangement: a) foster care - general; b) foster care - special; c) foster care - relatives; d) pre-adoptive placement; e) residential - general; f) residential - special; g) at home under care order; and h) other

Source: Child Care Interim Data Set, Department of Health and Children

Chronic Health Conditions and Hospitalisation

Definition: The ten most frequent conditions resulting in hospitalisation among children

Source: Hospital In-Patient Enquiry Statistics, Economic and Social Research Institute

Community Characteristics

Definition: The number of children aged 11, 13 and 15 who report to feel safe in the area where they live, expressed as a proportion of children in the same age groups

Source: Health Behaviour of School-Aged Children Survey, National University of Ireland, Galway

Crimes Committed by Children and Young People

Definition: The number of children referred to the Garda Juvenile Liaison Programme, expressed as a proportion of all children

Source: Annual Report, An Garda Siochana

Economic Security

Relative Poverty:

Definition: The number of children living in households with a household income below the national 60% median, equivalised using the modified OECD equivalence scale, expressed as a proportion of all children

Source: European Union Survey on Income and Living Conditions, Central Statistics Office

Consistent Poverty:

Definition: The number of children living in households with a household income below the national 70% median, equivalised using the modified OECD equivalence scale and experiencing basic deprivation, expressed as a proportion of all children

Source: European Union Survey on Income and Living Conditions, Central Statistics Office

Enrolment in Childhood Care and Education

Definition: The number of children under 13 in various early childhood care and education arrangements expressed as a proportion of all children in the same group. This can be sub-divided into: a) pre-school; b) compulsory school; c) centre-based care outside school hours; d) crèche or day-care; e) professional childminder; and f) family relative

Source: European Union Survey of Income and Living Conditions, Central Statistics Office

Enrolment in Education/Completion of School

Definition: The number of children who leave school (voluntarily or by exclusion) before the statutory school leaving age, expressed as a proportion of all children

Source: Post-Primary Pupil Database, Department of Education and Science

Environment and Places

Definition: The number of children aged 11, 13 and 15 who report that there are good places in their area to spend their free time, expressed as a proportion of children in the same age groups

Source: Health Behaviour of School-Aged Children Survey, National University of Ireland, Galway

Health of the Infant at Birth

Definition: The number of births within each 500g-weight interval, expressed as a proportion of all registered live and stillbirths. This can be sub-divided into: a) healthy birth weight (between 2,500 and 4,000 grams); b) low birth weight (less than 2,500 grams); and c) high birth weight (more than 4,000 grams)

Source: National Perinatal Reporting System, Economic and Social Research Institute
Definition: The distribution of timing of first antenatal visit by trimester of pregnancy for all women delivering live or stillborn babies. Trimesters are as follows: a) 1st trimester =< 15 weeks; b) 2nd trimester = 15 - 27 weeks; and c) 3rd trimester = 28 weeks or more

Source: National Perinatal Reporting System, Economic and Social Research Institute

Immunisation

Definition: The percentage uptake of D3/P3/T3/Hib3/Polio3 and Meningococcal C3 vaccinations at: a) 12 months; b) 24 months of age

Source: Immunisation Uptake Statistics for Ireland, National Disease Surveillance Centre

Definition: The percentage uptake of MMR1 vaccinations at 24 months of age

Source: Immunisation Uptake Statistics for Ireland, National Disease Surveillance Centre

Mental Health

Definition: The number of children referred to child and adolescent mental health services, expressed as a proportion of all children.

Source: Health Service Executive Statistics, Health Services Executive

Definition: The number of suicides among children in age categories 10-14, 15-17 and in total, expressed as a proportion of all children in the same age groups

Source: Vital Statistics, Central Statistics Office

Nutrition

Eating habits:

Definition: The number of children aged 11, 13 and 15 who report eating breakfast five or more days per week, expressed as a proportion of all children in the same age groups

Source: Health Behaviour of School-Aged Children Survey, National University of Ireland, Galway

Feeding practice:

Definition: The number of newborn babies who are: a) exclusively breastfed and; b) partially breastfed throughout the first 48 hours of age, expressed as a proportion of all newborn babies (to be developed further)

Source: National Perinatal Reporting System, Economic and Social Research Institute

Nutritional outcomes:

Definition: To be developed

Source: To be developed

Parental Time with Children

Definition: The number of children aged 15 who report that their parents: a) discuss how well they are doing at school; b) eat a main meal with them around a table; and c) spend time just talking with them more than once a week, expressed as a proportion of children in the same age group

Source: Programme for International Student Assessment Survey, Education Research Centre, Drumcondra

Participation in Decision-Making

Definition: The number of children aged 11, 13 and 15 who report that students at their school participate in making the school rules, expressed as a proportion of children in the same age groups

Source: Health Behaviour of School-Aged Children Survey, National University of Ireland, Galway

Pets and Animals

Definition: To be developed

Source: To be developed

Public Expenditure on Services for Children and Young People

Definition: Public expenditure on education as a percentage of GDP (to be developed further)

Source: Tuarascáil Staitistiúil, Department of Education and Science

Quality of Childhood Care and Education

Definition: To be developed

Source: To be developed

Relationship with Parents and Family

Definition: The number of children aged 11, 13 and 15 who report that they find it easy or very easy to talk with their: a) mother; and b) father when something is really bothering them, expressed as a proportion of all children in the same age groups

Source: Health Behaviour of School-Aged Children Survey, National University of Ireland, Galway

Relationships with Peers

Definition: The number of children aged 11, 13 and 15 who report to having been bullied at school, expressed as a proportion of children in the same age groups

Source: Health Behaviour of School-Aged Children Survey, National University of Ireland, Galway

Definition: The number of children aged 11, 13 and 15 who report to have three or more friends of the same gender, expressed as a proportion of children in the same age groups

Source: Health Behaviour of School-Aged Children Survey, National University of Ireland, Galway

Screening for Growth and Development

Definition: The percentage of mothers of new born children contacted by a Public Health Nurse (PHN) within 48 hours of hospital discharge

Source: Health Services National Performance Indicators, Department of Health and Children

Definition: The percentage uptake of developmental screening at seven to nine months

Source: Health Services National Performance Indicators, Department of Health and Children

Self-Esteem

Definition: The number of children in age categories 8-11 and 12-17 who report feeling happy with the way they are, expressed as a proportion of all children in the same age groups

Source: KIDSCREEN, Programme of Action for Children

Self-Reported Happiness

Definition: The number of children aged 11, 13 and 15 who report being happy with their life at present, expressed as a proportion of children in the same age groups

Source: Health Behaviour of School-Aged Children Survey, National University of Ireland, Galway

Sexual Health and Behaviour

Definition: The number of births to females in age categories 10-14 and 15-17 and in total, expressed as a proportion of all children in the same age groups

Source: Vital Statistics, Central Statistics Office

Things to Do

Definition: The number of children aged 11, 13 and 15 who report to be physically active for: a) at least two hours; and b) more than four hours per week, expressed as a proportion of children in the same age groups

Source: Health Behaviour of School-Aged Children Survey, National University of Ireland, Galway

Definition: The number of children aged 15 who report that reading is one of their favourite hobbies, expressed as a proportion of children in the same age group

Source: Programme for International Student Assessment Survey, Education Research Centre, Drumcondra

Use of Tobacco, Alcohol and Drugs

Definition: The number of children aged 11, 13 and 15 who report to smoke cigarettes: a) every day; and b) every week, expressed as a proportion of children in the same age groups

Source: Health Behaviour of School-Aged Children Survey, National University of Ireland, Galway

Definition: The number of children aged 15 who report to have had five or more alcoholic drinks in a row at least once in the last 30 days, expressed as a proportion of children in the same age group

Source: European Schools Project on Alcohol and Drugs Survey, St. Patrick's College, Drumcondra

Definition: The number of children aged 15 who report to have used any illicit drugs in their lifetime, expressed as a proportion of children in the same age groups. This can be sub-divided by type of drug used

Source: European Schools Project on Alcohol and Drugs Survey, St. Patrick's College, Drumcondra

Values and Respect

Definition: To be developed

Source: To be developed

SOCIO-DEMOGRAPHIC INDICATORS

Child Population

Definition: The number of children under 18, expressed as a proportion of the total population

Source: Census of the Population, Central Statistics Office

Family Structure

Definition: The number of children under 18 who live in family household units with only one parent or primary caregiver resident, expressed as a proportion of all children

Source: Census of the Population, Central Statistics Office

Parental Education Level Attained

Definition: The number of children under 18 whose parents have attained: a) primary; b) lower secondary; c) upper secondary; and d) third level education, expressed as a proportion of all children

Source: Census of the Population, Central Statistics Office

Child Mortality

Definition: The number of deaths among children under 18, expressed as a proportion of all children. This may be sub-divided by principal cause of death

Source: Vital Statistics, Central Statistics Office

Children and Young People with Additional Needs

Definition: The number of children under 18 registered as having an intellectual disability, expressed as a proportion of all children. This can be sub-divided by grade of disability: a) mild; b) moderate; c) severe; and d) profound

Source: National Intellectual Disability Database, Health Research Board

Definition: The number of children under 18 recorded as having a physical or sensory disability, expressed as a proportion of all children

Source: Census of the Population, Central Statistics Office

Definition: The number of: a) children seeking asylum, alone or as part of a family; b) non-national children; c) homeless children; and d) traveller children, expressed as a proportion of all children

Source: Census of the Population, Central Statistics Office and Child Care Interim Data Set, Department and Children

19

4. REFERENCES

1 **National Children's Strategy (2000)** *Our Children – Their Lives.* Dublin: The Stationery Office.

2 **Ben-Arieh, A., Hevener-Kaufman, N., Bowers-Andrews, A., Goerge, R.M., Joo-Lee, B. and Aber, J.L. (2001)** *Measuring and Monitoring Children's Well-Being.* Dordrecht, the Netherlands: Kluwer Academic Publishers.

3 **Moore, K.A. (1999)** *'Indicators of Child and Family Well-Being: The Good, the Bad and the Ugly'.* A Presentation to National Institutes of Health Office of Behavioural and Social Sciences Research.

4 **Fitzgerald, E. (2004)** *Counting Our Children: An Analysis of Official Data Sources on Children and Childhood in Ireland.* Dublin: Children's Research Centre, University of Dublin, Trinity College.

5 **Carroll, E. (2002)** *The Well-Being of Children: Four Papers Exploring Conceptual, Ethical and Measurement Issues.* Dublin: Irish Youth Foundation.

6 **McKeown K., Haasse, T. and Pratschke, J. (2001)** *Springboard: Promoting Family Well-Being Through Family Support Services.* Dublin: Department of Health and Children.

7 **McKeown, K., Pratschke, J. and Haase, T. (2003)** *Family Well-Being: What Makes a Difference.* Shannon: The Ceifin Centre.

8 **Costello, L. (1999)** *A Literature Review of Children's Well-Being.* Dublin: Combat Poverty Agency.

9 **Nolan, B. (2000)** *Child Poverty in Ireland.* Dublin: Combat Poverty Agency.

10 **New Policy Institute (2001)** *Poverty Reduction Indicators: A Discussion Paper.* Dublin: Combat Poverty Agency.

11 **Quinlan, A., Greally, T., Heslin, J., Nicholson, A., O'Reilly, C., O'Sullivan, M., Pelly, H. and Thornton, L. (2001)** *Towards the Development of Health Indicators for Irish Children.* Dublin: Best Health for Children.

12 **Department of Health and Children (2000)** *Child Care Interim Minimum Dataset.* Dublin: Department of Health and Children.

13 **Department of Health and Children (2001)** *The Health of Our Children: The Second Annual Report of the Chief Medical Officer.* Dublin: The Stationery Office.

14 **Department of Health and Children (2002a)** *Traveller Health: A National Strategy 2002-2005.* Dublin: The Stationery Office.

15 **Department of Health and Children (2002b)** *Health Services National Performance Indicators.* Dublin: Department of Health and Children.

16 **Rigby, K. and Kohler, L. (eds.)(2002)** *Child Health Indicators of Life and Development.* Luxembourg: European Commission.

17 **Kohler, L. and Rigby, M. (2003)** 'Indicators of Children's Development: Considerations When Constructing a Set of National Child Health Indicators for the European Union'. *Child: Care Health and Development,* 29 (6): 551-558.

18 **Zeitlin, J. and Wildman, K. (2003)** *PERISTAT: Indicators for Monitoring and Evaluating Perinatal Health in Europe.* Luxembourg: European Commission. Available at: http://europa.eu.int/comm/health/ph_projects/2000/monitoring/fp_monitoring_2000_frep_07_en.pdf [Accessed: 3rd August 2004].

19 **Zeitlin, J., Wildman, K., Bréart, G., Alexander, S., Barros, H., Blondel, B., Buitendijk, S., Gissler, M., MacFarlane, A. and the PERISTAT Scientific Advisory Committee (2003b)** 'PERISTAT: Indicators for Monitoring and Evaluating Perinatal Health in Europe'. *European Journal of Public Health,* 13 (3): 29-37.

20 **Zeitlin, J., Wildman, K., Bréart, G., Alexander, S., Barros, H., Blondel, B., Buitendijk, S., Gissler, M. and MacFarlane, A. (2003c)** 'Selecting an Indicator Set for Monitoring and Evaluating Perinatal Health in Europe: Criteria, Methods and Results from the PERISTAT Project'. *European Journal of Obstetrics and Gynaecology,* 111: S5-S14.

21 **Kelleher, C., Nic Gabhainn, S., Friel, S., Corrigan, H., Nolan, G., Sixsmith, J., Walsh, O. and Cooke, M. (2003)** *The National Health and Lifestyle Surveys* (II) *Survey of Lifestyle, Attitudes and Nutrition (SLÁN)* and the *Irish Health Behaviour in School-Aged Children Survey (HBSC).* Dublin: Department of Health and Children.

22 **Cosgrove, J., Shiel, G., Sofroniou, N., Zastrutzki, S. and Shortt, F. (2003)** *The OECD PISA 2003 Assessment of Mathematics, Reading literacy, Science and Cross-Curricular Problem Solving. Brief Summary of Key Findings for Ireland.* Dublin: Educational Research Centre. www.erc.ie/pisa/P03SummaryBrief.pdf [Accessed: 24th March 2005].

23 **National Statistics Board (2003)** *Developing Irish Social and Equality Statistics to Meet Policy Needs: Report of the Steering Group on Social and Equality Statistics.* Dublin: The Stationery Office.

24 **Pollard, E.L. and Lee, P. (2002)** 'Child Well-Being: A Systematic Review of the Literature'. *Social Indicators Research,* 61: 59-78.

25 **Bornstein, M.H., Davidson, L., Keyes, C.L.M., Moore, K. and the Centre for Child Well-Being (eds.) (2003)** *Well-Being: Positive Development Across the Life Course.* Mahwah, New Jersey: Lawrence Erlbaum Associates Publishers.

26 **Acton, G. (1994)** 'Well-Being as a Concept for Theory, Practice and Research'. *Online Journal of Knowledge Synthesis for Nursing,* 1-11.

27 **Gill, T.M. and Feinsten, A.R. (1994).** In Holmes, S. (2004) 'Assessing the Quality of Life: Reality or Impossible Dream?' *International Journal of Nursing Studies* (in press).

28 **Holmes, S. (2004)** 'Assessing the Quality of Life: 'Reality or Impossible Dream?' *International Journal of Nursing Studies* (in press).

29 **Dasgupta, P. (1999)** *Valuation and Evaluation: Measuring the Quality of Life and Evaluating Policy.* Stockholm: University of Cambridge and Beijer International Institute of Ecological Economics.

30 **Jensen, W., Myers, J., Sidorova, M., Duerr, M., Cragle, S., Brisolara, S., Berryhill, M., Lapp, B., Kehoe, D.A., Reed, B., Skillman, D.R., Englesby-Smith, J. and Wayda, M. (2002)** *Indicators of Well-Being Report: Shasta County Children Pre-Natal to Five and their Families.* Shasta County: First 5 Shasta, the Shasta Children and Family First Commission. Available at: http://www.ccfc.ca.gov/shasta/PDFs/Well-BeingRpt.pdf [Accessed: 3rd August 2003].

31 **Easterlin, R.A. (2003)** *Building a Better Theory of Well-Being.* Bonn, Germany: Institute of the Study for Labour.

32 **Smith, A.E. (2000)** 'Quality of Life: A Review'. *Education and Ageing,* 15 (3): 419-435.

33 **Strappazzon, L. (2001)** *Indicators of Well-Being: A Framework.* Paper Presented to the 45th Annual Australian Agricultural and Resource Economics Conference, Adelaide, January 2001.

34 **Treasury Board of Canada Secretariat (2000)** *Quality of Life: A Concept Paper: Defining, Measuring and Reporting Quality of Life for Canadians.* Ottawa: Treasury Board of Canada Secretariat.

35 **Veenhoven, R. (2000)** 'The Four Qualities of Life: Ordering Concepts and Measures of the Good Life'. *Journal of Happiness,* 1: 1-39.

36 **Gasper, D. (2004a)** *Human Well-Being: Concepts and Conceptualisations.* Discussion Paper No. 2004/06. Helsinki, Finland: United Nations University.

68968

[37] **Gasper, D. (2004b)** *Conceptualising Human Needs and Well-Being.* Paper for the International Workshop on Researching Well-Being in Developing Countries, Hanse Institute for Advanced Study, Delmenhorst, Germany, July 2004. Swindon: Economic and Social Research Council (ESRC) Research Group on Well-Being in Developing Countries.

[38] **Diener, E. (1984)** In Rask, K., Astedt-Kurki, P. and Paavilainen, E. (2003) 'Adolescent Subjective Well-Being and Family Dynamics'. *Scandinavian Journal of Caring Science,* 17: 129-138.

[39] **Ferrans, C.E. (1990)** In Holmes, S. (2004) 'Assessing the Quality of Life: Reality or Impossible Dream?' *International Journal of Nursing Studies* (in press).

[40] **Andrews, A., Ben-Arieh, A., Carlson, M., Damon, W., Dweck, C., Earls, F., Garcia-Coll, C., Gold, R., Halfon, N., Hart, R., Lerner, R.M., McEwen, B., Meaney, M., Offord, D., Patrick, D., Peck, M., Trickett, B., Weisner, T. and Zuckerman, B. (Ecology Working Group) (2002)** *Ecology of Child Well-Being: Advancing the Science and the Science-Practice Link.* Georgia: Centre for Child Well-Being.

[41] **Aber, L.J. and Jones, S. (1997)** *'Indicators of Positive Development in Early Childhood: Improving Concepts and Measures'.* In Hauser, R.M., Brown, B.V. and Prosser, W.R. (eds.) *Indicators of Children's Well-Being.* New York: Russell Sage Foundation.

[42] **Qvortrup, J. (1997)** *'Indicators of Childhood and the Intergenerational Dimension',* In Ben-Arieh, A. and Wintersberger, H. (eds.) (1997) *Monitoring and Measuring the State of Children - Beyond Survival.* Vienna: European Centre for Social Welfare Policy and Research.

[43] **Pollard, E.L., Davidson, L. and the Centre for Child Well-Being (2001)** *Action Research in Family and Early Childhood: Foundations of Child Well-Being.* Paris: UNESCO.

[44] **Moore, K.A. (1995)** *New Social Indicators of Child Well-Being.* Vienna: European Centre for Social Welfare Policy and Research.

[45] **Hogan, C. (2002)** In Reidy, M. and Winje, C. (2002) *Proceedings of the HHS ASPE State Youth Indicators Technical Assistance Workshop for States, Washington DC, April 2002.* Chicago: Chapin Hall Centre for Children, University of Chicago.

[46] **National Economic and Social Council (2002)** *National Progress Indicators for Sustainable Economic, Social and Environmental Development.* Dublin: National Economic and Social Council.

[47] **Maryland Partnership for Children, Youth and Families (2002)** *Maryland's Results for Well-Being.* Baltimore, Maryland: Maryland Partnership for Children, Youth and Families.

[48] **Brooks, A.M. and Hanafin, S. (2005)** *Measuring Child Well-Being: An Inventory of Key Indicators, Domains and Indicator Selection Criteria to Support the Development of a National Set of Child Well-Being Indicators.* Dublin: The Stationery Office.

[49] **NicGabhainn, S. and Sixsmith, J. (2005)** *Children's Understandings of Well-Being.* Dublin: The Stationery Office.

[50] **Hanafin, S. and Brooks, A.M. (2005a)** *The Delphi Technique: A Methodology to Support the Development of a National Set of Child Well-Being Indicators.* Dublin: The Stationery Office.

[51] **Hanafin, S. and Brooks, A.M. (2005b)** *The Development of a National Set of Child Well-Being Indicators.* Dublin: The Stationery Office.

[52] **Linstone, H.A. and Turoff, M. (eds.) (1975)** The *Delphi Method Techniques and Applications.* Massachusetts, Reading: Addison-Wesley.

[53] **Rowe, G. and Wright, G. (1999)** 'The Delphi Technique as a Forecasting Tool: Issues and Analysis'. *International Journal of Forecasting,* 15 353-375.

APPENDIX 1

PEOPLE INVITED TO TAKE PART ON THE PANEL OF EXPERTISE

Ms. Margaret Rogers	Barnardos
Ms. Liz Leonard	Barnardos
Mr. Heino Schonfeld	Centre for Early Childhood Development and Education
Dr. Saoirse NicGabhainn	Centre for Health Promotion Studies, National University of Ireland, Galway
Dr. Noírín Hayes	Centre for Social and Educational Research, Dublin Institute of Technology
Prof. Patricia Noonan-Walsh	Centre for the Study of Developmental Disabilities, University College Dublin
Ms. Mary Hargaden	Childcare Policy Unit, Department of Health and Children
Ms. Mary O'Connor	Children in Hospital Ireland
Mr. Ray Dooley	Children's Rights Alliance
Prof. Robbie Gilligan	Children's Research Centre, University of Dublin, Trinity College
Dr. Jean Whyte	Children's Research Centre, University of Dublin, Trinity College
Dr. Jim Walsh	Combat Poverty Agency
Ms. Catriona Dwan	Community Worker
Dr. Nollaig Byrne	Department of Child and Family Psychiatry, Mater Misericordiae Hospital, Dublin
Ms. Breda Naughton	Department of Education and Science
Mr. Gerry Hayes	Department of Justice, Equality and Law Reform
Ms. Sylda Langford	Department of Justice, Equality and Law Reform
Ms. Eiméar Fisher	Department of Justice, Equality and Law Reform
Mr. Frank Martin	Department of Law, National University of Ireland, Cork
Dr. Ursula Kilkelly	Department of Law, National University of Ireland, Cork
Dr. Anthony Staines	Department of Public Health and Epidemiology, University College Dublin
Mr. Heber McMahon	Department of Social and Family Affairs
Mr. Michael Rush	Department of Social Policy and Social Work, University College Dublin
Dr. Valerie Richardson	Department of Social Policy and Social Work, University College Dublin
Ms. Valerie O'Brien	Department of Social Policy and Social Work, University College Dublin
Dr. Helen Buckley	Department of Social Studies, University of Dublin, Trinity College
Dr. Colette McAuley	Department of Social Work, Queens University, Belfast
Dr. Rebecca King-O'Riain	Department of Sociology, National University of Ireland, Maynooth
Ms. Elaine Kelly	Department of the Taoiseach
Ms. Yvonne O'Neill	Eastern Regional Health Authority
Prof. Brian Nolan	Economic and Social Research Institute
Dr. Joan Hanafin	Education Department, National University of Ireland, Cork
Dr. Peter Archer	Education Research Centre, St. Patrick's College, Drumcondra
Ms. Liz Kerrins	End Child Poverty Coalition
Mr. Pat Bennett	Family Support Agency
Mr. Niall O'Baoill	Fatima Groups United
Ms. Olive McGovern	Health Promotion Unit, Department of Health and Children
Ms. Breda Cleary	Institute of Community Health Nursing
Mr. Owen Metcalfe	Institute of Public Health in Ireland
Ms. Frances Fletcher	Intellectual Disability Services, Department of Health and Children
Ms. Irene Gunning	IPPA, the Early Childhood Organisation
Ms. Catherine Carthy	Irish Association of Young People in Care

Dr. Ailis Ní Riain	Irish College of General Practitioners
Mr. Sean Cottrell	Irish Primary Principals Network
Ms. Michele Clarke	Irish Social Services Inspectorate
Mr. Paul Gilligan	Irish Society for the Prevention of Cruelty to Children
Mr. Liam O'Dwyer	Irish Youth Foundation
Ms. Margaret Burns	Jesuit Centre for Faith and Justice
Dr. Barney O'Reilly	Kerry Education Service
Ms. Liz O'Sullivan	Kildare Youth Service
Dr. Anne Good	National Disability Authority
Ms. Sarah Craig	National Economic and Social Forum
Mr. Feargal O'Neill	National Educational Psychological Service
Ms. Anne Colgan	National Parents Council
Ms. Christine McMaster	North Western Heath Board
Mr. Seamus McLoughlin	Department of Education and Science
Ms. Geraldine Brereton	One Family, The National Association of Single Parent Families
Ms. Maeve Crosbie	Parent
Ms. Ria Williams	Parent
Mr. Jim Symons	Parent
Ms. Breda Sammon	Parent
Ms. Carol Purcell	Parent
Ms. Janey Troy	Parent
Dr. Paula Byrne	Parent
Mr. David Brooks	Parent
Ms. Sandra Cahill	Parent
Ms. Susan Kenna	Parent
Ms. Deirdre Lynch	Parent
Mr. Kieran Ryan	Parent
Ms. Catríona de Bourca	Parent
Ms. Anna-May Harkin	Planning and Evaluation Unit, Department of Health and Children
Mr. Pat Dolan	Political Science and Sociology, National University of Ireland, Galway
Dr. Sean Denyer	Programme of Action for Children
Ms. Celia Keenaghan	Programme of Action for Children
Dr. Eilish Hennessy	Psychology Department, University College Dublin, Trinity College
Dr. Diane Hogan	Psychology Department, University of Dublin
Ms. Margaret Casey	Queen of Angels National School
Ms. Rosemary Horgan	Ronan Daly Jermyn Solicitors
Mr. Kieran McKeown	Social and Economic Research Consultant
Dr. John Pinkerton	Social Work Department, Queens University, Belfast
Dr. Deirdre Murray	South Eastern Health Board
Ms. Ann Godfrey	Southern Health and Social Services Board, Northern Ireland
Ms. Elizabeth Burke	Southern Health Board
Ms. Anne Halliday	St. John of God Kildare Services
Ms. Hilary Kenny	Trainer/ Consultant
Sr. Frances Murphy	Warrenmount Presentation Secondary School
Mr. Dermot Stokes	Youthreach

APPENDIX 2

LIST OF GOVERNMENT DEPARTMENTS, AGENCIES AND STAKEHOLDERS

Government Departments:

- Department of Education and Science
- Department of Health and Children
- Department of Justice, Equality and Law Reform
- Department of Social and Family Affairs
- Department of Community, Rural and Gaeltacht Affairs
- Department of the Environment, Heritage and Local Government

Agencies and Stakeholders:

- An Garda Síochana
- Centre for Early Childhood Development and Education
- Central Statistics Office
- Combat Poverty Agency
- Economic and Social Research Institute
- Irish Social Services Inspectorate
- Mental Health Commission
- National Advisory Council on Drugs
- National Alcohol Advisor
- National Breastfeeding Co-ordinator
- National Disability Authority
- National Disease Surveillance Centre
- National Education Welfare Board
- National Juvenile Office
- National Nutrition Surveillance Centre
- National Treatment Purchase Fund
- Programme of Action for Children

APPENDIX 3

OVERVIEW OF THE MAIN DATA SOURCES

Title:	Census of the Population
Source:	Central Statistics Office (www.cso.ie)
Description:	Population statistics including housing, employment, education and family structure.
Frequency:	Every five years
Title:	Childcare Interim Data Set
Source:	Department of Health and Children (www.doh.ie)
Description:	Statistics on children in care or at risk.
Frequency:	Annual
Title:	Education Welfare Board Database
Source:	National Education Welfare Board (www.newb.ie)
Description:	Statistics on children absent from school twenty or more days.
Frequency:	Annual
Title:	European Schools Project on Alcohol and Drugs (ESPAD) Survey
Source:	St. Patrick's College, Drumcondra (www.spd.dcu.ie)
Description:	European survey of the behaviours, knowledge and beliefs concerning cigarettes, alcohol, solvents and illegal drugs among 15-year-old children.
Frequency:	Every four years
Title:	European Union Survey on Income and Living Conditions (EU-SILC)
Source:	Central Statistics Office (www.cso.ie)
Description:	European survey on income, living conditions and basic deprivation.
Frequency:	Annual
Title:	Garda Annual Report
Source:	An Garda Siochana (www.garda.ie)
Description:	Crime statistics including arrests and diversions to the Garda Juvenile Liaison Programme.
Frequency:	Annual
Title:	Health Behaviour of School-Aged Children (HBSC) Survey
Source:	National University of Ireland, Galway (www.nuig.ie)
Description:	International survey of the health behaviours of 11-, 13-, and 15-year-old children covering areas such as general health, food and nutrition, exercise and alcohol consumption and children's perceptions of happiness.
Frequency:	Every four years
Title:	Health Services National Performance Indicators
Source:	Department of Health and Children (www.doh.ie)
Description:	Statistics on health and healthcare services including mental health, child and adolescent health and child care.
Frequency:	Annual
Title:	Hospital In-Patient Enquiry (HIPE)
Source:	Economic and Social Research Institute (www.esri.ie)
Description:	Statistics on hospital stays including date of birth, gender, marital status, medical card status, diagnosis, procedure and length of stay.
Frequency:	Annual

Title: Housing Needs Assessments published in the Quarterly Bulletin on Housing Statistics.
Source: Department of the Environment, Heritage and Local Government (www.environ.ie)
Description: Statistics on families on housing lists and homelessness.
Frequency: Every three years

Title: National Intellectual Disability Database
Source: Health Research Board (www.hrb.ie)
Description: Statistics on those with an intellectual disability (mild, moderate, severe and profound) in receipt of, or on a waiting list for, specialist services.
Frequency: Annual

Title: KIDSCREEN
Source: Programme of Action for Children (www.hse.ie)
Description: European survey of the Health-Related Quality of Life of 8-11-year-old and 12-17-year-old children.
Frequency: Currently being piloted

Title: National Disease Surveillance Statistics
Source: National Disease Surveillance Centre (www.ndsc.ie)
Description: Statistics on infectious diseases and vaccinations.
Frequency: Quarterly

Title: National Perinatal Reporting System
Source: Economic and Social Research Institute (www.esri.ie)
Description: Demographic statistics including stillbirths, perinatal and maternal deaths, mother and fathers' date of birth, nationality, occupation and marital status and basic clinical information including birth weight, period of gestation, type of feeding and congenital anomalies for every birth.
Frequency: Annual

Title: Post-Primary Pupil Database
Source: Department of Education and Science (www.education.ie)
Description: Statistics on pupil participation and retention rates.
Frequency: Annual

Title: Programme for International Student Assessment (PISA) Survey
Source: Education Research Centre, St. Patrick's College, Drumcondra (www.erc.ie)
Description: International survey of reading, mathematics and science achievement of 15-year old children.
Frequency: Every three years

Title: Tuarascáil Staitistiúil
Source: Department of Education and Science (www.education.ie)
Description: Statistics on schools and examinations.
Frequency: Annual

Title: Vital Statistics
Source: Central Statistics Office (www.cso.ie)
Description: Statistics on births, marriages, deaths.
Frequency: Quarterly

W-552-502

The Delphi Technique:
A Methodology to Support the Development of a National Set of Child Well-being Indicators

Sinéad Hanafin
Anne-Marie Brooks
June 2005

The National Children's Office,
1st Floor, St. Martin's House, Waterloo Road, Dublin 4
Tel: 353 1 2420000 Fax: 353 1 6641929
Email: nco@health.gov.ie Website: www.nco.ie

68962

Design: Penhouse Design www.penhouse.ie
Printed by: New Oceans

LIBRARY I.T. CARLOW
ACC. NO. 68962 DATE 31/5/12
305·23109417 PRICE €10·00
CLASS NO.
VENDOR DON

CONTENTS

01

DATE .... ACC NO. ....
PRICE .... CLASS NO. ....
VENDOR ....

TABLE OF TABLES

TABLE OF FIGURES

03

ACKNOWLEDGEMENTS

WE ARE GRATEFUL TO ALL THE PEOPLE WHO ASSISTED IN THE DEVELOPMENT OF THE NATIONAL SET OF CHILD WELL-BEING INDICATORS AND WOULD PARTICULARLY LIKE TO THANK:

- MS. EITHNE FITZGERALD FOR HER WORK ON DATA SOURCES ON CHILDREN'S LIVES;
- DR. SAOIRSE NIC GABHAINN AND MS. JANE SIXSMITH FOR THEIR CONTRIBUTION ON CHILDREN'S UNDERSTANDINGS OF WELL-BEING
- MEMBERS OF THE PANEL OF EXPERTISE WHO GAVE FREELY OF THEIR TIME AND KNOWLEDGE;
- INDIVIDUALS AND ORGANISATIONS WHO PROVIDED SPECIFIC DETAILS ABOUT INDIVIDUAL INDICATOR AREAS; AND
- PEOPLE WHO PROVIDED TECHNICAL AND OTHER SUPPORT FOR THE STUDY.

WE WERE FORTUNATE TO HAVE HAD AN ADVISORY GROUP WHO HELD CONSIDERABLE EXPERTISE IN DIFFERENT AREAS. THEIR WILLINGNESS TO SHARE THEIR EXPERIENCES AND KNOWLEDGE WITH US AND TO PROVIDE INSIGHTFUL GUIDANCE AT ALL TIMES WAS OF ENORMOUS BENEFIT IN UNDERTAKING THIS STUDY. THE MEMBERS OF THE ADVISORY GROUP WERE:

- DR. ED. CARROLL: INDEPENDENT RESEARCHER
- MS. DEIRDRE CULLEN: CENTRAL STATISTICS OFFICE
- MS. EITHNE FITZGERALD: NATIONAL DISABILITY AUTHORITY
- DR. MAEVE HENCHION: TEAGASC

05

1.0 INTRODUCTION

The Delphi technique is a research approach used to gain consensus through a series of rounds of questionnaire surveys, usually two or three, where information and results are fed back to panel members between each round. The first part of this report provides an overview of the Delphi technique as a research methodology. Key aspects of the Delphi technique including its origins, classifications, paradigmatic assumptions, purposes, advantages and disadvantages are explored. The second part of the report uses seven systematically identified studies, undertaken elsewhere, to rationalise options around key areas of contention. Specific areas for consideration here are: aims and objectives, sample selection, data collection, analysis and statistical interpretation, consensus, credibility, reliability and validity, and finally, ethical issues. Decisions taken in respect of the current Study, which had as its aim, achieving consensus around the development of a national set of child well-being indicators, are highlighted throughout.

1.1 OVERVIEW OF DELPHI TECHNIQUE

Delphi as a research methodology has been variously presented as a survey (Wang et al., 2003), procedure (Rogers and Lopez, 2002), method (Linstone and Turoff, 1975; Crisp et al., 1997) and technique (Broomfield and Humphries, 2001; Sharkey and Sharples, 2001; Snyder-Halpern, 2002; Campbell et al., 2004; Iavicoli et al., 2005). Here we refer to Delphi as a 'technique' because this appears to be the most commonly used terminology in the research literature. The Delphi technique is named after the ancient Greek oracle at Delphi who offered visions of the future to those who sought advice (Gupta and Clarke, 1996, p.185). There is general agreement that it was first used in technology forecasting studies initiated by the Research and Development (RAND) Corporation for the American military in 1944 (Gupta and Clarke, 1996). Since that time, it has become a popular way of harnessing opinion from people with expertise, although the technique itself and the purposes for which it has been used have been extensively modified by researchers over the years (Gupta and Clarke, 1996; Crisp et al., 1997).

Most authors draw on all (Wang et al., 2003) or some (Gupta and Clarke, 1996; Robertson and Mackinnon, 2002) of the definition set out by Linstone and Turoff (1975) who define the Delphi technique as:

> **'a method for structuring a group communication process so that the process is effective in allowing a group of individuals, as a whole, to deal with a complex problem'**
>
> (Linstone and Turoff, 1975, p.3).

This definition was used to provide methodological guidance for the development of a national set of child well-being indicators.

1.2 TYPES OF DELPHI

A number of different types of 'Delphi' studies have been identified. Indeed, Gupta and Clarke (1996) note that 'practitioners are often willing, and sometimes even eager, to modify Delphi' (Gupta and Clarke, 1996, p.189). They conclude that while some modifications are useful, others are random and undermine both the quality and credibility of the technique. Hasson et al. (2000) reports that 'Modified Delphi', 'Policy Delphi' and 'Real-time Delphi' have all been used, although the following categorisation, described by van Zolingen and Klaasen (2003), has broad appeal:

The Classical Delphi: This type of study is characterised by five features. They are: anonymity, iteration, controlled feedback, statistical group response and stability in responses among those with expertise on a specific issue. Participants in this type of Delphi have expertise and give opinions to arrive at stability in responses on specific issues.

The Policy Delphi: The aim in this situation is not to reach stability in responses among those with expertise but to generate policy alternatives by using a structured public dialogue. Here the Delphi is an instrument for policy development and promoting participation by obtaining as many divergent opinions as possible. It is characterised by 'selective anonymity', iteration, controlled feedback, polarised group response and structured conflict. Selective anonymity may mean that participants answer questions individually but may also come together in a group meeting.

The Decision Delphi: This type of Delphi is used for decision-making on social developments. Reality is created by a group of decision-makers rather than from the ad-hoc decision of only a small number of persons. Crucial to this type is the fact that decision-makers involved in the problem participate in the Delphi. They are selected according to their position in the hierarchy of decision-makers and the aim is to structure thinking so that consensus can be achieved. The characteristics are 'quasi-anonymity' (where people with expertise are mentioned by name and known to everybody from the beginning although questionnaire responses are anonymous).

> In this Study, the Delphi technique was used to structure thinking around key areas of child well-being so that consensus could be achieved with respect to a national set of child well-being indicators. This Study, therefore, adopted the approach of a 'Decision Delphi'.

1.3 PARADIGMATIC ASSUMPTIONS

Some consideration is given here to the assumptions underpinning the Delphi technique. On first examination, it appears that the epistemological basis for the Delphi technique favours the positivist paradigm. Such a paradigm assumes the position of the researcher within the research to be that of an objective and uninvolved observer (Robson, 1993) and it could be argued that this is the case for the Delphi technique. The objectivist position in the Delphi technique is supported through the utilisation of a quantitative approach to data collection and the application of single statistical measures to the identification of 'consensus'. The inclusion of 'experts' assumes an ontological position of single reality (that 'experts' agree on) and the reductionist approach to identification of the phenomenon under study could also be understood as adhering to positivistic principles (Blackburn, 1999; Monti and Tingen, 1999). Others, however, present the Delphi technique as subjective and qualitative in nature (Fitzsimmons and Fitzsimmons, 2001) and we present the case for this understanding below.

The aim of employing a Delphi technique is to achieve consensus through a process of iteration. The process itself is concerned with opinions, ideas and words (Stewart, 2001) and it is suggested here that the purpose of the methodology (to achieve consensus through group interaction) is in keeping with an interpretative paradigm. Group interaction in research is generally underpinned by an assumption that an individual's attitudes and beliefs do not form in a vacuum and that people need to take account of others' attitudes and understandings so that they can focus on their own (Marshall and Rossman, 1995; Reed and Roskell, 1997). Within an interpretative paradigm, there can be many differing paradigms including, for example, post-positivism, critical theory, constructivism and participatory/cooperative paradigm (Lincoln and Guba, 2000). Within this, constructivism, and particularly social constructivism, appears to have most to offer in terms of understanding the epistemological basis for the Delphi technique. Lincoln and Guba (1985), writing about constructivism as a research paradigm, for example, write that:

> **'Researchers in a variety of disciplines in the social sciences have been and are grappling with social constructivist approaches wherein the contribution of each individual in the context to the creation of a reality is recognised'**
> (Lincoln and Guba, 1985, p.82).

A key advantage of the Delphi technique is the potential it holds to recognise and acknowledge the contribution of each participant, and this was central to the development of a national set of child well-being indicators. While Schwandt (2000) writes that we are all constructivists if we believe that the mind is active in the construction of knowledge, social constructivists generally subscribe to an exogenic tradition of knowledge. Here the focus 'is on the arrangement of environmental inputs necessary to build up the internal representation' rather than on the person's intrinsic capacities for reason, logic or conceptual processing (Gergen, 1995, p.18). Within the Delphi technique, a process of individual feedback about group opinion with opportunities for respondents to change their position primarily on the basis of that feedback, provides a close fit with the assumptions set out above.

On the basis of the foregoing discussion, it is difficult to draw clear conclusions about paradigmatic assumptions underpinning all Delphi studies since it is reasonably clear that certain parts of the technique are more coherent with a constructivist paradigm and others more coherent with that of positivism. In this Study, we sought to achieve individual reconstructions that coalesced around consensus through providing opportunities for knowledgeable participants to interact with each other in a structured way. We were also committed to an ontological assumption of multiple realities.

> Consequently, we believed that social constructivism had something to offer to our understanding of Delphi and we therefore, underpinned the Study with features closely associated with that paradigm.

1.4 PURPOSE OF DELPHI TECHNIQUE

The main purpose of adopting a Delphi technique to decision-making is to provide a structured approach to collecting data in situations where the only available alternative may be an anecdotal or an entirely subjective approach (Broomfield and Humphries, 2001). The features of anonymity, iteration with controlled feedback, statistical group response and expert input can facilitate consensus where there is contradictory or insufficient information to make effective decisions (Linstone and Turoff, 1975; Goodman, 1987; Hasson et al., 2000; Snyder-Halpern, 2002). Other group approaches to reaching consensus were examined but were found to be less appropriate to the development of a set of national child well-being indicators. These included, for example, nominal groups (Carney et al., 1996), brain-storming (Hasson et al., 2000), focus groups (Morgan, 1997), analytic hierarchy process (AHP) technique (Lai et al., 2002) as well as the establishment of working groups. The main disadvantages with each of the above techniques was their risk of taking account only of the perceptions of the most outspoken or opinionated members of that group, or of only focusing on interesting or controversial elements (Fein et al., 1997).

The Delphi technique as a methodology has been in use for almost sixty years and the types of situations where it can be useful have been well described. Although some methodological issues remain outstanding, it is noted that the Delphi technique has been found to be particularly useful in the following situations:

1. WHERE A PROBLEM DOES NOT PERMIT THE APPLICATION OF PRECISE ANALYTICAL TECHNIQUES BUT CAN BENEFIT FROM SUBJECTIVE JUDGMENTS ON A COLLECTIVE BASIS;
2. WHERE THE RELEVANT SPECIALISTS ARE IN DIFFERENT FIELDS AND OCCUPATIONS AND NOT IN DIRECT COMMUNICATION;
3. WHERE THE NUMBER OF SPECIALISTS IS TOO LARGE TO EFFECTIVELY INTERACT IN A FACE-TO-FACE EXCHANGE AND TOO LITTLE TIME AND/OR FUNDS ARE AVAILABLE TO ORGANISE GROUP MEETINGS; AND
4. WHERE ETHICAL OR SOCIAL DILEMMAS DOMINATE ECONOMIC OR TECHNICAL ONES (LINSTONE AND TUROFF, 1975; GUPTA AND CLARKE, 1996).

It was clear in developing a national set of child well-being indicators that understandings could be significantly influenced by the particular area of expertise, experience or occupational position of a participant. There were therefore significant benefits in being able to harness subjective judgments of participants. Delphi technique has been found to be an appropriate mechanism for ensuring that emergent differences between, and within, key stakeholder groups (that can arise from differences in focus, situation and context) can be accounted for in a systematic way. The number of relevant people with expertise appeared too large to interact in a meaningful way through face-to-face exchange despite the very strong case for representation of as high a number of views as possible. Indeed, it was difficult to envisage a more appropriate way in which direct communication between the multiplicity of stakeholders concerned with child well-being could be facilitated.

1.5 ADVANTAGES OF ADOPTING A DELPHI TECHNIQUE

An overarching aim of the Delphi technique is to achieve consensus and, while further discussion of its conceptual basis takes place later in this paper, we understood consensus here to mean 'a general agreement' (Thompson, 1995) 'in constructing a hierarchy and making judgments' (Lai et al., 2002, p.135). It has been reported that the capacity of a group to reach consensus is influenced by:

- A tendency of low status group members to 'go along with' the opinion of group members with a higher status;
- A tendency of a group to exert pressure on its members to conform; and
- A tendency of a dominant group member to exert undue influence on the opinion of the group (Gupta and Clarke, 1996; Fein et al., 1997; van Zolingen and Klaassen, 2003).

Arising from these, the most obvious advantage of guaranteed anonymity in responding to questions is that it is likely to encourage opinions that are free of influences from others and are therefore more likely to be 'true' (Goodman, 1987; Snyder-Halpern, 2002). It has been suggested that anonymity encourages people with expertise to make statements on the basis of their personal knowledge and experience rather than a more 'cautious institutional position' (Gupta and Clarke, 1996, p.186). By adopting an iterative approach to data collection through questionnaires and feedback, however, the 'collective human intelligence capability' found in groups of people with expertise can be harnessed (Linstone and Turoff, 1975).

Other advantages relate to the use of questionnaires that have the capacity to capture a wide range of interrelated variables and multi-dimensional features (Gupta and Clarke, 1996) and enable a geographically dispersed group of experts to provide their understandings (Rogers and Lopez, 2002). Participants can complete the questionnaire at their leisure and this both reduces time pressures and allows for more reflection and contemplation of response (Linstone and Turroff, 1975). This, in turn, may increase the number and quality of contributions and can decrease respondent burden by allowing input at the participant's convenience. Snyder-Halpern (2002) summarises the 'primary' advantages of the Delphi technique as:

> **'(i)ts adaptability to diverse data collection strategies, decreased peer pressure secondary to anonymity and the ease of condensing opinions of many and varied experts into a few precise statements'**
>
> (Snyder-Halpern, 2002, p.185).

1.6 DISADVANTAGES OF ADOPTING A DELPHI TECHNIQUE

Disadvantages of the Delphi technique have also been identified and authors have questioned the reliability, validity and credibility of this research methodology. Sackman (1975), for example, has noted that anonymity may lead to a lack of accountability because response may not be traced back to the individual. In addition, it has been suggested that a consensus approach can lead to a diluted version of the best opinion and the result represents the 'lowest common denominator' (Powell, 2003, p.378). It could be argued, however, that all approaches (for example, working groups, nominal groups) to gaining consensus run this risk. Others have argued that this approach is time-consuming, labour-intensive and, therefore, expensive (Fitzsimmons and Fitzsimmons, 2001) although there is not agreement about this (Powell, 2003). A number of methodological issues arising in respect of Delphi have the capacity to threaten the credibility of the Study and these include issues around panel expertise, number of rounds, questionnaire development, analysis and achievement of consensus. These issues are considered in detail in Part Two of this document and decisions taken in respect of each with regard to this Study are highlighted.

1.7 SUMMARY

To summarise, the Delphi technique is a research approach to gaining consensus through the utilisation of questionnaires and the provision of feedback to participants who have expertise in key areas. While there are many potential types of Delphi techniques, three broad categories are generally in use and these are: classical, policy and decision. In this development, a 'decision Delphi' approach was employed. Advantages and disadvantages of the Delphi technique can be complementary. The adoption of an anonymous approach to data collection, for example, can facilitate positional openness but it may, at the same time, lead to a lack of accountability. The potential to harness a wide variety of views about different variables and across geographical areas has greater appeal than other alternatives, which may involve face-to-face interaction but, in doing so, some nuances may be lost. On balance, we considered that the advantages of this approach outweighed the disadvantages for our particular situation.

Some consideration has been given to the epistemological basis of the Delphi technique and, while the literature around this area is conflicting, we are suggesting here that many of its assumptions in terms of purpose and process are in keeping with that of social constructivism. Consequently, we understand the 'decision Delphi' technique to be primarily situated within an interpretative paradigm and this provided guidance for us in undertaking the Study.

Figure 1 provides a summary of the main elements of the Study undertaken in the development of a national set of child well-being indicators. Components included are panel composition and expertise, number of rounds and outcomes

Figure 1: Key Elements of the Study

2.0 OVERVIEW

Key issues of contention relating to the use of a Delphi technique in the development of a national set of child well-being indicators are now considered using material from Delphi studies undertaken (n = 7) elsewhere on indicator development. These issues are situated within the context of the aims and objectives, conceptual framework and key methodological challenges arising in the development of a national set of child well-being indicators. Particular attention is paid to the identification of expertise, number of rounds, consensus, questionnaire development and data collection, analysis and mechanisms for ensuring credibility in the current Study. Conclusions reached and actions taken in respect of this Study are highlighted.

Seven studies are used throughout this section to rationalise options selected, particularly where contentious issues arise. These studies were chosen in a systematic way using the principles of mini-review set out by Griffiths et al. (2002). The papers were identified through database searches of Medline (1966-2003), Embase (1980 - 2003), Cinahl (1982-2003), Eric (1988-2003), Social Work Abstracts (1977-2003) and Econlit (1988-2003) using two key words, 'Delphi' and 'indicator'. Because of the large number of abstracts generated (more than 3,000 in one database alone), it was necessary to place limitations on the material and these are identified below. Criteria for inclusion were that the study:

1. FOCUSED ONLY ON INDICATOR DEVELOPMENT;
2. REPORTED ON THE RESEARCH ITSELF;
3. PUBLISHED IN ENGLISH; AND
4. PUBLISHED FROM 1995.

A bibliographic review published in 1995 (Gupta and Clarke, 1996) reported that the three most popular areas for Delphi applications were health, education and business. Consequently, in identifying studies for illustrative purposes, we took random examples from health (Cambell et al., 2000; Wang et al., 2003; Schuster et al., 1997), education (Rogers and Lopez, 2002; van Zolingen and Klaasen, 2003) and business (Miller, 2001; Snyder-Halpern, 2002). This facilitated maximum variability across different disciplines, an important factor given the diverse backgrounds of the participants in this Study.

We accept that the criteria used for final inclusion of studies has limitations in respect of the material identified but we are, nevertheless, reasonably confident that the papers identified were sufficiently comprehensive to provide an overview of key issues. Table 1 sets out the main elements of each of the key studies.

Table 1: Overview of Key Studies

	AUTHOR	MAIN FOCUS	FOCUS
1	Campbell et al. (2000)	'Prescribing' indicators for general practice	Health
2	Rogers and Lopez (2002)	Cross-cultural school psychology competencies	Education
3	Schuster et al. (1997)	Quality of health care measures for children and adolescents	Health
4	Van Zolingen and Klaassen (2003)	Key qualifications in senior secondary vocational education	Education
5	Snyder-Halpern (2002)	Indicators of organisational readiness for clinical information technology innovation	Organisational development
6	Millar (2001)	Indicators for sustainable tourism	Organisational focus
7	Wang et al. (2003)	Reproductive health indicators for China's rural areas	Health

2.1 AIM AND OBJECTIVES

The National Children's Strategy (2000) identifies a set of actions emerging from Goal Two: 'children's lives will be better understood'. The key action to which this Study relates is the development of a set of 'child well-being indicators' as a basis for the production of a biennial report to be known as the 'State of the Nation's Children'. The development of the national set of child well-being indicators is underpinned by the commitment within the Strategy to the 'whole child perspective'. The aim of this Study was:

'To reach consensus about a national set of child well-being indicators that can be used as the basis for the biennial report 'the State of the Nation's Children'.

The objectives of this Study are, as follows:

- To gain consensus about indicators that take account of key aspects of the 'whole child perspective' as set out in the National Children's Strategy (2000);
- To gain consensus about indicators that can facilitate comparisons between the Irish and international context regarding child well-being; and
- To gain consensus about indicators that meet key selection criteria.

2.2 CONCEPTUAL UNDERPINNING: A WHOLE CHILD PERSPECTIVE

The 'whole child perspective', first set out in the National Children's Strategy (2000) was used to provide a conceptual underpinning for this Study. This perspective situates the child within a socio-ecological context and has, therefore, been informed by the work of Bronfenbrenner (1979, 1993, 1995) and others concerned with the context of children's lives (for example, Ford and Lerner, 1992). This commitment to the context of the child's life is explicitly reflected within the two domains of 'children's relationships' and 'formal and informal supports'. Ward's (1995, 1998) work on outcomes around which children's lives can be understood provides a mechanism for taking account of the innate capacity of the child and, within this, nine key dimensions are identified. The perspective is underpinned by the key principles of non-discrimination, best interests of the child, survival and development and respect for the voice of the child that emerge from the UN Convention on the Rights of the Child (1989). The 'whole child perspective' sets out three broad domains and these are:

1. CHILDREN'S OWN CAPACITY;
2. CHILDREN'S RELATIONSHIPS; AND
3. FORMAL AND INFORMAL SUPPORTS.

Children's own capacity: The National Children's Strategy (2000) identifies nine dimensions of childhood and these are named:

- Physical and mental well-being;
- Emotional and behavioural well-being;
- Intellectual capacity;
- Spiritual and moral well-being;
- Identity;
- Self care;
- Family relationships;
- Social and peer relationships; and
- Social presentation.

The National Children's Strategy (2000) notes that it is helpful to consider the outcomes children achieve at each stage of development as 'expressions', which develop over time and which eventually provide the capacity for coping with adulthood (National Children's Strategy, 2000, p.25).

Any single dimension presented above could form a legitimate focus for indicator development on children. Here, however, our intention is to focus on Irish children in a holistic way and consequently, in addition to understanding individual dimensions we are also concerned with how dimensions interact with each other and how they may influence and, are in turn, influenced by the other two substantive domains (children's relationships and formal and informal supports).

Children's Relationships: This domain sets out the complex set of relationships which are recognised as essential for a satisfying and successful childhood. These relationships range from the family (the primary source of care) all the way up to the State, which acts as the ultimate guarantor of their rights.

Formal and informal supports: This domain is concerned with the essential services and supports that are provided for children through the primary social networks of family, extended family and community (informal supports), and through formal support services provided by the voluntary sector, commercial sector, the State and its agencies. These provide the conduit through which children draw the support and services they need and benefit from.

The holistic nature of the 'whole child perspective' leads to a recognition that while each of the three domains set out above are important in their own right, it is only by taking account of the inter and intra-domain relationships that a full and comprehensive understanding of children's lives can be achieved. A graphic representation of the 'whole child perspective' is presented in Figure 2.

Figure 2: The Whole Child Perspective

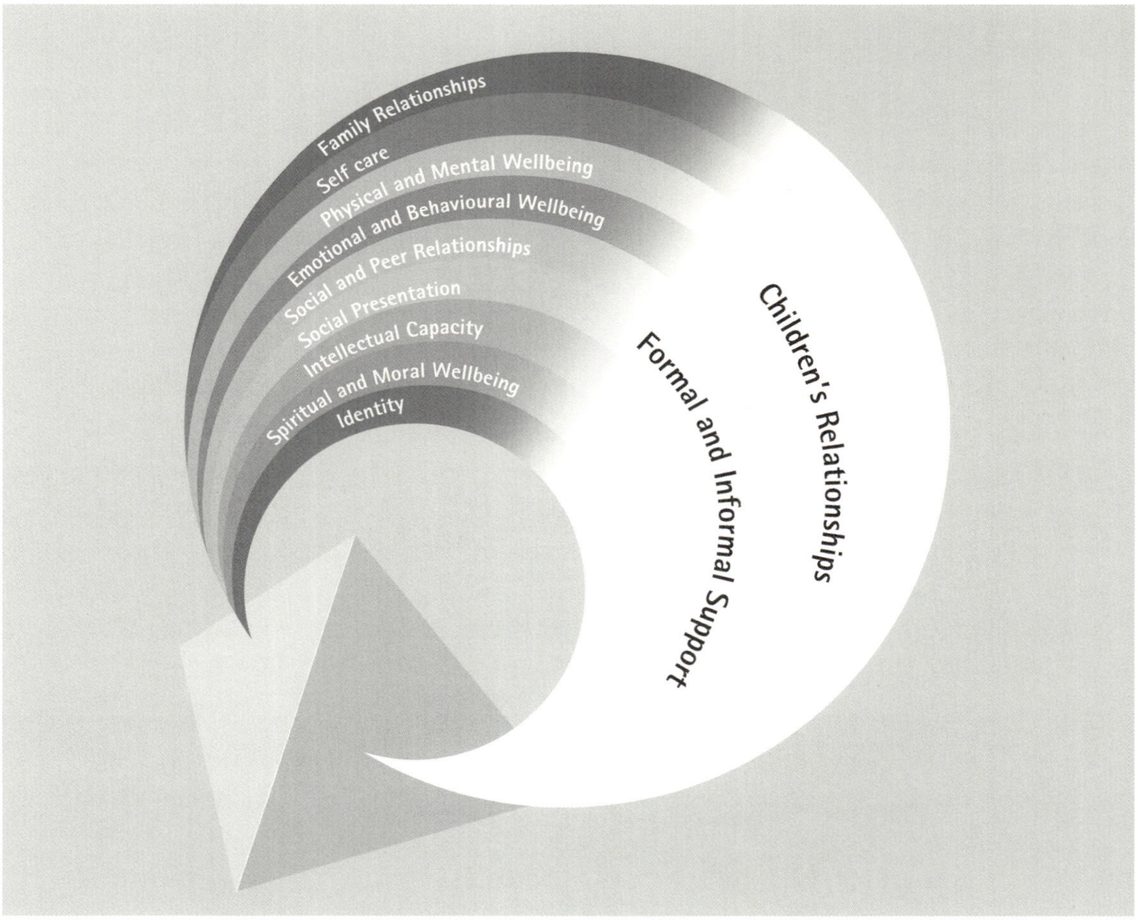

The extent to which indicators about all three domains and their inter-relationships would be identified as part of the national set of child well-being indicators was not pre-determined in this Study. Members of the panel of expertise were, however, asked to keep the three broad domains of the 'whole child perspective' in mind when making decisions about key areas for inclusion in the indicator set.

Work already undertaken in the Irish context highlights the difficulties in reaching a definition of child well-being (Carroll, 2002). For the purposes of guiding this Study, we adopted the definition set out by Andrews et al. (2002) as:

'Healthy and successful individual functioning (involving physiological, psychological and behavioural levels of organisation), positive social relationships (with family members, peers, adult caregivers, and community and societal institutions, for instance, school and faith and civic organisations), and a social ecology that provides safety (e.g., freedom from interpersonal violence, war and crime), human and civil rights, social justice and participation in civil society' (Andrews et al., 2002, p.103).

Methodological Issues Emerging

This section of the document outlines the Study method and focuses, in particular, on issues relating to sampling, data collection, analysis and statistical interpretation, credibility, reliability and validity, and ethical issues arising in respect of the Study.

2.3 SAMPLING

Delphi's claim to credibility lies in its ability to draw on expertise (Miller, 2001) and this is promoted by purposeful selection of 'experts' for inclusion to the panel rather than relying on random sampling. The term 'expert' is contested (Hasson et al., 2000), however, and it has been suggested that this title is misleading (McKenna, 1994). Cognisant of this debate, we used the terms 'panel of expertise' and 'participants' in this Study rather than 'experts'.

There is some agreement that key features of the participants involved in Delphi studies included both 'willingness' and 'ability' to make a valid contribution to the subject under examination (Goodman, 1987). These two factors need to be balanced with the potential for bias. Rowe et al., cited in van Zolingen and Klaassen (2003), suggest that researchers may create a study bias if they only:

A. SELECT RESPONDENTS THAT ARE EASILY AVAILABLE;

B. SELECT RESPONDENTS WHOSE REPUTATIONS ARE KNOWN TO THE RESEARCHER;

C. SELECT RESPONDENTS THAT MEET A MINIMAL NUMBER OF CRITERIA OF FAMILIARITY WITH THE FIELD OF THE RESEARCH PROBLEM; AND

D. SELECT RESPONDENTS ON THE BASIS OF SELF-RATINGS OF THEIR EXPERTISE.

An additional problem has been noted by van Zolingen and Klaassen (2003), who suggest that participants willing to take part in the Delphi technique may be more favourable to the method. This, in turn, may mean they are more inclined to agree with other panel members than those having a less adaptable attitude. Consideration is now given to ways in which other research studies have determined eligibility for inclusion on panels of expertise and these are summarised in Table 2.

Table 2: Key Issues Relating to Expert Panels

	AUTHOR	N: PANEL SIZE	EXPERT ELIGIBILITY
1	Campbell et al. (2000)	N = 305	All pharmaceutical and medical advisors in the UK
2	Rogers and Lopez (2002)	N = 65 including practitioners, faculty and administrators	Two of five criteria: 1. Authorship 2. Conference presentation 3. Member of chair of committee 4. Employed in practice or supervision with five years experience 5. Employed as faculty member with specific interest in area
3	Schuster et al. (1997)	N = 18 Two panels 9 members on each	Paediatric panel: Nominations from various academies - all physicians Women's panel: Nominations from various academies - all physicians Representation from different clinical practice settings, community and academic medicine and geographic regions
4	Van Zolingen and Klaassen (2003)	N = 53 4 stakeholder groups	Two years experience in their function Extensive knowledge of the content of the functions, qualification, connections and carers For teachers: Had worked on curriculum development committee, was a senior teacher
5	Snyder-Halpern (2002)	N = 34	Volunteers identified through online membership directory of specific group Employed in US based healthcare organisation Held position that reflected direct involvement with clinical information systems
6	Millar (2001)	N = 74	'Informed academics and consultants' Had published in the area of sustainability in previous two years in one of 4 major journals
7	Wang et al. (2003)	N = 123 Two panels Chinese (N = 63) International experts (N = 60)	No information on Chinese Others identified through Ford Foundation reproductive health programme. Background: Public health, social science, health acre and women's studies. Had rural experience

The details presented in Table 2 illustrate the many diverse ways in which 'expert' can be defined and mechanisms for identification of participants have ranged from 'volunteers' to 'nominations' to acknowledgement of 'experience and knowledge'. Exact and explicit criteria are set for inclusion in the panel for some studies (Rogers and Lopez, 2002) while, for others, 'expertness' is assumed on the basis of membership of a particular group (Campbell et al., 2000) or organisation (Snyder-Halpern, 2002). In the case of the study undertaken by Schuster et al. (1997), nominations were sought from various academies of paediatric and adolescent medicine (Panel 1), and family physicians and obstetricians (panel 2). Rogers and Lopez (2002) included practitioners, faculty and administrators (N = 65) in their study of developing indicators of cross-cultural school psychology competencies. They set out very explicit selection criteria for inclusion in their study as 'expert' and these criteria are identified in the example below, which referred to school psychologists who had expertise in the provision of psychological services to racially, culturally and/or linguistically diverse populations. The expertise of the panel members was defined in terms of professional accomplishments in multiple domains of professional functioning relevant to psychological service delivery with diverse clients and two of the following five criteria had to be met:

- Primary or secondary author of two or more school psychology publications concerning racially, ethnically, culturally and linguistically diverse clients;
- Presented three or more presentations on relevant cross-cultural topics at national school psychology conferences;
- Member or Chair of an APA division 16 (school psychology) or NASP committee about delivering services to racially, ethnically, culturally and linguistically diverse clients;
- Employed as a practising or supervising school psychologist with at least five years experience working primarily with racially, ethnically, culturally and linguistically diverse clients; and
- Employed as a school psychology faculty member at a school psychology program that emphasised multi-cultural or bilingual training.

In other studies less formal criteria were identified and a snowball type approach was adopted. Wang et al. (2003), for example, report 'the majority of the Chinese panel experts were identified by the study team, while most of the international experts were chosen with the help of the Ford Foundation reproductive health program officers' (Wang et al., 2003, p.218).

2.3.1 Number of Participants and Panels

There is no precise mechanism for identifying the number of individuals or the number of panels for inclusion in any individual study (Williams and Webb, 1994). It has been suggested that the size of the panel may vary according to the topics covered, the nature of different viewpoints included, and the time and money available (van Zolingen and Klaassen, 2003). One or more panels can be formed. Van Zolingen and Klaassen (2003), for example, included four different stakeholder groups in one panel while Wang et al. (2003) included two panels differentiated by location (Chinese experts N = 63; international experts N = 60). Schuster et al. (1997) formed two panels (although each panel included only nine experts). In other studies single panels were formed, although there was substantial variation in the numbers of experts included. Campbell et al. (2000), for example, included more than three hundred experts in their study while Rogers and Lopez (2002) included sixty-five. There does not, therefore, appear to be an optimum number of panels or indeed, panel members.

In the context of the current Study, the multi-dimensional nature of the 'whole child perspective', coupled with a desire to create a 'national' set of indicators meant that two options arose in respect of the panel of expertise. These were:

- That a single panel of expertise, heterogeneous in formal knowledge and experiential base, could be developed; or,
- That a number of separate panels could be developed each of which could focus on a particular dimension or aspect of the 'whole child perspective'.

Advantages and disadvantages of adopting one or more panels are set out below in Table 3.

Table 3: Advantages and Disadvantages of Single and Multiple Panels

ADVANTAGES MULTIPLE PANEL	DISADVANTAGES MULTIPLE PANEL
■ The pool of expertise for any individual area would be larger ■ A more inclusive approach to stakeholders could be adopted and this could be advantageous in terms of 'buy-in' ■ Stakeholders would only be involved in identifying indicators that they have specific areas of expertise	■ May be conceptually inappropriate because the unifying feature of the 'whole child perspective' is the underlying commitment to understanding children in a holistic way ■ The breadth of focus of any individual panel may be difficult to determine ■ The complexity of the study would increase exponentially ■ Anonymity may be difficult to maintain ■ The balance between selecting experts who would be relatively impartial and yet have information that reflects current knowledge may be difficult to strike ■ It is possible that having initially adopted a reductionist approach that the complexity and number of 'experts' involved in different panels may lead to several practical problems in the subsequent integration of the material
ADVANTAGES SINGLE PANEL	**DISADVANTAGES SINGLE PANEL**
■ The identification of each indicator would be situated within the context of the overall 'whole child perspective' and this may have a synergetic quality ■ The study would be less complex than that of multiple panels ■ The focus of the development would be on the 'whole child perspective' and consequently it may be easier to strike the balance between impartiality and expertise ■ The expertise held by individual panel members in particular areas could be shared across all panel members throughout the course of the study rather than being predetermined by the study organisers	■ It may not be possible to include the same number in the panel so the subsequent level of 'buy-in' may be lower ■ Panalists may respond to areas where they do not have expertise and this may invalidate the results ■ It may not be possible to reach consensus because the diversity of the panel experts may be too great

2.3.2 Panel of Expertise for the Study

Understanding children's lives in a holistic way was centrally important to the development of the national set of child well-being indicators. We were, therefore, committed to reaching consensus across many different areas of their lives. Consequently, it seemed logical to have a single panel of expertise because this could protect against fragmentation and lack of coherence within the indicator set. This, in turn, led to some difficulties in determining the extent to which specific indicators, which would require considerable knowledge of the most appropriate indicator, should be agreed by all panel members. In order to surmount this difficulty, we used the Delphi technique to identify the key areas for inclusion in the indicator set rather than the individual indicators themselves. When key areas were identified, organisations or people with specific expertise in an individual area were asked to recommend the most appropriate indicator for inclusion.

The potential for identifying members for inclusion on the panel of expertise through systematic sampling was given some consideration. We examined ways in which, for example, policy makers from the Statutory Departments with responsibility for children's lives could be identified. We found, however, that although there are six main Departments, there are many sub-divisions and agencies that could have something to contribute. Within the Department of Health and Children, for example, there are more than fifty separate organisations as well as the main Department. Although a full list of each of these was compiled, with a view to creating a sampling frame, it was clear that such an approach was unwieldy and unlikely to result in a panel of expertise.

Problems also arose in respect of the academic community because of the absence of a central database in the Republic of Ireland for academics or researchers with an interest in children's issues. Nevertheless, we did make efforts to identify those who had published in the area of children's research through, for example, individual institutional databases that identify publications from researchers / lecturers working in their university and other on-line portals, for example, 'Expertise Ireland'. Again, we concluded that the likelihood of achieving a comprehensive relevant sampling frame would be beyond the scope of this Study. Within the Non-Governmental Organisation sector there is an umbrella group for children's rights (the Children's Rights Alliance (CRA)), that brings together more than seventy organisations who work with, or on behalf of, children. This organisation was subsequently invited to nominate three people. In light of the difficulties highlighted above, and in view of some concerns about the ability to capture relevant expertise, it was decided that a systematic approach to sampling was not an option.

In 2003, the National Children's Office established a Research Development Advisory Group (RDAG) and this Group comprises eighteen researchers, policy makers and service providers which have a specialist expertise in areas of children's lives. We were fortunate and grateful to be able to use this Group as the basis for the panel of expertise along with nominees from the Children's Rights Alliance. Using snowball sampling, each member of the Group was asked to identify two further people known to have expertise. In order to ensure an appropriate mix of expertise, each Group member was asked to nominate persons from a sector other than their own. This meant, for example, that a policy maker would nominate a researcher and service provider, while a researcher would nominate a policy maker and service provider. In addition to this Group, parents were also included and these were also identified using a snowball approach where members of the Advisory Group were asked to identify parents from different backgrounds and from different geographic areas. National parents' organisations such as the National Parents Council and the IPPA, the Early Childhood Organisation, were also contacted and given an opportunity to nominate people. The final panel of expertise comprised eighty-seven people and we are confident that the overall composition of the panel provided is a good reflection of the diversity of children's lives.

In keeping with Goal One of the National Children' Strategy (2000), 'children will have a voice in matters which affect them and their views will be given due weight in accordance with their age and maturity' (National Children' Strategy, 2000, p.30), we also considered ways in which children could be included in the process. We concluded, following discussion with personnel involved in the area of children's participation, that the most appropriate way to ensure children's views were represented was by commissioning a study on 'children's understandings of well-being'. This Study was undertaken by Dr. Saoirse Nic Gabhainn and Jane Sixsmith and was similar to this Study, underpinned by a commitment to recognising the influence of social interaction in achieving consensus. The overall single panel of expertise is set out in Table 4 and a full list of participants is set out in Appendix 1.

Table 4: Composition of the Panel of Expertise

	FREQUENCY	PERCENT	VALID PERCENT	CUMULATIVE PERCENT
Parents	11	15.9	15.9	15.9
Policy makers	25	36.2	36.2	52.2
Researchers	21	30.4	30.4	82.6
Service Providers	12	17.4	17.4	100.0
Total	69	100.0	100.0	

2.4 DATA COLLECTION

Loss of participants from the study can be problematic in situations where data is collected at more than one point in time (Henekens and Buring 1987; Farrington 1990; Courtenay and Mekkelholt, 1997). The cumulative effects of repeated contacts with participants can lead to respondent burden and this in turn has the potential to create difficulties around bias.

A number of key mechanisms have been identified as helpful in decreasing attrition between rounds and these include:

- Ensuring participants are fully informed about the study (Hasson et al., 2000);
- Having short follow-up periods between study rounds (Taylor and Lynn, 1996); and
- Issuing reminders by e-mail, telephone and personal contact (van Zolingen and Klaassen, 2003).

While these mechanisms can also be used to increase low response rates for questionnaire surveys where there is only one questionnaire round (Robson, 1993; Cohen and Manion, 1994), it is important in a Delphi study that these efforts take place at each round of the Study.

Prior to the start of the data collection, each nominee was contacted and an opportunity was provided for them to clarify issues relating to the Study. In addition, a comprehensive review of literature about the Delphi technique was made available on the National Children's Office website (www.nco.ie) so that participants could, if they wished, get a more in-depth understanding about how the Study would proceed. In addition, three reminders were sent to each participant. Issues of timing were also considered at each Study round so that questionnaires were not issued at an important holiday time or at a time where it was likely that participants were more busy than normal. These mechanisms assisted in ensuring good response rates for each round.

2.4.1 Response rates

> Response rates varied between seventy-two and eighty-four percent.

The first questionnaire round had a response rate of eighty percent (N = 69). Only participants that had taken part in the first round were invited to take part in the second questionnaire round as the purpose here was to ensure that participants had an opportunity to change their initial response on the basis of feedback received. The response rate for the second round was eighty-four percent (N = 58) and this was considered satisfactory. The final questionnaire was concerned with overall levels of satisfaction with both the indicator set identified and with the Delphi process. Consequently, participants who had taken part at any stage in the process were invited to give their opinions and, as two participants had withdrawn, the valid response rate for this round was seventy-two percent (N = 48).

2.4.2 Questionnaire Development

Some authors using the Delphi technique have reported extensively on their questionnaire (Millar, 2001) while others have only indicated broad areas of inclusion. Miller (2001), for example, presents a clear outline of key questions asked about each specific indicator in their work on sustainable tourism and this is set out below in Figure 3.

Figure 3: Questionnaire Format for Indicators (Millar, 2001)

NAME OF INDICATOR: ____________________
TYPE OF INDICATOR: ____________________
PAGE NUMBER (IN EXPLANATORY BOOKLET): ____________________

	YES	NO	SEE NOTES
1 Is the indicator applicable?			
2 Is the indicator a complete indicator?			
3 Is the indicator applicable to all types of tourism?			
4 Is the data for the indicator easily obtained?			
5 Is the calculation required for the indicator simple?			
6 Is the indicator understandable?			
7 Is the data objective, quantifiable and reliable?			
8 Does the indicator point towards sustainable development?			
9 Can the indicator be measured on an ongoing basis?			

Others report using a smaller number of questions for each indicator. Campbell et al. (2000), for example, in a study of quality indicators report three questions for each indicator. Respondents in that study were asked 'to rate each indicator against two continuous 1-9 integer scales':

- 'Is this indicator a useful measure of cost minimization?'
- 'Is this indicator a useful measure of quality?'.

In developing each questionnaire, we adhered to good practices and were particularly mindful of issues raised about the length of the questionnaire, the importance of clearly formulated unambiguous questions and the implications of having a heterogeneous group of respondents (van Zolingen and Klaassen, 2003). The heterogeneous nature of the panel of expertise in this Study meant that respondents did not have expertise in each specific indicator area. One potential way of taking this into account was to use the information provided in the demographic / expertise section to include or exclude respondents. This subjective approach may, however, have led to problems of interpretation. Munier and Rondé (2001), for example, asked respondents to declare their knowledge on a given subject based on four clearly defined levels (very good, good, limited and null) using very precise definitions set out below:

- 'Very good' knowledge implies that the 'expert currently devotes himself to research on this precise topic or closely related topic';
- 'Good knowledge' suggests that the 'expert devoted himself in the past to this research and continues to follow very closely the work of his colleagues';
- 'Limited knowledge' means the 'expert is satisfied with reading articles, newspapers and reviews or has contacts with specialists'; and
- 'Null knowledge' suggests that the 'expert is not informed in the field'.

An analysis of responses by all fields (78,486) showed that only 3 percent reported having 'very good' knowledge, 7 percent having 'good' knowledge and almost two-thirds (63 percent) had 'null' knowledge. Adopting this type of approach, therefore have led to difficulties in ensuring there were adequate numbers of respondents for each indicator.

> In this Study, we took the view that all participants on the panel of expertise, by virtue of their involvement in children's lives, would have some knowledge of the key areas for inclusion and this would allow for the holistic nature of children's lives to be captured. More specific detail was required when identifying the actual indicators themselves, and at that point, only those with specific knowledge in that particular area would be involved. This accommodated the difference in levels of expertise when identifying specific details of each individual indicator. In the final round, study participants were asked to rate their level of satisfaction with the overall set rather than with individual indicators within the set.

2.4.3 Pilot Study

The situation around pilot testing in respect of the Delphi technique is unclear. Powell (2003), for example, argues that 'pilot testing is optional although it may be useful to identify ambiguities and improve the feasibility of administration' (Powell, 2003, p. 378). In view of the importance of this Study to future policy-making and developments around children's lives, we undertook substantial pre-testing and a two-round pilot study with people (N = 10) who did not take part in the main Study. We believe it was worthwhile doing this and a number of changes were made as a result including, for example:

1. CHANGES TO THE LAYOUT OF THE QUESTIONNAIRE;
2. CHANGES TO THE CONTENT OF THE QUESTIONNAIRE, PARTICULARLY IN THE PROVISION OF INFORMATION ABOUT CHILD WELL-BEING AND INDICATOR SETS;
3. QUESTION WORDING WAS CHANGED TO INCORPORATE AN EVENT LIST FOR THE INDICATOR AREAS, WHICH GREATLY ASSISTED CLARITY;
4. DE-GROUPING OF INDICATORS, WHEREAS INITIALLY INDICATORS WERE GROUPED ACCORDING TO BROAD THEMATIC AREAS, SUCH AS,

68962.

'EDUCATION' AND 'ECONOMICS', RESULTS FROM THE PILOT STUDY SUGGESTED THIS WAS NOT HELPFUL. THE SEQUENCING OF THE INDICATOR AREAS WAS SUBSEQUENTLY CHANGED TO AN ALPHABETICAL FORMAT;

5. FORMAT OF RESPONSE TO THE QUESTIONNAIRE AS A RESULT OF THE PILOT STUDY, AND DISCUSSION WITH THE ADVISORY GROUP, A RATING SCALE (FROM 0–10, WHERE 0 IS LEAST IMPORTANT AND 10 IS MOST IMPORTANT) WAS USED. THIS WAS BECAUSE THERE WERE TOO MANY KEY AREAS INITIALLY TO RANK (APPROXIMATELY 60). IN ADDITION, THE ADOPTION OF A RATING APPROACH ALLOWED FOR THE USE OF MEASURES OF DISPERSION (e.g. STANDARD DEVIATION) WHICH WERE CENTRAL TO THE IDENTIFICATION OF STABILITY BETWEEN ROUNDS.

The pilot study also facilitated a link with the study on 'children's understanding of well-being' and both research teams met on completion of their respective pilot studies.

2.4.4 Round One

In the classical Delphi technique, the first round adopts an inductive approach where participants are invited to generate ideas and are given complete freedom in their responses (Hasson et al., 2000). This allows panel members to identify an infinite range of possibilities and although this has many advantages in terms of comprehensiveness, it can be problematic where the respondents are heterogeneous in knowledge, expertise and experience. In addition, this inductive-type approach has been criticised on the basis of its inability to produce the level of information that a thorough literature review would (Millar, 2001).

In this Study, we considered the appropriateness of an open-ended approach to the first round but believed that, on balance, it was more efficient to adopt a semi-structured approach for the following reasons:

1) A key objective of this Study was 'to identify indicators that would facilitate comparisons between the Irish and international context regarding child well-being'. We considered it necessary, therefore, to examine indicators used elsewhere so that such comparability would be achievable;
2) The complexity of indicators used to describe 'well-being' means that many different definitions can be used to describe the same phenomenon. We were anxious, therefore, to set out clear definitions around each indicator so that ambiguity was decreased and specific data sources could, if available, be identified.

Two sequential processes preceded the development of the first questionnaire.

- First, a systematic search of indicator sets commonly used elsewhere was undertaken and more than 2,500 indicators were identified. Although some of these indicators were clearly of less relevance to the Irish situation (for example, an indicator of 'percentage of children carrying guns to school'), and some were almost identical to each other, it was decided not to exclude any indicator at that point (Brooks and Hanafin, 2005).
- Second, an expert in the area of data sources of child statistics was contracted by the National Children's Office to examine the feasibility of each of the indicators identified. These indicators were then categorised according to whether data sources were or were not available (Fitzgerald, 2004).

On the basis of the work already completed, a semi-structured approach was adopted and some fifty-six key areas, agreed with the Advisory Group were presented to participants in an 'event list' format. Participants were then asked to rate each one on a scale of 0-10 (where 0 = not important and 10 = very important). Participants were also given an opportunity to identify additional areas if they wished and to make any other comments. Finally, demographic information about each participant was also collected on the first questionnaire round. This type of approach has been used by others (for example, Schuster et al., 1997; Millar, 2001; Rogers and Lopez, 2002; van Zolingen and Klaassen, 2003) and it has been reported that an 'event list', similar to that used, is more preferable than a blank piece of paper because it provided participants with a context in which to provide their responses (Snyder-Halpern, 2002).

The first questionnaire (Appendix 2) was divided into three parts. Part One asked respondents to identify their demographic and 'expertise' characteristics, while Part Two presented an event list with fifty-six key areas. These areas were identified on the basis of the work already completed and with the assistance of the Advisory Group. Part Three of the questionnaire allowed respondents to make comments and identify any areas they felt were not covered.

2.4.5 Round Two

In keeping with the Delphi technique, preliminary analysis of responses from Round One took place prior to Round Two and the findings formed the basis for the second questionnaire (Appendix 3). The Round Two questionnaire provided a prioritised list of key areas with a drop down list of those that had been excluded as a result of the first round prioritisation. An analysis of first round answers in respect of key areas identified by participants was also included in the second round. Participants were given an opportunity to provide feedback on the prioritised areas and were also asked to identify three areas not prioritised in the first round that they felt should be included in the final set.

2.4.6 Consultation Regarding Key Indicators

On completion of Round Two, key areas for inclusion in the indicator set had been identified and the next step in the process was to identify the most appropriate indicator(s) for each. At this stage of the process, a set of indicator selection criteria first suggested by Moore (1997) and later adapted by Carroll (2002) for the Irish context had been identified and agreed with the Advisory Group. These are shown in Table 5 below.

Table 5: Selection Criteria for Indicators of Child Well-Being

1. Comprehensive coverage: Indicators should assess well-being across a broad array of outcomes, behaviour and processes.
2. Children of all ages: Age-appropriate indicators are needed at every age from birth through adolescence and covering transition into adulthood.
3. Clear and comprehensible: Indicators should be easily and readily understood by the public.
4. Positive outcomes: Indicators should assess positive as well as negative aspects of well-being.
5. Forward-looking: Indicators should be collected now that anticipate the future and provide baseline data for subsequent trends.
6. Rigorous methods: Coverage of the population or event being monitored should be complete or very high and data collection measures should be rigorous and consistent over time.
7. Geographically detailed: Indicators should be developed not only at the national level, but also at the state and local level.
8. Cost-efficient: Although investments in data about US children have been insufficient, strategies to expand and improve the data system need to be thoughtful, well-planned and economically efficient.
9. Reflective of social goals: Some indicators should allow us to track progress in meeting national, state and local goals for child well-being.

In addition to these criteria, three other key concerns guided the selection of the indicators. These were that the indicators chosen would:

- Be capable of drawing international comparisons, where possible;
- Comprise a balanced collection of objective and subjective measures; and
- Assess both well-being and well-becoming.

A thorough examination of the inventory of indicators (Appendix 4) was then undertaken using the selection criteria as a framework for analysis. Specific indicators were then identified for each key area and where possible these included indicators from existing international (for example, CHILD and PERISTAT) and national (for example, Department of Health and Children interim data set, the Department of Education and Science Education Statistics) indicator sets.

On completion of this, a consultation process then took place with relevant Government Departments and Agencies and others with expertise in data about child well-being in Ireland. The National Advisory Council on Drugs, for example, was consulted about the most appropriate indicator to adopt for use of alcohol, and the National Nutrition Surveillance Centre was consulted about the most appropriate indicator of children's nutrition. This consultation was particularly useful when there were a number of potential indicators that could be used, since each area had to be limited, where possible, to only one specific indicator. A full list of these Government Departments and Agencies is given in Appendix 5.

The selection of indicators, particularly for the more subjective areas such as self-esteem and relationship with parents and family, also relied on the existing data sources available. The inventory of child well-being indicators demonstrated the paucity of both subjective and positive indicators in use in other countries; therefore, for many of these areas, existing data sources were examined for potential indicators. In cases where indicators could not be found to measure a key area, this was noted and indicator development in the key area advocated. This was the case, for example, for 'pets/animals' and the 'quality of early childhood care and education'. The indicators were then discussed with the Advisory Group, which provided an opportunity to ensure that, as far as possible, the overall set met the selection criteria.

2.4.7 Round Three

Analysis of material from Round Two, the consultative process with various agencies, organisations and Government Departments regarding the specific indicators within the set, the selection criteria and discussions with the Advisory Board all contributed to the development of the third round questionnaire (Appendix 6). This questionnaire presented the specific indicators and a number of key selection criteria. Participants were asked to indicate their level of overall satisfaction with the indicator set using the key selection criteria as well as their satisfaction generally with the indicator set. Comments were also invited in respect of the Delphi technique itself and any other emergent issues.

2.4.8 Integration of Data from the Study on 'Children's Understandings of Well-Being'

The importance of giving children a voice in the development of the national set of child well-being indicators was operationalised at every stage. On completion of each stage of the process, discussions and written communication took place between the researchers engaged on the Delphi study and those carrying out the study on children's understanding of well-being. It was clear from these discussions that there was much common ground and agreement between key areas in the literature and findings emerging from the Study of 'children's understandings of well-being'. At the pilot study stage, however, there were two clear exceptions to this and these were:

A. THE IMPORTANCE CHILDREN ASSIGNED TO 'PETS/ANIMALS' IN THE CONTEXT OF THEIR OWN WELL-BEING; AND

B. THE IMPORTANCE ATTACHED TO 'BEDROOMS AND SLEEP'.

Although there were indicators available about hours of sleep, no indicator had previously been documented about pets/animals in the extant literature on child well-being. In response to these findings, two key areas were included in the first round of the Delphi study and these were 'pets/animals' and 'hours of sleep'. Interestingly, however, the area 'pets/animals' achieved the lowest mean average rating (4.71) of all key areas presented to the panel of expertise and was therefore deemed to be the lowest priority area. 'Hours of sleep' as a key area was prioritised as forty-eight (fourth lowest) with a mean average score of 6.55.

At the time of development of the second round questionnaire for the Delphi technique, the study with children had been completed and it was possible, therefore to get further elaboration about the 'meanings' children assigned to 'pets/animals' and 'bedrooms and sleep' as well as other areas that had emerged. 'Bedrooms and Sleep' as a category was excluded from the second round because it was clear from the main study with children that the meaning intended was not around sleep but rather the bedroom as a 'place to go'. This meaning could also be accommodated under the key areas 'things to do' and 'environment/places to go'. A number of different themes had also emerged in the area 'pets/animals' and these were:

- Giving Love;
- Receiving Love;
- Companionship;
- Emotional Coping;
- Activities;
- Responsibility;
- Pride; and
- Exercise.

Given the breadth of difference among these themes, it was decided that this key area was warranted as an area in its own right and consequently, the area was again included in the second round despite not having been prioritised in the first.

Two further areas were also included in the second questionnaire round and these were 'environment/places' and 'things to do'. Again there were multiple understandings underpinning each. In respect of 'environment/places', for example, these included aspects of the natural, built, home and oversees environment that were underpinned by 'belonging', 'aesthetics', 'serenity', 'contexts for activities', 'life-giving' and 'work'. 'Things to do' as an indicator area was underpinned by themes such as 'fun', 'learning', 'belonging', 'coping', 'health enhancing', 'pride', 'sharing' and 'connecting with the world'.

Since the category 'pets/animals' has never been used as a key area of child well-being prior to this, it was not possible to select an indicator that would meet the criteria set out for inclusion. It is planned, however, to develop an indicator in this area. It was possible to include indicators for 'things to do' and the 'environment and places'.

2.4.9 Method of Data Collection

A number of issues arose in respect of the mechanisms through which the questionnaires should be distributed to the panel of expertise. Snyder-Halpern et al. (2003), for example, compared mailed vs. internet applications of the Delphi technique and found that while there were both advantages and disadvantages to using e-mail, there was a very good case to be made for this type of approach to data collection. A summary of advantages and disadvantages as well as key issues emerging in respect of this method of data collection, identified by Snyder-Halpern et al. (2003) are set out in Table 6.

Table 6: Advantages and Disadvantages of E-mail Use

ADVANTAGES	DISADVANTAGES
Recruitment was cheaper and quicker	Disadvantages mainly technological and include:
Cost savings were substantial	Unexpected changes of e-mail application
Legibility of responses	Unreliability of panellist e-mail capabilities, resulting in some panellists being unable to participate in some rounds
Ease of data entry, resulting in decreased data entry time and errors	Some respondents were unable to retrieve e-mail attachments in their original format
Decrease in response turnaround time	Some respondents had incompatibility with Excel or MS word applications.
Ability to track transmission status (for example, for incorrect addresses)	Problems with mime encryption

The ease, convenience and comprehensiveness of an 'on-line' mechanism made this type of approach a very attractive option in this Study and we were influenced in this by the high levels of Internet access available to most participants (Central Statistics Office, 2004). Nevertheless, we also ensured that people who did not have ready access to the Internet would be facilitated and a hard copy of the questionnaire was sent to anybody who wanted it.

The main approach used for data collection was on-line completion of the questionnaires. This was done using the software package Keypoint© and technical support was provided by the Information Technology section at the Department of Health and Children.

Keypoint software was particularly appropriate for this Study because it combines questionnaire generation, data collection, analysis and presentation in a single package. This meant that it was possible to provide feedback relatively quickly and therefore shortened the length of time between rounds. In addition to on-line access, the software allowed for questionnaires to be printed, published on a client's own website, sent as an e-mail or through the provision of a host server. In general, questionnaires were completed through the host server although where participants requested, printed copies were provided.

In keeping with good practices in this area, participants of the Study were sent an e-mail providing explicit instructions for completion of the questionnaire, contact details should they have any difficulties, and a direct link to the host service were provided (Snyder-Halpern et al., 2003).

2.5 ANALYSIS, ITERATION AND CONSENSUS

2.5.1 Analysis

Analysis that takes place in a Delphi study has two purposes. First, analysis should provide feedback between rounds for respondents and, second, it should be able to identify when consensus has been reached. There does not, however, appear to be agreement about the best method of mathematical aggregation (Murphy et al., 1998). In Rowe and Wright's (1999) systematic review of literature on Delphi technique, a number of different descriptive statistics were used. These included median, mode, percentages for each event, ranks, upper and lower quartile ranges, regression weights or induced (if-then) rules, and statistical average of points for each factor. Qualitative material was also examined and in a number of studies 'reasons' were analysed and given to respondents as feedback.

Data from other studies in respect of analysis and consensus is set out in Table 7.

Table 7: Analysis and Identification of Consensus in Key Studies

	AUTHOR	MAIN FOCUS	STATISTICS	CONSENSUS
1	Campbell et al. (2000)	'Prescribing' indicators for general practice	Percentages for each indicator	Disagreement defined as 30% or more scores in both the bottom (1-3) and top (6-9) tertile
2	Rogers and Lopez (2002)	Cross-cultural school psychology competencies	Item means and standard deviations Median Range	'The percentage of panellist ratings that fell within the established range of consensus +/- 1.64SD on round 2' (p. 127)
3	Schuster et al. (1997)	Quality of health care measures for children and adolescents	Number of votes in each category (1-9) for each indicator	Consensus not required because each panellist has a vote for each indicator (p1086). Disagreement defined as at least 3 votes in the 1-3 range and at least 3 votes in the 7-9 range.
4	Van Zolingen and Klaassen (2003)	Key qualifications in senior secondary vocational education	Information file - no additional information	Qualitative understanding: 'opinions did not differ in many cases' (p. 337)
5	Snyder-Halpern (2002)	Indicators of organisational readiness for clinical information technology innovation	Seven member coding team in thematic analysis of responses	Inter-relater agreement = 43% or greater i.e. 3/7 or greater
6	Millar (2001)	Indicators for sustainable tourism	Percentage agree/ disagree mean standard deviation	Qualitative: using words like 'general agreement', 'disharmony', 'spread of opinion', 'disagreement', 'divisive'
7	Wang et al. (2003)	Reproductive health indicators for China's rural areas		Not explicit

Table 7 identifies the main statistics reported on in a small number of studies. In general, statistics presented included:

- percentages;
- standard deviations;
- means;
- medians; and
- ranges.

While cautioning that these statistics assume an interval scale, Greatorex and Dexter (2000) concluded that the mean, a measure of central tendency, can be understood to represent group opinion. The standard deviation (a measure of spread), they suggest, can then be understood as a representation of the amount of disagreement within the panel. If the standard deviation is low, then the panel is in agreement, and the converse is also true. If the standard deviation is high, the panel is in disagreement. In a systematic examination of consensus development methods and their use in clinical guideline development, however, Murphy et al. (1998) argue that the median and the inter-quartile range are more robust than the mean and standard deviation.

In this Study, we used the mean and standard deviation as the main statistical measures in Round One.

This was particularly useful in facilitating a reduction in the number of key areas for inclusion in the indicator set. The cut-off level was determined by relative rating and the twenty-five key areas with the highest mean average rating were included in the indicator set. This approach was used in conjunction with the standard deviation, which provided a measure of dispersion.

In Round Two and Three, percentages were also used to identify if consensus had been reached. A ninety percent level of agreement was considered the optimum level of agreement in these instances (Zeitlin et al., 2003).

2.5.2 Feedback

Iteration is a key feature of the Delphi technique and feedback on questionnaire analysis is provided to each respondent at each round. Feedback has been defined as:

> **'The means by which information is passed between panellists so that individual judgement may be improved and debiasing may occur'**
>
> (Rowe and Wright, 1999, p. 370).

Levels of feedback vary and may be provided in a number of different ways. The purpose of feedback is to allow each expert to revise his or her own judgement in light of the judgement of others (Munier and Rondé, 2001). Others have suggested that feedback be provided in the form of a median or inter-quartile range, and that experts who continue to give extreme views are asked to provide a rationale (van Zolingen and Klaassen, 2003). Crisp et al. (1997) notes that one of the most common forms of feedback is measures of central tendency (mean, median), which may or may not be accompanied by a measure of dispersion (standard deviation).

The timing of feedback is also an issue and it has been suggested that the quality of the Delphi study increases as the time between filling in a questionnaire and the next one being mailed becomes shorter (Waldron, cited in van Zolingen and Klaassen, 2003).

We provided both individualised and group feedback in Rounds Two and Three so that members of the panel of expertise were able to situate their responses within the broader context.

2.5.3 Consensus

Consensus has been identified as one of the most contentious components of the Delphi technique and debates have centred on the position of consensus in such a study. The aim of the Delphi technique is to achieve consensus but this is not a straightforward concept and is generally poorly explained (Williams and Webb, 1994). The *Longman Dictionary of Contemporary English* (Thompson, 1987) defines consensus as 'a general agreement; the opinion of most people in a group' (*Longman Dictionary of Contemporary English,* 1987, p. 216). Although some authors have presented qualitative judgements of consensus (e.g. Millar, 2001), in general an empirical approach is taken. Consensus is usually determined through statistically measuring the variance in responses across rounds. Less variance is understood to mean greater consensus (Rowe and Wright, 1999), although this has itself been the subject of some controversy. Bardecki (1984), cited in Rowe and Wright (1999), reported that respondents with more extreme views were more likely to drop out of the study than participants with more moderate views. The conclusion drawn was that the decrease in variance can be a consequence of attrition rather than consensus.

Munier and Rondé (2001), among others, suggest that the possibility that participants may simply alter their estimates in order to conform to the group (conformance), without actually changing their opinions (consensus), must be considered. Their own work in testing the influence of expert knowledge on consensus suggests, however, that consensus is the more likely explanation for decreased variance. Their conclusion that 'it can be theoretically demonstrated that the median response of the entire group should move towards the true value' supports a move towards consensus rather than conformance (Munier and Rondé, 2001, p. 1548). Some authors have undertaken 'post group consensus', which concerns the extent to which individuals on completion of the Delphi technique agreed with the final group aggregate, their own final round estimates, or the estimates of other participants (Rowe and Wright, 1999).

Studies focussing on the number of rounds needed in a Delphi survey to achieve consensus suggest that most changes occur in the transition from the first to the second round (van Zolingen and Klaassen, 2003). The number of rounds in the modified technique may be decreased to as few as two, if panellists have been provided with an event list, and if early group consensus is achieved (Snyder-Halpern, 2002). Other authors have focussed on participant burden as a problem and suggest that when the number of rounds exceeds four, the response rates can be very low. Table 7 sets out definitions of consensus used in studies elsewhere.

2.6 PARTICIPANTS' VIEWS OF THE DELPHI TECHNIQUE

The third round questionnaire asked participants for their views about the Delphi technique itself. Participants focused in particular on the process of the study as well as the advantages and disadvantages. More than ninety-six percent of participants indicated they were either 'satisfied' or 'very satisfied' with the approach and these very high levels of satisfaction with the process used to develop the indicators are presented in Table 8.

Table 8: Overall satisfaction with the process of development

	FREQUENCY	PERCENT
Very dissatisfied	0	2.1
Dissatisfied	1	2.1
Satisfied	24	50
Very Satisfied	22	45.8

2.6.1 Advantages of Adopting a Delphi Technique

Four main advantages were associated with the high level of satisfaction identified and these were categorised as:

1. INCLUSIVE AND CONSULTATIVE;
2. COMPREHENSIVE;
3. RIGOROUS AND SYSTEMATIC; AND
4. EFFICIENT.

Inclusiveness and Consultative

Participants noted that this type of approach gathers a wide range of responses and enables the inclusion of 'many interests', 'multiple stakeholders', 'partners', 'professionals', and 'diverse backgrounds'. The large numbers involved in the panel of expertise facilitated the 'accommodation of a wide number of views', which would not have been possible in a face-to-face interaction. The sense of 'inclusiveness' and 'ownership' of the final set of indicators for those involved was also identified as important as participants had been able to have an input at each stage of the process. As one respondent noted, the main advantage was that it allowed:

'Consultation with what was a broad spectrum of people involved in one way or another with children, including children themselves, and in research grounded in the outcomes of what is really happening for children'.

Comprehensive

The importance of getting a comprehensive overview of children's lives was critical to the conceptual underpinning of this development. Participants indicated that this had been possible and was achieved using the Delphi technique. Ninety-five percent of participants indicated they were 'satisfied' or 'very satisfied' with the comprehensiveness of the overall set. While the breadth of the indicators was representative of the participants, there was general agreement that the Delphi technique had ensured that a more 'rounded response, which reflects the wide range of influences on children and their lives' was achieved. The difficulties for each sector in seeing beyond their own areas were noted and one participant wrote that:

'(G)etting a balance that will suit all is very difficult. Therefore your approach is probably the most practical'.

Rigorous and Systematic

Participants reported that the Delphi technique allows for a more systematic approach that was 'open and transparent' and 'scientific and rigorous'. It was felt that this would enhance the status of the findings and would be very important when the statistics for each area of children's lives were being collected and presented to a wider audience. The ways in which the Delphi technique allowed for prioritisation of the key areas was considered particularly useful although such prioritisation remained difficult. One participant wrote:

'The necessity for weighting of some indicators against others in the tiered process was very useful to the finalisation of the indicators. It was easy to see the justification for the inclusion/exclusion of certain indicators at the later parts of the process'.

Others noted that it was a less biased way of getting people's views than working groups or other types of meetings, and that the approach used ensured 'dominance by one ideology or set of values' was avoided. Not all participants agreed with this point. It was noted that within the panel of expertise, it was still possible for bias to occur if there were more participants from one area of children's lives (for example, health or education) over another.

Efficiency

The final aspect of the Delphi technique identified as being advantageous was the efficiency of the approach. Participants felt the shorter time required (compared with other approaches), the ease of participation and general user-friendliness of the approach was important. The approach was reported to be 'very focused' and 'took less time than meetings'. In addition, it got over the problem of 'endless debates' about what should or should not be included and 'avoided tortuous discussions'. As one participant wrote:

> **On-line collaboration and development of questionnaires permits input from a wider field of contributors who themselves are not burdened by trying to attend meetings to progress their contributions'.**

2.6.2 Disadvantages

Participants were also asked to identify disadvantages associated with this method and while some of those identified could also be attributed to other approaches to consensus (for example, the 'watering down of indicators', 'bias because of only taking account of the views of those who decide to take part'), specific issues were raised in respect of the lack of face-to-face interaction between participants. Three issues emerged in this regard and these were:

1. INCOMPLETE UNDERSTANDING OF THE RATIONALE OF OTHERS;
2. LACK OF GROUP EFFECTS; AND
3. DIFFERING UNDERSTANDINGS OF KEY STAKEHOLDERS.

Understanding Rationales

A small number of participants noted that it was difficult sometimes to understand why other participants on the panel of expertise did, or did not, prioritise particular indicator areas. This, coupled with the wide variety of stakeholders, meant that a strong 'argument for the inclusion of an indicator may be lost in the process' and opportunities for justifying its inclusion were not available. Others noted that they did not have a clear statement or understanding of the rationale of the well-being project and that made it difficult at times to rank the dimensions and indicators. As one participant noted:

> **'The disadvantage is that we just get a glimpse and do not know what decision-making process lies behind it'.**

Group Interaction

A number of participants noted that there were disadvantages to not getting the effect of 'group interaction'. Some participants wrote they would have welcomed the possibility for 'dialogue and discussion', and 'anecdotal discussion and interaction' about 'grey areas and value-laden areas'. This, it was felt, would have led to 'healthy debate and discussion'. Another participant noted that:

> **'One would miss the buzz that comes from brainstorming although obviously someone was there to pull together all the ideas and sort them efficiently'.**

It was suggested that the process of individuals completing questionnaires in isolation did not allow for the development of ideas / discussion of issues such as happens in face-to-face group approaches. This was felt to be a drawback particularly because some respondents had greater expertise in some areas compared with others. As one participant wrote:

> **'Completion of some areas difficult because of lack of knowledge, experience etc. ....e.g., my opinions about infant measures are limited but I have commented on these as much as on areas where my views more developed, such as education'.**

The lack of opportunity to discuss the selection and advantages, as well as 'deficiencies of individual indicators' with anyone else in the group was felt by one participant to be a significant disadvantage.

Different Perspectives

The final area identified as problematic by participants was mediating different stakeholder understandings. Given the wide range of participants and their varying backgrounds, it was noted that 'different participants understand key terms and concepts differently'. The lack of face-to-face interaction between participants meant that it was not possible to identify whether this was the case and, if it were, to come to a general agreement about a particular area. Two participants felt it would have been useful to have had a seminar 'to discuss the theoretical and policy context and hear the views of other stakeholders', which might have led to 'a deeper understanding about the 'whole child perspective'.

2.6.3 Conclusion

There was overwhelming support for the use of the Delphi technique in developing the national set of child well-being indicators with ninety-six percent of participants either satisfied or very satisfied with the approach taken. The main advantages associated with using this approach related to its ability to be inclusive of a very broad number of views and stakeholders. This, in turn, led to a comprehensive and broader representation of children's lives. The approach itself was felt to be rigorous and systematic where, at each round, there was transparency and openness in how areas were identified for inclusion. It was also felt to be an efficient method for harnessing group opinions and there were significant time-savings for many participants.

2.7 CREDIBILITY OF THE STUDY

Since Sackman's (1975) initial critique of the Delphi technique and Linstone and Turoff's (1975) claim that this method is more 'art than science', a substantial literature has developed about the credibility of Delphi as a research method. Criticisms of the Delphi technique eloquently summed up by Gupta and Clarke (1996) include:

> **'Conceptual and methodological inadequacies, potential for sloppy execution, crudely designed questionnaires, poor choice of experts, unreliable result analysis, limited value of feedback and consensus, and instability of responses among consecutive Delphi rounds'**
>
> (Gupta and Clarke, 1996, p. 187).

In essence, there is potential for compromising credibility at all stages of a Delphi study. Some authors have argued that the Delphi technique is an interpretative research approach and should be judged accordingly (Keeney et al., 2001). This, however, is problematic because, although there is some agreement that the terminology and criteria used to judge qualitative enquiry should differ from that of quantitative studies, there is little agreement around the precise criteria that should be used (Emden and Sandelowski, 1999; Lincoln and Guba, 2000; Cutcliffe and McKenna, 2002). According to Powell (2003), a decision trail should be set in a way that provides sufficient evidence to defend the appropriateness of the method to address the problem selected, choice of expert panel, data collection procedures, identification of justifiable consensus levels, and means of dissemination and implementation.

Some of these areas have also been identified by others, operating from a more positivist paradigm (e.g. van Zolingen and Klaassen, 2003). They have suggested that compromises to the validity and reliability of a Delphi study arise from the value-led nature of feedback and consensus and the instability of responses. These areas are, in turn, influenced by the number of experts, their average expertise and the average inter-correlation of their judgements. These authors argue for setting specific guidelines around each of these areas, so that the reliability of a Delphi study (or whether a replication of a Delphi study would give the same results with a different panel) can be judged.

Others have suggested that the credibility of a Delphi study rests on whether it is effective in aiding decision-making. The extent to which this is the case has been subject to some examination. One systematic review of empirical studies (N = 25) comparing Delphi study with standard interacting groups concluded, with some caution, that Delphi groups outperform groups in decision-making and forecasting (Rowe and Wright, 1999).

Throughout this document, we have identified areas of potential compromise in the carrying out of this Study and have presented a literature on areas around which methodological decisions subsequently taken were based. We view this as the conception of a decision trail and suggest that responses and decisions taken on the basis of questions raised provide a mechanism for making judgements about the credibility of the Study.

In addition, we engaged with a small group of advisors, each with a different area of expertise and these advisors were critical to the on-going oversight and methodological rigour of the Study. These advisors were:

- Dr. Ed. Carroll, Independent researcher
- Ms. Deirdre Cullen, Central Statistics Office
- Ms. Eithne Fitzgerald, National Disability Authority
- Dr. Maeve Henchion, Teagasc

This Group, each of whom had a particular expertise in an area relevant to the Study, provided guidance and support for us while, at the same time, providing a monitoring mechanism to ensure transparency in the conduct of the Study. We believe this further supports the credibility of the Study.

2.8 Ethical Issues

Ethical issues 'saturate all stages of the research process' and start with the researcher's choice of topic and method (Punch, 1998, p. 281). We believe it was ethical to adopt a Delphi technique to identify the national set of child well-being indicators. First, this technique facilitated the engagement of more expertise than any other group method. In addition, this type of study facilitated 'fair' representation of the views of each participant because each participant had an equal opportunity to have their views taken into account. Alternative mechanisms for reaching consensus would not have provided as transparent a decision trail for each indicator, and the capacity of the Delphi technique to achieve this meant that the rationale for inclusion and exclusion of indicators could be clearly stated. This is likely to lead to greater acceptance of the findings than other methods.

The potential for harm in this Study was relatively low, because participants were mature adults and, as each were chosen on the basis of their expertise, they were not considered vulnerable. Nevertheless, other ethical issues revolving around consent, privacy and confidentiality of data were also considered and informed consent was achieved at each stage of the Study. Participants were informed about the purpose of the Study, the procedures to be followed, the anticipated time commitment, and contact details for the Principal Investigators if they wished to ask any questions about the Study. They were of course free to withdraw from the Study at any time.

In the research context, the right to privacy can be violated during the course of an investigation or after a study has been completed. In this case, every effort was made to protect the privacy of the participants. Two ways of protecting privacy are through confidentiality and anonymity. The essence of anonymity is that information provided by participants should in no way reveal their identity (Cohen et al., 2000), and such anonymity is a central feature of the Delphi technique. Individual names or positions were not directly linked to individual responses in the questionnaire feedback. Requirements under data protection legislation were also complied with.

In summary, this Study actively subscribed to principles of mutual respect, non-coercion and non-manipulation, the support of democratic values, and the belief that every research act implies moral and ethical decisions (Denzin and Lincoln, 1994). These principles were used to guide each part of the Study and at all stages, issues relating to consent, privacy, and confidentiality were key features.

2.9 CONCLUSION

To conclude, this report has presented an overview of the methodological issues arising in the course of the development of a national set of child well-being indicators. Part One of the report provides an overview of the Delphi technique itself and considers issues relating to categorisations, advantages, disadvantages, purpose, processes, and epistemological underpinnings of the Delphi technique. In the current development, the adoption of the Delphi technique enabled the collation of a large number of varying viewpoints across a diverse panel of expertise and a nationally geographical area. In addition, it provided a mechanism through which each person had an equal opportunity to contribute. This would not have been possible with such large numbers in a face-to-face interaction.

Part Two of the report uses seven systematically identified studies, undertaken elsewhere, to provide guidance about key areas of contention in respect of the Delphi technique including methodological concerns such as sampling, panel expertise, questionnaire development for each round, data collection, analysis and consensus. Consideration was given to each of these areas and decisions taken in respect of this Study clearly identified throughout the report. Issues relating to study credibility have been made explicit and this report in itself contributes to the audit trail.

The final set comprises forty-two child well-being indicators across thirty-five areas (Appendix 7) and data from the final questionnaire round shows that ninety percent of participants (N=43), were either satisfied or very satisfied with that outcome. There were also high levels of agreement that the indicator set met various selection criteria with responses suggesting agreement ranged between eighty-three percent (for enough measures of 'children of all ages') and ninety-seven percent (the overall set is comprehensiveness). Finally, ninety-six percent of participants reported they were 'satisfied' (fifty percent) or 'very satisfied' (forty-six percent) with the process of development. We are concluding therefore, that the Delphi technique is an appropriate and acceptable mechanism to achieve consensus when developing sets of indicators.

SPEEDO

35

3.0 REFERENCES

Andrews, A., Ben-Arieh, A., Carlson, M., Damon, W., Dweck, C., Earls, F., Garcia-Coll, C., Gold, R., Halfon, N., Hart, R., Lerner, R.M., McEwen, B., Meaney, M., Offord, D., Patrick, D., Peck, M., Trickett, B., Weisner, T. and Zuckerman, B. (Ecology Working Group) (2002) *Ecology of Child Well-Being: Advancing the Science and the Science-Practice Link.* Georgia: Centre for Child Well-Being.

Blackburn, S. (1999) *Think.* Oxford: Oxford University Press.

Bronfenbrenner, U. (1979) *The Ecology of Human Development.* Cambridge, MA: Harvard University Press.

Bronfenbrenner, U. (1993) *The Ecology of Cognitive Development: Research Models and Fugitive Findings.* In: Wozniak, R.H. and Fischer, K.W. (eds.) *Development in Context Acting and Thinking in Specific Environments.* NewJersey: Lawrence Erlbaum Associates Inc. Publishers: 3-44.

Bronfenbrenner, U. (1995) *Developmental Ecology through Space and Time: A Future Perspective.* In: Moen, P., Elder, Jr G.H. and Luscher, K. *Examining Lives in Context: Perspectives on the Ecology of Human Development.* Washington DC: American Psychological Association: 619-647.

Brooks, A.M. and Hanafin, S. (2005) *Measuring Child Well-Being: An Inventory of Key Indicators, Domains and Indicator Selection Criteria to Support the Development of a National Set of Child Well-Being Indicators.* Dublin: The Stationery Office.

Broomfield, D. and Humphries, G.M. (2001) Using the Delphi Technique to Identify the Cancer Education Requirements of General Practitioners. *Medical Education,* 35: 928-937.

Campbell, S.M., Cantrill, J.A. and Roberts, D. (2000) Prescribing Indicators for UK General Practice: Delphi Consultation Study. *BMJ,* 321: 425-428.

Campbell, S.M., Shield, T., Rogers, A. and Gask, L. (2004) How do Stakeholder Groups Vary in a Delphi Technique About Primary Mental Health Care and What Factors Influence their Ratings? *Qual Saf Health Care,* 13 (6): 428-34.

Carney, O., McIntosh, J. and Worth, A. (1996) The Use of the Nominal Group Technique in Research with Community Nurses. *Journal of Advanced Nursing,* 23: 1024-1029.

Carroll, E. (2002) *The Well-being of Children: Four Papers Exploring Conceptual, Ethical and Measurement Issues.* Dublin: Irish Youth Foundation.

Central Statistics Office (2004) *Information Society Statistics – Ireland 2004.* Dublin: The Stationery Office. Available at: http://www.cso.ie/newsevents/documents/ictireland 2004.pdf [Accessed: 14th January 2005].

Cohen, L. and Manion, L. (1994) *Research Methods in Education (4th Edition).* London: Routledge Falmer.

Cohen, L., Manion, L. and Morrison, K. (2000) *Research Methods in Education (5th Edition).* London: Routledge Falmer.

Courtenay, G. and Mekkelholt, P. (1997) *England and Wales Youth Cohort Study Handbook: The First Ten Years.* London: Department for Education and Employment.

Crisp, J., Pelletier, D., Duffuield, C., Adams, A. and Nagy, S. (1997) The Delphi Method? *Nursing Research,* 46(2): 116-118.

Cutcliffe, J.R. and McKenna, H.P. (2002) When do we Know that we Know? Considering the Truth of Research Findings and the Craft of Qualitative Research. *International Journal of Nursing Studies,* 39: 611-618.

Denzin, N.K. and Lincoln, Y.S. (1994) Introduction: Entering the Field of Qualitative Research. In: Denzin, N.K. and Lincoln, Y.S. (eds.) *Handbook of Qualitative Research.* London: Sage: 1-17.

Emden, C. and Sandelowski, M. (1999) The Good, the Bad and the Relative, Part Two: Goodness and the Criterion Problem in Qualitative Research. *International Journal of Nursing Practice,* 5: 2-7.

Farrington, D.J., Gallagher, B., Morley, L., St. Ledger, R. and West, D.J. (1990) Minimizing Attrition in Longitudinal Research: Methods of Tracing and Securing Cooperation in a 24-year Follow-up Study. In: Magnusson, D. and Bergman, L. (eds.) *Data Quality in Longitudinal Research.* Cambridge: Cambridge University Press.

Fein, J.A., Lavelle, J.M., Ginsburgt, K.R. and Giardino, A.P. (1997) A Methodology to Maximize Resident Input in Improving a Paediatric Rotation. *Arch Pediatr Adolesc Med,* 151: 840-844.

Fitzgerald, E. (2004) *Counting Our Children: An Analysis of Official Data Sources on Children and Childhood in Ireland.* Dublin: Children's Research Centre, University of Dublin, Trinity College.

Fitzsimmons, J.A. and Fitzsimmons, M.J. (eds.) (2001) *Service Management: Operations, Strategy and Information Technology (4th Edition).* Boston: McGraw-Hill.

Ford, D.H. and Lerner, R.M. (1992) *Developmental Systems Theory: An Integrative Approach.* Newbury Park, CA: Sage.

Gergen, K.J. (1995) Social Construction and the Educational Process. In: Steffe, L. and Gale, J. (eds.) *Constructivism in Education.* Hove, UK: Lawrence Erlbaum Associates: 17-40.

Goodman, C.M. (1987) The Delphi Technique: A Critique. *Journal of Advanced Nursing,* 12: 729-734.

Greatorex, J. and Dexter, T. (2000) An Accessible Analytical Approach for Investigating What Happens Between the Rounds of a Delphi Study. *Journal of Advanced Nursing,* 32(4): 1016-1024.

Griffiths, P. (2002) Evidence Informing Practice: Introducing the Mini-Review. *British Journal of Community Nursing,* 7(1): 38-40.

Guba, E.G. and Lincoln, Y.S. (1994) Competing Paradigms in Qualitative Research. In: Denzin, N.K. and Lincoln, Y.S. (eds.) *Handbook of Qualitative Research.* London: Sage: 105-117.

Gupta, U.G. and Clarke, R.E. (1996) Theory and Applications of the Delphi Technique: A Bibliography (1975-1994) *Technological Forecasting and Social Change,* 53: 185-211.

Hasson, F., Keeney, S. and McKenna, H. (2000) Research Guidelines for the Delphi Survey Technique. *Journal of Advanced Nursing,* 32(4): 1008-1015.

Hennekens, C. and Buring, S.D. (1987) *Epidemiology in Medicine.* Boston: Little, Brown and Company.

Iavicoli, S., Rondinone, B., Marinaccio, A. and Fingerhut, M. (2005) Identification of Research Priorities in Occupational Health. *Occup Environ Med,* 62 (2):71-2.

Keeney, S., Hasson, F. and McKenna, H.P. (2001) A Critical Review of the Delphi Technique as a Research Methodology for Nursing. *International Journal of Nursing Studies,* 38: 195-200.

Lai, V.S., Wong, B.K. and Cehung, W. (2002) Group Decision-Making in a Multiple Criteria Environment: A Case Using the AHP in Software Selection. *European Journal of Operational Research,* 137: 134-144.

Lincoln, Y.S. and Guba, E.G. (1985) *Naturalistic Inquiry.* London: Sage.

Lincoln, Y.S. and Guba, E.G. (2000) Paradigmatic Controversies, Contradictions, and Emerging Confluences. In: Denzin, N.K. and Lincoln, Y.S. (eds.) *Handbook of Qualitative Research.* London: Sage: 163-188.

Linstone, H.A. and Turoff, M. (eds.) (1975) *The Delphi Method Techniques and Applications.* Massachusetts, Reading: Addison-Wesley.

Marshall, C. and Rossman, G.B. (1995) *Designing Qualitative Research (2nd Edition).* London: Sage.

McKenna, H. (1994) The Delphi Technique: A Worthwhile Research Approach for Nursing? *Journal of Advanced Nursing,* 19: 1221-1225.

Millar, G. (2001) The Development of Indicators for Sustainable Tourism: Results of a Delphi Survey of Tourism Researchers. *Tourism Management,* 22: 351-362.

Monti, E.J. and Tingen, M.S. (1999) Multiple Paradigms of Nursing Science. *Advances in Nursing Science, 21(4): 64-80.*

Moore, K.A. (1997) Criteria for Indicators of Child Well-Being. In: Hauser, R.M., Brown, B.V. and Prosser, W.R. (eds.) *Indicators of Children's Well-Being.* New York: Russell Sage Foundation.

Morgan, D.L. (1997) *Focus Groups as Qualitative Research (2nd Edition).* London: Sage.

Munier, F. and Rondé, P. (2001) The Role of Knowledge Codification in the Emergence of Consensus Under Uncertainty: Empirical Analysis and Policy Implications. *Research Policy,* 20: 1537-1551.

Murphy, M.K., Black, N.A., Lamping, D.L., McKee, C.M., Sanderson, C.D.B., Askham, J. and Marteau, T. (1998) *Consensus Development Methods and their Use in Clinical Guideline Development: A Review.* United Kingdom: Health Technology Assessment 2(3) http://www.hta.nhsweb.nhs.uk/pdfexecs/summ203.pdf [Accessed: 13th September 2003].

National Children's Strategy (2000) *Our Children – Their Lives.* Dublin: The Stationery Office.

Orna, E. and Stevens, G. (1995) *Managing Information for Research.* Buckingham: Open University Press.

Powell, C. (2003) The Delphi Technique: Myths and Realities. *Journal of Advanced Nursing,* 41(4): 376-382.

Punch, K. (1998) *Introduction to Social Research.* London: Sage.

Reed, J. and Roskell, V. (1997) Focus Groups: Issues of Analysis and Interpretation. *Journal of Advanced Nursing,* 26: 765-771.

Robertson, H.A. and MacKinnon, N.J. (2002) Development of a List of Consensus-Approved Clinical Indicators of Preventable Drug-Related Morbidity in Older Adults. *Clinical Therapeutics,* 24(10): 1595-1613.

Robson, C. (1993) *Real World Research.* Oxford: Blackwell Publishing.

Rogers, M.R. and Lopez, E.C. (2002) Identifying Critical Cross-Cultural School Psychology Competencies. *Journal of School Psychology*, 40(2): 115-141.

Rowe, G. and Wright, G. (1999) The Delphi Technique as a Forecasting Tool: Issues and Analysis. *International Journal of Forecasting,* 15: 353-375.

Sackman, H. (1975) *Delphi Critique.* Massachusetts, Lexington: Lexington Books.

Schuster, M.A., Asch, S.M., McGlynn, E.A., Kerr, E., Hardy, A.M. and Gifford, D.S. (1997) Development of a Quality of Care Measurement System for Children and Adolescents: Methodological Considerations and Comparisons with a System for Adult Women. *Arch Pediatr Adolesc Med*, 151: 1085-1092.

Schwandt, T.A. (2000) Three Epistemological Stances for Qualitative Inquiry. In: Denzin, N.K. and Lincoln, Y.S. (eds.) *Handbook of Qualitative Research (2nd Edition).* London: Sage: 189-213.

Sharkey, S.B. and Sharples, A.Y. (2001) An Approach to Consensus Building Using the Delphi Technique: Developing a Learning Resource in Mental Health. *Nurse Education Today,* 21: 398-408.

Snyder-Halpern, R. (2002) Indicators of Organizational Readiness for Clinical Information Technology Systems Innovation: A Delphi Study. *International Journal of Medical Informatics,* 63: 179-204.

Snyder-Halpern, R., Thompson, C. and Schaffer, J. (2003) Comparison of Mailed vs. Internet Applications of the Delphi Technique in Clinical Informatics Research http://www.amia.org/pubs/symposia/D200120.PDF [Accessed: 4th July 2004].

Stewart, J. (2001) Is the Delphi Technique a Qualitative Method? *Medical Education,* 35: 922-923.

Taylor, S. and Lynn, P. (1996) *England and Wales Youth Cohort Study (YCS) The Effect of Time Between Contacts, Questionnaire Length, Personalisation and Other Factors on Response to the YCS.* London: Department for Education and Employment.

Thompson, D. (1995) *The Concise Oxford Dictionary of Current English.* Oxford: Clarendon Press.

van Zolingen, S.J. and Klaassen, C.A. (2003) Selection Processes in a Delphi Study about Key Qualifications in Senior Secondary Vocational Education. *Technological Forecasting and Social Change,* 70: 317-340.

Wang, C.C., Wang, Y., Zhang, K., Fang, J., Liu, W., Luo, S., Tang, S., Wang, S. and Lu, V.C. (2003) Reproductive Health Indicators for China's Rural Areas. *Social Science and Medicine,* 57(2): 217-225.

Ward, H. (1998) Using a Child Development Model to Assess the Outcomes of Social Work Interventions with Families. *Children & Society,* 12: 202-211.

Ward, H. (eds.) (1995) *Looking After Children: Research into Practice. The Second Report to the Department of Health on Assessing Outcomes in Child Care.* London: HMSO.

Williams, P.L. and Webb, C. (1994) The Delphi Technique: A Methodological Discussion. *Journal of Advanced Nursing,* 19: 180-186.

Zeitlin, J., Wildman, K., Breart, G., Alexander, S., Barros, H., Blondel, B., Buitendijk, S., Gissler, M., MacFarlane, A. and the PERISTAT Scientific Advisory Committee (2003) PERISTAT: Indicators for Monitoring and Evaluating Perinatal Health in Europe. *European Journal of Public Health,* 13 (3): 29-37.

40

41

APPENDIX 1

PEOPLE INVITED TO TAKE PART IN THE PANEL OF EXPERTISE

Ms. Margaret Rogers	Barnardos
Ms. Liz Leonard	Barnardos
Mr. Heino Schonfeld	Centre for Early Childhood Development and Education
Dr. Saoirse NicGabhainn	Centre for Health Promotion Studies, National University of Ireland, Galway
Dr. Noírín Hayes	Centre for Social and Educational Research, Dublin Institute of Technology
Prof. Patricia Noonan-Walsh	Centre for the Study of Developmental Disabilities, University College Dublin
Ms. Mary Hargaden	Childcare Policy Unit, Department of Health and Children
Ms. Mary O'Connor	Children in Hospital Ireland
Mr. Ray Dooley	Children's Rights Alliance
Prof. Robbie Gilligan	Children's Research Centre, University of Dublin, Trinity College
Dr. Jean Whyte	Children's Research Centre, University of Dublin, Trinity College
Dr. Jim Walsh	Combat Poverty Agency
Ms. Catriona Dwan	Community Worker
Dr. Nollaig Byrne	Department of Child and Family Psychiatry, Mater Misericordiae Hospital, Dublin
Ms. Breda Naughton	Department of Education and Science
Mr. Gerry Hayes	Department of Justice, Equality and Law Reform
Ms. Sylda Langford	Department of Justice, Equality and Law Reform
Ms. Eiméar Fisher	Department of Justice, Equality and Law Reform
Mr. Frank Martin	Department of Law, National University of Ireland, Cork
Dr. Ursula Kilkelly	Department of Law, National University of Ireland, Cork
Dr. Anthony Staines	Department of Public Health and Epidemiology, University College Dublin
Mr. Heber McMahon	Department of Social and Family Affairs
Mr. Michael Rush	Department of Social Policy and Social Work, University College Dublin
Dr. Valerie Richardson	Department of Social Policy and Social Work, University College Dublin
Ms. Valerie O'Brien	Department of Social Policy and Social Work, University College Dublin
Dr. Helen Buckley	Department of Social Studies, University of Dublin, Trinity College
Dr. Colette McAuley	Department of Social Work, Queens University, Belfast
Dr. Rebecca King-O'Riain	Department of Sociology, National University of Ireland, Maynooth

Ms. Elaine Kelly	Department of the Taoiseach
Ms. Yvonne O'Neill	Eastern Regional Health Authority
Prof. Brian Nolan	Economic and Social Research Institute
Dr. Joan Hanafin	Education Department, National University of Ireland, Cork
Dr. Peter Archer	Education Research Centre, St. Patrick's College, Drumcondra
Ms. Liz Kerrins	End Child Poverty Coalition
Mr. Pat Bennett	Family Support Agency
Mr. Niall O'Baoill	Fatima Groups United
Ms. Olive McGovern	Health Promotion Unit, Department of Health and Children
Ms. Breda Cleary	Institute of Community Health Nursing
Mr. Owen Metcalfe	Institute of Public Health in Ireland
Ms. Frances Fletcher	Intellectual Disability Services, Department of Health and Children
Ms. Irene Gunning	IPPA, the Early Childhood Organisation
Ms. Catherine Carthy	Irish Association of Young People in Care
Dr. Ailis Ní Riain	Irish College of General Practitioners
Mr. Sean Cottrell	Irish Primary Principals Network
Ms. Michele Clarke	Irish Social Services Inspectorate
Mr. Paul Gilligan	Irish Society for the Prevention of Cruelty to Children
Mr. Liam O'Dwyer	Irish Youth Foundation
Ms. Margaret Burns	Jesuit Centre for Faith and Justice
Dr. Barney O'Reilly	Kerry Education Service
Ms. Liz O'Sullivan	Kildare Youth Service
Dr. Anne Good	National Disability Authority
Ms. Sarah Craig	National Economic and Social Forum
Mr. Feargal O'Neill	National Educational Psychological Service
Ms. Anne Colgan	National Parents Council
Ms. Christine McMaster	North Western Heath Board
Mr. Seamus McLoughlin	Department of Education and Science
Ms. Geraldine Brereton	One Family, The National Association of Single Parent Families
Ms. Maeve Crosbie	Parent
Ms. Ria Williams	Parent
Mr. Jim Symons	Parent
Ms. Breda Sammon	Parent
Ms. Carol Purcell	Parent
Ms. Janey Troy	Parent
Dr. Paula Byrne	Parent
Mr. David Brooks	Parent
Ms. Sandra Cahill	Parent
Ms. Susan Kenna	Parent
Ms. Deirdre Lynch	Parent
Mr. Kieran Ryan	Parent

Ms. Catríona de Bourca	Parent
Ms. Anna-May Harkin	Planning and Evaluation Unit, Department of Health and Children
Mr. Pat Dolan	Political Science and Sociology, National University of Ireland, Galway
Dr. Sean Denyer	Programme of Action for Children
Ms. Celia Keenaghan	Programme of Action for Children
Dr. Eilish Hennessy	Psychology Department, University College Dublin
Dr. Diane Hogan	Psychology Department, University of Dublin, Trinity College
Ms. Margaret Casey	Queen of Angels National School
Ms. Rosemary Horgan	Ronan Daly Jermyn Solicitors
Mr. Kieran McKeown	Social and Economic Research Consultant
Dr. John Pinkerton	Social Work Department, Queens University, Belfast
Dr. Deirdre Murray	South Eastern Health Board
Ms. Ann Godfrey	Southern Health and Social Services Board, Northern Ireland
Ms. Elizabeth Burke	Southern Health Board
Ms. Anne Halliday	St. John of God Kildare Services
Ms. Hilary Kenny	Trainer/Consultant
Sr. Frances Murphy	Warrenmount Presentation Secondary School
Mr. Dermot Stokes	Youthreach

45

APPENDIX 2

ROUND ONE QUESTIONNAIRE

THE DEVELOPMENT OF A NATIONAL SET OF CHILD WELL-BEING INDICATORS USING THE DELPHI TECHNIQUE

Research Division, NCO

Thank you for agreeing to participate in this Study, which is concerned with getting agreement on the key areas of children's lives that the national set of child well-being indicators should measure.

This questionnaire is divided into two sections. Section 1 presents a series of background questions, which will provide a context for analysing your responses. Section 2 presents 56 potential areas for inclusion in the national set of child well-being indicators. You are asked to rate the relative importance of each of these areas out of 10, where 0 = low priority for inclusion and 10 = high priority for inclusion in the final indicator set (half points are permitted). For example, if you think an indicator relating to abuse and maltreatment is high priority, you could rate it 9 out of 10. Alternatively, if you think it is a low priority indicator, you could rate it 3.5 out of 10.

A child well-being indicator is a measure that assesses well-being at 'a point in time, over time and across geographic areas and population groups' (Moore, 1999). For the purpose of this Study, please consider the following broad definition of well-being:

> 'Healthy and successful individual functioning (involving physiological, psychological and behavioural levels of organisation), positive social relationships (with family members, peers, adult caregivers, and community and societal institutions, for instance, school and faith and civic organisations), and a social ecology that provides safety (e.g., freedom from interpersonal violence, war and crime), human and civil rights, social justice and participation in civil society'. (Andrew et al., 2002, p.103)

Please also note that, to conform with the spirit and principles of the United Nations Convention on the Rights of the Child (1989) and the National Children's Strategy (2000), the following definition of a child has been adopted by the National Children's Office - 'every human being below the age of eighteen years'.

Therefore, it is hoped that age appropriate indicators are identified, which assess well-being in its broadest sense (as outlined above) at every age from birth through adolescence and, where possible, across time, geographic areas and population groups.

Please return your completed questionnaire by **Friday, 9th April 2004**. Your response will remain confidential and will not, at any time, be disclosed to other participants in this Study. You will receive the results from this questionnaire at round two of the Study.

Thank you for your time and assistance.

Sinéad Hanafin, PhD, Head of Research, National Children's Office
Anne-Marie Brooks, Research Officer, National Children's Office

SECTION 1: BACKGROUND INFORMATION

A) Name: ____________________

B) In what capacity are you responding to this questionnaire?

- ☐ Policy maker
- ☐ Researcher/ Academic
- ☐ Practitioner/ Service Provider
- ☐ Parent
- ☐ Other

If your work relates to children, please answer questions c-i:

C) Which organisation, if any, do you represent? ____________________

____

D) Which of the following describes the main focus of your work?

- ☐ Child health
- ☐ Child education
- ☐ Childcare
- ☐ Child protection
- ☐ Children participation
- ☐ Juvenile justice
- ☐ Other

E) Does your work relate to all children of all ages?

- ☐ Yes
- ☐ No

F) If no, please specify your target group: ____________________

____

G) How many years have you been working in this area? ____________________

H) Aside from relevant experience, do you hold any qualification you consider relevant to child well-being?

- ☐ Yes
- ☐ No

I) If yes, please specify: ____________________

FOR PARENTS ONLY:

J) How many children do you have:
Under 18 years __________

Over 18 years __________

SECTION 2: Indicators of Child Well-Being Relating to:	\10
1. Abuse and maltreatment (e.g. neglect, physical abuse, sexual abuse, emotional abuse)	
2. Academic attainment (e.g. reading, mathematics, science skills, results of State Examinations)	
3. Academic commitment (e.g. homework habits, attitudes towards learning and school)	
4. Attendance at school (e.g. absenteeism, truancy, disciplinary absences)	
5. Availability, accessibility, affordability and quality of housing for families with children	
6. Availability, accessibility, affordability, quality of, and participation in, arts, cultural and play facilities (inc. natural environment) by children and young people	
7. Availability, accessibility, affordability, quality and utilisation of basic health services for children and young people	
8. Availability, accessibility, affordability, quality and utilisation of child care services (informal and formal)	
9. Availability, accessibility, affordability, quality of, and enrolment in, early childhood education programmes (e.g. pre-school, kindergarten, nursery school)	
10. Availability, accessibility, affordability, quality and utilisation of educational resources (e.g. computer, library, books)	
11. Breast-feeding	
12. Children and young people dependent on supplementary welfare and/or charitable donations (e.g. back to school clothing and footwear allowance)	
13. Children and young people in care (e.g. foster care, residential care, pre-adoptive care)	
14. Children and young people with additional needs (e.g. homeless children, asylum seeking children, children with disabilities, children involved in divorce)	
15. Chronic health conditions (e.g. cystic fibrosis, diabetes, asthma, cancer)	
16. Community characteristics (e.g. community crime, community poverty level, community facilities such as church, community centres, police station)	
17. Completion of school (e.g. early school leavers)	
18. Crimes committed by children and young people	
19. Crimes committed on children and young people	

continued on next page >

20. Dental health	
21. Economic security (e.g. children in poverty, secure parental employment, food insecurity)	
22. Enrolment in education (e.g. enrolment in pre-primary, primary, secondary and tertiary education)	
23. Health of the infant at birth (e.g. birth weight, birth defects, prematurity)	
24. Helping others and volunteering (e.g. helping family, helping friends, helping out in the community)	
25. Hospitalisation	
26. Hours of sleep	
27. Immunisation (e.g. vaccinations against measles, mumps, rubella, polio)	
28. Injuries (e.g. burns, poisonings, fractures, road traffic accidents)	
29. Mental health (e.g. attempted suicide, referrals to mental health services, ability to cope)	
30. Nutrition (e.g. healthy diet, eating disorders)	
31. Parental or family characteristics (e.g. parental education level, use of tobacco, alcohol or drugs)	
32. Parental time with children (e.g. reading to children, involvement in activities with children)	
33. Participation in decision-making (e.g. involvement in student councils, ability to influence decisions in matters which affect them)	
34. Participation in out-of-school activities (e.g. scouting groups, community sports programmes)	
35. Participation in school activities (e.g. school athletics, school music, debating)	
36. Pastimes (e.g. reading, television viewing, physical activities, computer games)	
37. Permanency and stability in the lives of children and young people (e.g. moving house, moving school)	
38. Pets	
39. Pre-natal behaviour (e.g. attendance for pre-natal care, use of tobacco, alcohol or drugs during pregnancy, folic acid intake)	
40. Public expenditure on services for children and young people (e.g. expenditure on education, health, childcare, child protection)	

continued on next page >

41. Relationships with parents and family (e.g. parental attachment, parental style, parental rules and guidance)	
42. Relationships with peers (e.g. friends in school and the community, bullying, dating)	
43. Relationships with significant others (i.e. other adults excluding parents or relatives such as teachers and youth leaders)	
44. Safe mobility and transport of children and young people (e.g. seat belt use, helmet use, exposure to drunk driving)	
45. School characteristics (e.g. teacher-pupil ratio, school services)	
46. School readiness (i.e. readiness of child to enter school at age 4/5)	
47. Screening for growth and development (e.g. hearing, vision, gross motor development, fine motor development)	
48. Self-esteem (e.g. confidence, belief in one's ability)	
49. Self-reported happiness	
50. Self-reported health status	
51. Sexual health and behaviour (e.g. sexually transmitted diseases, number of sexual partners, contraceptive use, unprotected intercourse)	
52. Spirituality and religion (e.g. religious service attendance)	
53. Use of tobacco, alcohol or drugs (age at first use, current use, frequent use, binge-drinking)	
54. Values and respect (e.g. respecting others, non-discrimination)	
55. Youth employment	
56. Weight and height (e.g. birth weight, moderately or severely underweight for age, obesity)	

57. Please comment on your responses.

____

____

____

58. Are there any additional areas that you feel should be included in the national set of child well-being indicators?

☐ Yes

☐ No

59. If yes, please identify those areas now, indicating why you feel they should be included.

____

THANK YOU FOR YOUR TIME AND ASSISTANCE.

APPENDIX 3

ROUND TWO QUESTIONNAIRE

THE DEVELOPMENT OF A NATIONAL SET OF CHILD WELL-BEING INDICATORS USING THE DELPHI TECHNIQUE

Research Division, NCO

Thank you for returning your completed questionnaire for this Study on child well-being indicators. You will recall that the purpose of this questionnaire was to generate agreement on the most important areas (approximately thirty) of children's lives that should be examined by the national set of child well-being indicators and we are delighted to report that there was a high level of agreement among the panel in this regard.

The results from this questionnaire have now been incorporated into a second questionnaire, which we now ask you to complete. The purpose of the second questionnaire is to establish if you are in agreement with the panel on the key areas that have been prioritised and also to seek some clarification and further feedback from you on several issues.

If agreement can be reached on the most important areas at this point, we will work with various agencies to identify and select the specific indicators to be used for each. Please note that we also intend to incorporate a number of general demographic indicators and policy indicators into the national set of child well-being indicators for context. It is anticipated that this work will be completed by Autumn 2004, at which time the results and final indicator set will be presented to you.

In completing this questionnaire, we draw your attention once again to the definition of well-being, which has been adopted for the purpose of this Study:

> **'Healthy and successful individual functioning, positive social relationships and a social ecology that provides safety, human and civil rights, social justice and participation in civil society'.**
> (Andrew et al., 2002, p.103)

When you have completed this questionnaire, click on the submit button and your response will be forwarded to the National Children's Office. You will be unable to submit incomplete responses or more than one questionnaire. Completed questionnaires must be submitted by **Monday, 21st June 2004**. Please note that your response will continue to remain confidential and will not, at any time, be disclosed to other participants in this Study.

If you experience any difficulties completing this questionnaire, please do not hesitate to contact Ms. Anne-Marie Brooks at (01) 242 0007. In the event that you experience difficulties completing this questionnaire on-line, a copy has also been sent to you in the post.

Thank you once again for your time and assistance and I look forward to receiving your response.

Sinéad Hanafin, PhD, Head of Research, National Children's Office
Anne-Marie Brooks, Research Officer, National Children's Office

1. The following 26 areas have been prioritised by the panel as areas that should be examined in the indicator set. Please indicate if you are in agreement with the panel opinion by ticking the appropriate box.

a. Abuse and maltreatment	☐ Yes	☐ No
b. Availability, accessibility, affordability, quality and utilisation of basic health services for children and young people	☐ Yes	☐ No
c. Economic security	☐ Yes	☐ No
d. Mental health	☐ Yes	☐ No
e. Relationships with parents and family	☐ Yes	☐ No
f. Availability, accessibility, affordability and quality of housing for families with children	☐ Yes	☐ No
g. Public expenditure on services for children and young people	☐ Yes	☐ No
h. Self-esteem	☐ Yes	☐ No
i. Crimes committed on children and young people	☐ Yes	☐ No
j. Children and young people with additional needs	☐ Yes	☐ No
k. Nutrition	☐ Yes	☐ No
l. Relationships with peers	☐ Yes	☐ No
m. Screening for growth and development	☐ Yes	☐ No
n. Completion of school	☐ Yes	☐ No
o. Enrolment in education	☐ Yes	☐ No
p. Children and young people in care	☐ Yes	☐ No
q. Sexual health and behaviour	☐ Yes	☐ No
r. Health of the infant at birth	☐ Yes	☐ No
s. Self-reported happiness	☐ Yes	☐ No
t. Chronic health conditions	☐ Yes	☐ No
u. Parental time with children	☐ Yes	☐ No
v. Immunisation	☐ Yes	☐ No
w. Use of tobacco, alcohol or drugs	☐ Yes	☐ No
x. Attendance at school	☐ Yes	☐ No
y. Availability, accessibility, affordability, quality and utilisation of child care services (informal/formal)	☐ Yes	☐ No
z. Values and respect	☐ Yes	☐ No

2. If you agree that the following key areas should be examined, we would now like you to identify one specific dimension from each. For example, if you think the indicator set should examine the affordability of basic health services as opposed to the quality of basic health services, we ask you to tick this preference.

a. Basic health services:

- ☐ Availability
- ☐ Accessibility
- ☐ Affordability
- ☐ Quality
- ☐ Utilisation

b. Child care services:

- ☐ Availability
- ☐ Accessibility
- ☐ Affordability
- ☐ Quality
- ☐ Utilisation

c. Housing:

- ☐ Availability
- ☐ Accessibility
- ☐ Affordability
- ☐ Quality

3. The areas that were not prioritised in the first round of this Study are listed below. If you feel strongly that any of these key areas should be examined in the indicator set, please identify the area and the reason you would like to see it included. You should select no more than three.

- Academic attainment
- Academic commitment
- Availability, accessibility, affordability, quality of, and enrolment in early childhood education
- Availability, accessibility, affordability, quality and utilisation of educational resources
- Breast-feeding
- Children and young people dependent on supplementary welfare and/or charitable donations
- Community characteristics
- Crimes committed by children and young people
- Dental health
- Helping others and volunteering
- Hospitalisation
- Hours of sleep
- Injuries
- Parental and/or family characteristics
- Participation in decision-making
- Participation in out-of-school activities
- Participation in school activities
- Permanency and stability in the lives of children and young people
- Pre-natal behaviour
- Relationships with significant others
- Safe mobility and transport of children and young people
- School characteristics
- School readiness
- Self-reported health status
- Spirituality and religion
- Youth employment
- Weight and height

a. **1st choice:** ______________________________

b. **2nd choice:** ______________________________

c. **3rd choice:** ______________________________

4. In developing this national set of child well-being indicators, the National Children's Office have also commissioned a study of children's understandings of well-being. The findings from this Study have shown that the areas prioritised by the children who participated in the Study are broadly similar to those prioritised by this panel. However, the children have prioritised three additional areas as follows:

- **Pets/animals:** children described 'pet/animals' as important contributors to their well-being in terms of, for example, giving and receiving love, having a companion and responsibility.
- **Things to do:** children described 'things to do' as important contributors to their well-being in terms of, for example, having fun, learning, enhancing health and making friends.
- **Environment/places:** children described 'environment/places' as important contributors to their well-being in terms of, for example, belonging and providing a context for activities.

Consequently, in keeping with Goal 1 of the National Children's Strategy that *'children will have a voice in matters which affect them and their views will be given due weight in accordance with their age and maturity',* the National Children's Office intend also to examine these areas in the final indicator set.

Are there any comments that you would like to make on these additional areas identified by the children?

5a. Do you have any general comments to make on the key areas that have been prioritised for inclusion in the national set of child well-being indicators?

5b. Name:

THANK YOU FOR YOUR TIME AND ASSISTANCE.

57

APPENDIX 4

LIST OF REPORTS IN THE INVENTORY

1. **Alaska Department of Health and Human Services (2000)** *Building Blocks: The Next Steps for Supporting Alaska's Young Children and Their Families.* Available at: http://www.gov.state.ak.us/children/nominations.html [Accessed: 4th March 2003].

2. **Al-Yaman, F., Bryant, M. and Sargeant, H. (2002)** *Australia's Children: Their Health and Well-Being 2002.* Canberra: Australian Institute of Health and Welfare. Available at: http://www.aihw.gov.au/publications/phe/ac02/ac02.pdf [Accessed: 14th January 2005].

3. **Annie E. Casey Foundation (2002)** *Children at Risk: State Trends 1990-2000: A PRB/ KIDS COUNT Special Report.* Baltimore, Maryland: Annie E. Casey Foundation. Available at: http://www.aecf.org/kidscount/c2ss/pdfs/entire_book.pdf [Accessed: 10th February 2003].

4. **Annie E. Casey Foundation (2003)** *Kidscount Data Book.* Baltimore, Maryland: Annie E. Casey Foundation. Available at: http://www.aecf.org/kidscount/databook/ [Accessed: 10th February 2003].

5. **Ben-Arieh, A., Hevener-Kaufman, N., Bowers-Andrews, A., Goerge, R.M., Joo-Lee, B. and Aber, J.L. (2001)** *Measuring and Monitoring Children's Well-Being.* Dordrecht, the Netherlands: Kluwer Academic Publishers.

6. **Bradshaw, J. (ed.) (2002)** *The Well-Being of Children in the UK.* London: Save the Children.

7. **Bradshaw, J. and Barnes, H. (1999)** *How do Nations Monitor the Well-Being of their Children? Paper to the LIS Child Poverty Conference Luxembourg 30th September 1999 - 2nd October 1999.* Heslington, York: Social Policy Research Unit, University of York. Available at: http://www.lisproject.org/links/cpconf/bradshaw.pdf [Accessed: 10th February 2003].

8. **Brownell, M., Martens, P., Kozyrskyj, A., Fergusson, P., Lerfald, J., Mayer, T., Derksen, S. and Friesen, D. (2001)** *Assessing the Health of Children in Manitoba: A Population-Based Study.* Manitoba: Manitoba Centre for Health Policy and Evaluation, Department of Community Health Sciences Faculty of Medicine, University of Manitoba. Available at: http://www.umanitoba.ca/centres/mchp/reports/child_pdfs.htm [Accessed: 3rd August 2004].

9. **Centre for Epidemiology, Indicators, Research and Evaluation (2000)** *The Health Status and Well-Being of Children and Youths in Western Sydney.* Western Sydney: Western Sydney Area Health Service. Available at: http://203.32.142.101/services/dsdph/EIRE/Publicat/HEALTH_S.PDF [Accessed: 21st May 2003].

10. **Child Trends (2003)** *Child Trends Data Bank.* Washington DC: Child Trends. Available at: http://www.childtrendsdatabank.org/ [Accessed: 14th April 2003].

11. **Children's Defence Fund (2003)** *Minnesota Kids A Closer Look: 2003 Data Book.* Minnesota: Children's Defence Fund. Available at: http://www.cdf-mn.org/PDF/KidsCountData_03/DataBook_2003.pdf [Accessed: 3rd August 2004].

12. **Combat Poverty Agency (2000)** *Submission on the National Children's Strategy.* Dublin: Combat Poverty Agency.

13. **Commission for Children and Young People (2002)** *Children and Young People in Queensland - A Snap Shot.* Queensland: Commission for Children and Young People. Available at: http://www.childcomm.qld.gov.au/publications/reports.htm [Accessed: 21st May 2003].

14. **Costello, L. (1999)** *A Literature Review of Children's Well-Being.* Dublin: Combat Poverty Agency.

15. **Department for Work and Pensions (2002)** *Opportunity for All: Fourth Annual Report.* London: HMSO. Available at: http://www.dwp.gov.uk/ofa/reports/2003/ pdf/report.pdf [Accessed: 10th February 2003].

16. **Department of Health and Children (2001)** *The Health of Our Children: The Second Annual Report of the Chief Medical Officer.* Dublin: The Stationery Office.

17. **El Tawila, S. (1997)** *Child Well-Being in Egypt.* Cairo: Social Research Centre, American University. Available at: http://www.childinfo.org/mics/Cntry_files/ Egyintro.pdf [Accessed: 10th February 2003].

18. **Federal Interagency Programme on Child and Family Statistics (2002)** *America's Children – Key National Indicators of Child Well-Being.* Washington DC: US Government Printing Office. Available at: http://www.childstats.gov/ac2002/ pdf/ac2002.pdf [Accessed: 10th February 2003].

19. **Government of Canada (2002)** *The Well-Being of Canada's Young Children.* Ottawa: Human Resources Development Canada and Health Canada. Available at: http://socialunion.gc.ca/ecd/2002/reportb-e.pdf [Accessed: 10th February 2003].

20. **Gutmann, B. and Hamilton, J. (2001)** *Trends in the Well-Being of America's Children and Youth 2001.* Washington DC: Office of the Assistant Secretary for Planning and Evaluation, U.S. Department of Health and Human Services. Available at: http://aspe.hhs.gov/hsp/01trends/ [Accessed: 10th February 2003].

21. **Hauser, R.M., Brown, B.V. and Prosser, W.R. (eds.) (1997)** *Indicators of Children's Well-Being.* New York: Russell Sage Foundation.

22. **Howell, F., Howell, P.R. and Gipson Wells, J. (1998)** *Indicators of the Well-Being of Mississippi Children.* Mississippi: Social Science Research Centre, Mississippi State University. Available at: http://www.ssrc.msstate.edu/publications/srrs98-1.pdf [Accessed: 3rd August 2003].

23. **Jensen, W., Myers, J., Sidorova, M., Duerr, M., Cragle, S., Brisolara, S., Berryhill, M., Lapp, B., Kehoe, D.A., Reed, B., Skillman, D.R., Englesby-Smith, J. and Wayda, M. (2002)** *Indicators of Well-Being Report: Shasta County Children Pre-Natal to Five and their Families.* Shasta County: First 5 Shasta, the Shasta Children and Family First Commission. Available at: http://www.ccfc.ca.gov/ shasta/PDFs/Well-BeingRpt.pdf [Accessed: 3rd August 2003].

24. **Maryland Partnership for Children, Youth and Families (2002)** *Maryland's Results for Well-Being. Baltimore,* Maryland: Maryland Partnership for Children, Youth and Families. Available at: http://www.ocyf.state.md.us/ [Accessed: 10th February 2003].

25. **Maternal and Child Health Bureau (2002)** Child Health USA: 2002. Washington DC: Maternal and Child Health Bureau, U.S. Department of Health and Human Services. Available at: http://mchb.hrsa.gov/chusa02/index.htm [Accessed: 3rd August 2003].

26. **Micklewright, J. and Stewart, K. (1999)** *Is the Well-Being of Children Converging in the European Union? Paper to the LIS Child Poverty Conference Luxembourg 30th September 1999 - 2nd October 1999.* Florence: UNICEF International Child Development Centre. Available at: http://www.lisproject.org/links/cpconf/ micklewright.pdf [Accessed: 10th February 2003].

27. **Mid-Western Health Board (2001)** *Health and Well-Being of Children in the Mid-West: Report of the Director of Public Health.* Limerick: Mid-Western Health Board.

28. **Ministry of Children and Family Development (2000)** *Indicators of Early Childhood Health and Well-Being in British Columbia: A Baseline Report.* British Columbia: Ministry of Children and Family Development. Available at: http://www.mcf.gov.bc.ca/publications/measure_success/final_indicators_document.pdf [Accessed: 10th February 2003].

29. **Ministry of Social Development (2004)** *Children and Young People: Indicators of Well-Being in New Zealand.* Available at: http://www.msd.govt.nz/documents/work-areas/csre/children-young-people-indicators-wellbeing-nz.pdf [Accessed: 14th January 2005].

30. **Minnesota Department of Human Services (2000)** *Measuring Our Performance and the Well-Being of Children: Indicators to Help Strengthen Minnesota's Child Welfare System.* Minnesota: Department of Human Services. Available at: http://www.dhs.state.mn.us/main/groups/children/documents/pub/DHS_id_007125.pdf [Accessed: 10th February 2003].

31. **Murphey, D. (2004)** *The Social Well-Being of Vermonters: A Report on Outcomes for Vermont Citizens.* Waterbury, Vermont: Vermont Agency of Human Services, Planning Division. Available at: http://www.ahs.state.vt.us/publs/docs/04swb/ 04SWB.pdf [Accessed: 14th January 2005].

32. **North Carolina Child Advocacy Institute (2002)** *NC Children's Index: A Profile of Leading Indicators on the Health and Well-Being of North Carolina's Children.* Raleigh, North Carolina: North Carolina Child Advocacy Institute. Available at: http://www.ncchild.org/CI2004/INDEX_02_WEB.pdf [Accessed: 10th February 2003].

33. **North Carolina Child Advocacy Institute and North Carolina Institute of Medicine (2002)** *North Carolina Child Health Report Card.* Raleigh, North Carolina: North Carolina Child Advocacy Institute and Durham, North Carolina: North Carolina Institute of Medicine. Available at: http://www.nciom.org/docs/ card2002.pdf [Accessed: 10th February 2003].

34. **Olivier, D.J. (2004)** *The State of the Child in Pennsylvania – 2004: State of the Child in Pennsylvania Fact Book Series.* Harrisburg, Pennsylvania: Pennsylvania KIDS COUNT. Available at: http://www.papartnerships.org/stateofthechild.asp [Accessed: 14th January 2005].

35. **Organisation for Economic Co-operation and Development (OECD) (1998)** *Methodology Sheets for Development Indicators: Methodological Notes and Indicator Sheets.* Paris: OECD. Available at: http://www.oecd.org/dataoecd/3/45/1896978.pdf [Accessed: 10th February 2003].

36. **Peterborough County - City Health Unit (2003)** *The First Nine Years: A Profile of Perinatal and Child Health in Peterborough County and City.* Peterborough: Peterborough County - City Health Unit. Available at: http://pcchu.peterborough.on.ca/First_Nine_Years_Second_Edition.PDF [Accessed: 3rd August 2004].

37. **Rahman, M., Palmer, G. and Kenway, P. (2001)** *Monitoring Poverty and Social Exclusion.* York, North Yorkshire: Joseph Rowntree Foundation. Available at: http://www.jrf.org.uk/knowledge/findings/socialpolicy/d31.asp [Accessed: 10th February 2003].

38. **Region of Peel Health Department (2002)** *Child Health Report: A Peel Health Status Report.* Peel: Region of Peel Health Department. Available at: http://www.region.peel.on.ca/health/health-status-report/pdfs-child/CH_report.pdf [Accessed: 3rd August 2004].

39. **Reidy, M. and Winje, C. (2002)** *Youth Indicators in Use in States as of September 2002: New York.* Chicago: Chapin Hall Centre for Children, University of Chicago. Available at: http://www.chapinhall.org/PDFDownload_new.asp?tk=1229292&ar= 1343&L2=65&L3=120 [Accessed: 13th May 2003].

40. **Reidy, M. and Winje, C. (2002)** *Youth Indicators in Use in States as of September 2002: Wyoming.* Chicago: Chapin Hall Centre for Children, University of Chicago. Available at: http://www.chapinhall.org/PDFDownload_new.asp?tk=1229292&ar= 1343&L2=65&L3=120 [Accessed: 13th May 2003].

41. **Reidy, M. and Winje, C. (2002)** *Youth Indicators in Use in States as of September 2002: Kansas.* Chicago: Chapin Hall Centre for Children, University of Chicago. Available at: http://www.chapinhall.org/PDFDownload_new.asp?tk=1229292&ar= 1343&L2=65&L3=120 [Accessed: 13th May 2003].

42. **Reidy, M. and Winje, C. (2002)** *Youth Indicators in Use in States as of September 2002: Iowa.* Chicago: Chapin Hall Centre for Children, University of Chicago. Available at: http://www.chapinhall.org/PDFDownload_new.asp?tk=1229292&ar= 1343&L2=65&L3=120 [Accessed: 13th May 2003].

43. **Reidy, M. and Winje, C. (2002)** *Youth Indicators in Use in States as of September 2002: Illinois.* Chicago: Chapin Hall Centre for Children, University of Chicago. Available at: http://www.chapinhall.org/PDFDownload_new.asp?tk=1229292&ar= 1343&L2=65&L3=120 [Accessed: 13th May 2003].

44. **Reidy, M. and Winje, C. (2002)** *Youth Indicators in Use in States as of September 2002: Missouri.* Chicago: Chapin Hall Centre for Children, University of Chicago.. Available at: http://www.chapinhall.org/PDFDownload_new.asp?tk=1229292&ar= 1343&L2=65&L3=120 [Accessed: 13th May 2003].

45. **Reidy, M. and Winje, C. (2002)** *Youth Indicators in Use in States as of September 2002: Maine.* Chicago: Chapin Hall Centre for Children, University of Chicago. Available at: http://www.chapinhall.org/PDFDownload_new.asp?tk=1229292&ar= 1343&L2=65&L3=120 [Accessed: 13th May 2003].

46. **Reidy, M. and Winje, C. (2002)** *Youth Indicators in Use in States as of September 2002: Georgia.* Chicago: Chapin Hall Centre for Children, University of Chicago. Available at: http://www.chapinhall.org/PDFDownload_new.asp?tk=1229292&ar= 1343&L2=65&L3=120 [Accessed: 13th May 2003].

47. **Report Card Working Group (2003)** *Toronto Report Card on Children: Volume 5. Toronto: Report Card Working Group.* Available at: http://www.city.toronto.on.ca/children/report/repcard5/repcard5.htm [Accessed: 3rd August 2004].

48. **Rigby, K. and Kohler, L. (eds.)(2002)** *Child Health Indicators of Life and Development.* Luxembourg: European Commission. Available at: http://europa.eu.int/comm/health/ph_projects/000/monitoring/fp_monitoring_2000_exs_08_en.pdf [Accessed: 10th February 2003].

49. **Smith, K.E., Bass, L.E. and Fields, J. M. (1998)** *Child Well-Being Indicators From the Survey of Income and Program Participation (SIPP): Working Paper 24.* Washington DC: Population Division, U.S. Bureau of the Census. Available at: http://www.census.gov/population/www/documentation/twps0024/twps0024.html [Accessed: 13th May 2003].

50. **Snyder, T. and Shafer, L. (1996)** *Youth Indicators 1996: Trends in the Well-Being of American Youth.* Washington DC: U.S. Department of Education, National Centre for Education Statistics. Available at: http://nces.ed.gov/pubs98/yi/youth.pdf [Accessed: 10th February 2003].

51. ***South Carolina KIDSCOUNT Report (2003)*** Available at: http://www.sckidscount.org/report03/SC_kc03.pdf [Accessed: 3rd August 2004].

52. **Tamburlini, G., Ronfani, L. and Buzzetti, R. (2001)** 'Development of a Child Health Indicator System in Italy'. *European Journal of Public Health,* 11 (1): 11-17.

53. **Tennessee Commission on Children and Youth (2002)** *The State of the Child in Tennessee.* Nashville, Tennessee: Tennessee Commission on Children and Youth. Available at: http://www.state.tn.us/tccy/kc02.pdf [Accessed: 13th May 2003].

54. **U.S. Department of Commerce (2003)** *A Child's Day: 2000 (Selected Indicators of Child Well-Being).* Washington DC: U.S. Department of Commerce, U.S. Census Bureau. Available at: http://www.census.gov/prod/2003pubs/p70-89.pdf [Accessed: 3rd August 2004].

55. **UNICEF (2001)** *A Decade of Transition: Regional Monitoring Report No. 8.* Florence: UNICEF Innocenti Research Centre. Available at: http://www.unicef-icdc.org/publications/pdf/monee8/eng/monee8_annex.pdf [Accessed: 14th April 2003].

i **Amanniyazova, L. (2000)** *Family Welfare in Turkmenistan: Trends and Indicators.* Ashgabat: National Institute of Statistics and Prognosis. Available at: http://www.unicef-icdc.org/research/ESP/CountryReports2000_01/ Turkmen00.pdf [Accessed: 14th April 2003].

ii **Banovec, T. (2000)** *Trends and Indicators on Child and Family Well-Being in Slovenia, 1989-1999.* Ljubljana: Statistical Office. Available at: http://www.uniceficdc.org/research/ESP/CountryReports2000_01/ Slovenia00.pdf [Accessed: 14th April 2003].

iii **Chirca, C. (2000)** *Trends and Indicators on Child and Family Well-Being in Romania.* Bucharest: National Institute for Statistics and Economic Studies. Available at: http://www.unicef-icdc.org/research/ESP/CountryReports2000_01/ Romania00.pdf [Accessed: 14th April 2003].

iv **Eidukiene, V. (2000)** *Child and Family Well-Being in Lithuania. Lithuania: Department of Statistics.* Available at: http://www.unicef-icdc.org/research/ESP/CountryReports2000_01/Lithuania00.pdf [Accessed: 14th April 2003].

v **Galazka, Z. (2000)** *Trends and Indicators on Child and Family Well-Being in Poland.* Warsaw: Central Statistical Office. Available at: http://www.unicef-icdc.org/research/ESP/CountryReports2000_01/Poland00.pdf [Accessed: 14th April 2003].

vi **Gardashkhanova, M. (2000)** *Trends and Indicators on Family and Children Well-Being in Azerbaijan.* Baku: State Statistical Committee. Available at: http://www.unicef-icdc.org/research/ESP/CountryReports2000_01/ Azerbaijan00.pdf [Accessed: 14th April 2003].

vii **Gasyuk, G. (2000)** *Trends and Indicators of the Child and Family Welfare in the Republic of Belarus (1990-1999).* Minsk: Ministry of Statistics and Analysis. Available at: http://www.unicef-icdc.org/research/ESP/CountryReports2000_01/Belarus00eng.pdf [Accessed: 14th April 2003].

viii **Gogishvili, T. (2000)** *Trends and Family Well-Being in Georgia.* Georgia: State Department for Statistics of Georgia. Available at: http://www.unicef-icdc.org/research/ESP/CountryReports2000_01/Georgia00fam.pdf [Accessed: 14th April 2003].

ix **Kalachova, I. (2000)** *Child and Family Welfare in Ukraine: Trends and Indicators. Kiev: State Committee for Statistics.* Available at: http://www.unicef-icdc.org/research/ESP/CountryReports2000_01/ Ukraine00.pdf [Accessed: 14th April 2003].

x **Kask, U. (2000)** *Trends and Indicators on Child Well-Being in Estonia.* Estonia: Statistical Office. Available at: http://www.unicef-icdc.org/research/ESP/Country Reports2000_01/Estonia00.pdf [Accessed: 14th April 2003].

xi **Koichumanova, K. (2000)** *Family and Child Welfare Trends in the Transition Period in Kyrgyzstan.* Bishkek: National Statistical Committee. Available at: http://www.unicef-icdc.org/research/ESP/CountryReports2000_01/ Kyrgyz00eng.pdf [Accessed: 14th April 2003].

xii **Lakatos, J. (2000)** *Poverty and Welfare Trends Over the 1990's in Hungary.* Budapest: Hungarian Central Statistical Office. Available at: http://www.unicef-icdc.org/research/ESP/CountryReports2000_01/ Hungary00.pdf [Accessed: 14th April 2003].

xiii **Magloutchiants, J. (2000)** *Trends and Indicators on Child and Family Well-Being in Armenia.* Yerevan: Department of Statistics State Register and Analysis. Available at: http://www.unicef-icdc.org/research/ESP/ CountryReports2000_01/ Armenia00.pdf [Accessed: 14th April 2003].

xiv **Mukhammadieva, B. (2000)** *Child and Family Welfare in Tajikistan: The Main Trends and Indicators.* Dushanbe: State Statistics Agency. Available at: http://www.unicef-icdc.org/research/ESP/CountryReports2000_01/ Tajik00.pdf [Accessed: 14th April 2003].

xv **Musabekov, E. (2000)** *Child and Family Welfare: Trends and Indicators in the Republic of Kazakhstan.* Almaty: National Statistics Agency. Available at: http://www.unicef-icdc.org/research/ESP/CountryReports2000_01/ Kazak00.pdf [Accessed: 14th April 2003].

xvi **Novak, J. (2000)** *Trends and Indicators on Child and Family Well-Being in the Czech Republic.* Prague: Czech Statistical Office. Available at: http://www.unicef-icdc.org/research/ESP/CountryReports2000_01/ CzechRep00.pdf [Accessed: 14th April 2003].

xvii **Placintar, E. (2000)** *Trends and Indicators on Child and Family Well-Being in Slovakia.* Bratislava: Statistical Office. Available at: http://www.unicef-icdc.org/research/ESP/CountryReports2000_01/Slovakia00.pdf [Accessed: 14th April 2003].

xviii **Puskovic, D. (2000)** *Poverty and Welfare Trends Over the 1990's in the FR Yugoslavia.* Belgrade: Federal Statistical Office. Available at: http:// www.unicef-icdc.org/research/ESP/CountryReports2000_01/ FRYugos00.pdf [Accessed: 14th April 2003].

xix **Tafi, J. (2000)** *Poverty and Welfare Over the 1990's in the Republic of Moldova: Indicators of Status and Trends.* Chisinau: Department for Statistical and Sociological Analysis. Available at: http://www.unicef-icdc.org/research/ESP/CountryReports2000_01/Moldova00.pdf [Accessed: 14th April 2003].

xx **Tzvetkova-Anguelova, J. (2000)** *Trends and Indicators on Child and Family Well-Being in Bulgaria.* Sofia: National Statistical Institute. Available at: http://www.unicef-icdc.org/research/ESP/CountryReports2000_01/ Bulgaria00.pdf [Accessed: 14th April 2003].

xxi **Vaskis, E. (2000)** *Trends and Indicators on Child and Family Well-Being in Latvia.* Riga: Central Statistical Bureau. Available at: http://www.unicef-icdc.org/research/ESP/CountryReports2000_01/Latvia00.pdf [Accessed: 14th April 2003].

xxii **Zbarskaya, I. (2000)** *Child and Family Welfare in Russia: Trends and Indicators.* Goskomstat of Russia: State Committee of the Russian Federation on Statistics. Available at: http://www.unicef-icdc.org/research/ESP/CountryReports2000_01/ Russia00.pdf [Accessed: 14th April 2003].

56. **UNICEF (2005)** *The State of the World's Children.* New York: UNICEF. Available at: http://www.unicef.org/sowc05/english/index.html [Accessed: 14th January 2005].

57. **United Nations Educational, Scientific and Cultural Organisation (UNESCO) (1995)** *Early Childhood Care and Education: Basic Indicators on Young Children.* Paris: UNESCO. Available at: http://unesdoc.unesco.org/images/0010/001036/ 103655e.pdf [Accessed: 14th April 2003].

58. **Zeitlin, J. and Wildman, K. (2003)** *PERISTAT: Indicators for Monitoring and Evaluating Perinatal Health in Europe.* Luxembourg: European Commission. Available at: http://europa.eu.int/comm/health/ph_projects/2000/monitoring/ fp_monitoring_2000_frep_07_en.pdf [Accessed: 3rd August 2004].

65

APPENDIX 5

LIST OF GOVERNMENT DEPARTMENTS, AGENCIES AND STAKEHOLDERS

Government Departments:

- Department of Education and Science
- Department of Health and Children
- Department of Justice, Equality and Law Reform
- Department of Social and Family Affairs
- Department of Community, Rural and Gaeltacht Affairs
- Department of the Environment, Heritage and Local Government

Agencies and Stakeholders:

- An Garda Síochana
- Centre for Early Childhood Development and Education
- Central Statistics Office
- Combat Poverty Agency
- Economic and Social Research Institute
- Irish Social Services Inspectorate
- Mental Health Commission
- National Advisory Council on Drugs
- National Alcohol Advisor
- National Breast-feeding Co-ordinator
- National Disability Authority
- National Disease Surveillance Centre
- National Education Welfare Board
- National Juvenile Office
- National Nutrition Surveillance Centre
- National Treatment Purchase Fund
- Programme of Action for Children

67

APPENDIX 6

ROUND THREE QUESTIONNAIRE
THE DEVELOPMENT OF A NATIONAL SET OF CHILD WELL-BEING INDICATORS USING THE DELPHI TECHNIQUE

Research Division, NCO

Thank you for participating in the Delphi Study, which was set up to assist with the development of the national set of child well-being indicators. We are delighted to report that, as a result of this Study, the following key areas have been prioritised for inclusion in this indicator set:

- Abuse and maltreatment
- Crimes committed on children and young people
- Accessibility of basic health services
- Economic security
- Mental health
- Relationships with parents and family
- Availability of housing for families with children
- Public expenditure on services
- Self-esteem
- Nutrition
- Relationships with peers
- Screening for growth and development
- Enrolment in education
- Completion of school
- Children and young people in care
- Sexual health and behaviour
- Health of the infant at birth
- Self-reported happiness
- Chronic health conditions
- Parental time with children
- Immunisation
- Use of tobacco, alcohol or drugs
- Attendance at school
- Quality of early childhood care and education
- Values and respect
- Pets and animals
- Things to do
- Environment and places
- Crimes committed by children and young people
- Community characteristics
- Participation in decision-making
- Children and young people with additional needs

Since our last contact, we have been in touch with several Government Departments and Agencies in an attempt to select the best indicator(s) for each key area prioritised by you. We have now identified 41 indicators of child well-being, which will form the national set of child well-being indicators together with a select number of demographic indicators, which are also presented to you overleaf.

We would appreciate it if you could now look at the overall set of child well-being indicators and complete the questionnaire that follows. This questionnaire invites your feedback on how the indicator set was developed and also on how satisfied you are with the indicator set itself. Pages 2 to 5 of the questionnaire presents the indicators selected, and pages 6 and 7 present a series of questions for completion. To move between pages on the questionnaire simply click on the back (<) or forward (>) buttons.

When you have completed this questionnaire, click on forward button (>) and this will bring you to a new page, which will invite you to submit your response. To do this simply click on the submit button and your response will be forwarded to the National Children's Office. You will be unable to submit incomplete responses or more than one questionnaire. Completed questionnaires must be submitted by **Monday, 18th October 2004**. Please note that your response will continue to remain confidential and will not, at any time, be disclosed to other participants in this Study.

If you experience any difficulties completing this questionnaire, please do not hesitate to contact Ms. Anne-Marie Brooks at (01) 242 0007. In the event that you experience difficulties completing this questionnaire on-line, a copy has also been sent to you in the post.

We would like also to take this opportunity to thank you for your time and continued assistance with developing this indicator set. We look forward to receiving your feedback.

Sinéad Hanafin, PhD, Head of Research, National Children's Office
Anne-Marie Brooks, Research Officer, National Children's Office

Areas	Well-Being Indicators
Abuse and maltreatment/crimes committed on children and young people	The number of children referred to the Child Protection Notification System, expressed as a proportion of all children. This can be sub-divided by most serious type of harm: a) physical; b) emotional; c) sexual; and d) neglect. The number of children subject to substantiated notification, expressed as a proportion of all children. This can be sub-divided by most serious type of harm: a) physical; b) emotional; c) sexual; and d) neglect.
Accessibility of basic health services for children and young people	The number of children on hospital waiting lists for in-patient admission, expressed as a proportion of all children.
Economic security	Relative poverty: The number of children living in households with a household income below the national 60% median, equivalised using the modified OECD equivalence scale, expressed as a proportion of all children. Consistent poverty: The number of children living in households with a household income below the national 70% median, equivalised using the modified OECD equivalence scale, and experiencing basic deprivation, expressed as a proportion of all children.
Mental health	The number of children referred to child and adolescent mental health services, expressed as a proportion of all children. The number of suicides among children in age categories 10- 14, 15-17 and in total, expressed as a proportion of all children in the same age groups.
Relationship with parents and family	The number of children aged 11, 13 and 15 who report that they find it easy or very easy to talk with their a) mother; and b) father when something is really bothering them, expressed as a proportion of all children in the same age groups.
Availability of housing for families with children	The number of children in families on a local-authority housing waiting list, expressed as a proportion of all children.
Public expenditure on services for children and young people	Public expenditure on education as a percentage of GDP (to be developed further).
Self-esteem	The number of children in age categories 8-11 and 12-17 who report feeling happy with the way they are, expressed as a proportion of all children.
Attendance at school	The number of children who are absent from school for 20 days or more in the school year, expressed as a proportion of all children.
Nutrition	Eating Habits: The number of children aged 11, 13 and 15 who report to eat breakfast five or more days per week, expressed as a proportion of all children in the same age groups. Feeding practice: The number of newborn babies who are a) exclusively breastfed; and b) partially breastfed throughout the first 48 hours of age, expressed as a proportion of all newborn babies. Nutritional Outcomes: To be developed.
Relationships with peers	The number of children aged 11, 13 and 15 who report to having been bullied in their lifetime, expressed as a proportion of all children in the same age groups. The number of children aged 11, 13 and 15 who report to have three or more close friends of the same gender, expressed as a proportion of all children in the same age groups.

Screening for growth development	The percentage uptake of developmental screening at seven to nine months.
Enrolment in education/ completion of school	The number of children who leave school (voluntarily or by exclusion) before the statutory school-leaving age, expressed as a proportion of all children.
Children and young people in care	The number of children who are in the care of the Health Services Executive (HSE), expressed as a proportion of all children. This can be sub-divided by type of care arrangement: a) foster care - general; b) foster care - special; c) foster care - relatives; d) pre-adoptive placement; e) residential - general; f) residential - special; g) at home under care order; and h) other.
Sexual health and behaviour	The number of births to children in age categories 10-14, 15-17 and in total, expressed as a proportion of all children in the same age groups.
Health of the infant at birth	The number of births within each 500g weight interval, expressed as a proportion of all registered live and stillbirths. This can be sub-divided into: a) healthy birth weight (between 2,500 and 4,000 grams); b) low birth weight (less than 2,500 grams); and c) high birth weight (more than 4,000 grams). The distribution of timing of first antenatal visit by trimester of pregnancy for all women delivering live or stillborn babies. Trimesters are as follows: a) 1st trimester = < 15 weeks; b) 2nd trimester = 15-27 weeks; and c) 3rd trimester = 28 weeks or more.
Self-reported happiness	The number of children aged 11, 13 and 15 who report being happy with their life at present, expressed as a proportion of all children in the same age groups.
Chronic health conditions/ morbidity	The ten most frequent conditions resulting in hospitalisation among children.
Parental time with children	The number of children aged 15 who report that their parents: a) discuss how well they are doing at school; b) eat a main meal with them around a table; and c) spend time just talking to them more than once a week, expressed as a proportion of all children in the same age group.
Immunisation	The percentage uptake of D3/P3/T3/Hib3/Polio3 and Meningococcal C3 vaccinations at a) 12 months; and b) 24 months of age. The percentage uptake of MMR1 vaccinations at 24 months of age.
Use of alcohol, tobacco and drugs	The number of children aged 11, 13 and 15 who report to smoke cigarettes a) every day; and b) every week, expressed as a proportion of all children in the same age groups. The number of children aged 15 who report to have had five or more alcoholic beverages in a row at least once in the last 30 days, expressed as a proportion of all children in the same age group. The number of children aged 15 who report to have used any illicit drugs in their lifetime, expressed as a proportion of all children in the same age group. This can be sub-divided by type of drug used.
Enrolment in early childhood care and education	The number of children under 13 in various childcare/education arrangements, expressed as a proportion of all children in the same age group. This can be sub-divided into: a) pre-school; b) compulsory school; c) centre-based service outside school hours; d) crèche or day care; e) professional child minder; and f) family relative.

Quality of early childhood care and education	To be developed
Values and respect	To be developed
Pets and animals	To be developed
Things to do	The number of children aged 11, 13 and 15 who report to be physically active for a) at least two hours; and b) more than four hours per week, expressed as a proportion of all children in the same age groups. The number of children aged 15 who report that reading is one of their favourite hobbies, expressed as a proportion of all children in the same age group.
Environment and places	The number of children aged 11, 13 and 15 who report that there are good places in their area to spend their free time, expressed as a proportion of all children in the same age groups.
Community characteristics	The number of children aged 11, 13 and 15 who report to feel safe in the area where they live, expressed as a proportion of all children in the same age groups.
Participation in decision-making	The number of children aged 11, 13 and 15 who report that students at their school participate in making the school rules, expressed as a proportion of all children in the same age groups.
Crimes committed by children and young people	The number of children referred to the Garda Juvenile Diversion Programme, expressed as a proportion of all children.

Areas	Socio-Demographic Indicators
Child population	The number of children under 18, expressed as a proportion of the total population.
Family structure	The number of children under 18, who live in family household units with only one parent or primary care-giver resident, expressed as a proportion of all children.
Parental education level attained	The number of children under 18, whose parents have attained: a) primary; b) lower secondary; c) upper secondary; and d) third level education, expressed as a proportion of all children.
Child mortality	The number of deaths among children under 18, expressed as a proportion of all children. This may be sub-divided by principal cause of death.
Children and young people with additional needs	The number of children under 18, registered as having an intellectual disability, expressed as a proportion of all children. This can be sub-divided by grade of disability: a) mild; b) moderate; c) severe; and d) profound. The number of children under 18, recorded as having a physical or sensory disability, expressed as a proportion of all children. The number of: a) children seeking asylum, alone or as part of a family; b) non-national children; c) homeless children; and d) traveller children, expressed as a proportion of all children.

All indicators may also be sub-divided by:

a) Male, female, where appropriate
b) Age categories 0-4, 5-9, 10-14 and 15-17, where appropriate
c) Socio-economic group, where appropriate
d) Geographic location, where appropriate

THE NATIONAL SET OF CHILD WELL-BEING INDICATORS 1.a The following statements are concerned with the selection criteria, which were adopted to guide the development and selection of this indicator set. Please state the extent to which you agree or disagree that the selection criteria was adhered to by ticking the relevant box.					
	STRONGLY AGREE	AGREE	DISAGREE	STRONGLY DISAGREE	DON'T KNOW
COMPREHENSIVE This indicator set includes measures that assess well-being across a broad range of issues such as physical well-being, peer and social relationships, family relationships, emotional and behavioural well-being.					
CHILDREN OF ALL AGES This indicator set includes enough measures for children of every age, from birth through to adolescence. For example, it includes measures such as breast-feeding and birth weight, which relates to infants. It also includes measures such as early school-leaving and participation in decision-making, which relates to older children.					
CLEAR This indicator set includes measures that are easily and readily understood.					
POSITIVE AND NEGATIVE This indicator set includes enough negative measures and enough positive measures of well-being. For example, it includes measures on problem behaviour and negative circumstances such as binge-drinking and child abuse. It also includes measures on pro-social behaviour and positive circumstances such as participation in decision-making and positive family functioning.					
REFLECTIVE OF SOCIAL GOALS This indicator set allows us to track our progress in meeting national goals for child well-being such as, for example, goals to reduce the number of early school-leavers and goals to increase the incidence of breast-feeding and childhood immunisations.					
OBJECTIVE AND SUBJECTIVE This indicator set includes enough objective measures and enough subjective measures of well-being. For example, it includes objective measures of well-being such as poverty and chronic health conditions. It also includes subjective measures based on children's personal assessments of their circumstances such as self-reported happiness.					
WELL-BEING AND WELL-BECOMING This indicator set includes enough measures that look at the current well-being of children and also includes enough measures that look at factors that are likely to affect well-being in adult life. For example, it includes a measure on early school leaving, which is one of the most significant determinants of poverty in adulthood.					

1b. Please provide some feedback on your responses.

1c. Overall, how satisfied are you with the National Set of Child Well-Being Indicators?

☐ Very satisfied ☐ Satisfied ☐ Dissatisfied ☐ Very dissatisfied

THE DELPHI STUDY

It would be helpful for us to have some general feedback about this Study. Your comments would be greatly appreciated.

2a. Overall, how satisfied were you with the approach taken to develop this indicator set?

☐ Very satisfied ☐ Satisfied ☐ Dissatisfied ☐ Very dissatisfied

2b. What do you see as the main advantages in taking this type of approach?

2c. What do you see as the main disadvantages in taking this type of approach?

2d. Did you have any difficulties completing the questionnaires?

☐ Yes

☐ No

2e. If yes, please tell us a little about the difficulties you experienced.

2f. Are there any further comments that you would like to make?

2g. Name: ____________________

THANK YOU FOR YOUR TIME AND ASSISTANCE.

74

75

CHILD WELL-BEING INDICATORS

Abuse and Maltreatment

Definition: The number of children referred to the Child Protection Notification System, expressed as a proportion of all children. This can be sub-divided by most serious type of harm: a) physical; b) emotional; c) sexual; and d) neglect

Source: Child Care Interim Data Set, Department of Health and Children

Definition: The number of children subject to substantiated notification, expressed as a proportion of all children. This can be sub-divided by most serious type of harm: a) physical; b) emotional; c) sexual; and d) neglect

Source: Child Care Interim Data Set, Department of Health and Children

Accessibility of Basic Health Services for Children and Young People

Definition: The number of children on hospital waiting lists for in-patient admission, expressed as a proportion of all children

Source: Health Services National Performance Indicators, Department of Health and Children

Attendance at School

Definition: The number of children who are absent from school for 20 days or more in the school year, expressed as a proportion of all children

Source: Education Welfare Board Database, National Education Welfare Board

Availability of Housing for Families with Children

Definition: The number of children in families on a local-authority housing waiting list, expressed as a proportion of all children

Source: Housing Needs Assessments published in the Quarterly Bulletin on Housing Statistics, Department of the Environment, Heritage and Local Government

Children and Young People in Care

Definition: The number of children who are in the care of the Health Services Executive (HSE), expressed as a proportion of all children. This can be sub-divided by type of care arrangement: a) foster care - general; b) foster care - special; c) foster care - relatives; d) pre-adoptive placement; e) residential - general; f) residential - special; g) at home under care order; and h) other

Source: Child Care Interim Data Set, Department of Health and Children

Chronic Health Conditions and Hospitalisation

Definition: The ten most frequent conditions resulting in hospitalisation among children

Source: Hospital In-Patient Enquiry Statistics, Economic and Social Research Institute

Community Characteristics

Definition: The number of children aged 11, 13 and 15 who report to feel safe in the area where they live, expressed as a proportion of children in the same age groups

Source: Health Behaviour of School-Aged Children Survey, National University of Ireland, Galway

Crimes Committed by Children and Young People

Definition: The number of children referred to the Garda Juvenile Liaison Programme, expressed as a proportion of all children

Source: Annual Report, An Garda Siochana

Economic Security

Relative Poverty:

Definition: The number of children living in households with a household income below the national 60% median, equivalised using the modified OECD equivalence scale, expressed as a proportion of all children

Source: European Union Survey on Income and Living Conditions, Central Statistics Office

Consistent Poverty:

Definition: The number of children living in households with a household income below the national 70% median, equivalised using the modified OECD equivalence scale and experiencing basic deprivation, expressed as a proportion of all children

Source: European Union Survey on Income and Living Conditions, Central Statistics Office

Enrolment in Childhood Care and Education

Definition: The number of children under 13 in various early childhood care and education arrangements expressed as a proportion of all children in the same group. This can be sub-divided into: a) pre-school; b) compulsory school; c) centre-based care outside school hours; d) crèche or day-care; e) professional childminder; and f) family relative

Source: European Union Survey of Income and Living Conditions, Central Statistics Office

Enrolment in Education/Completion of School

Definition: The number of children who leave school (voluntarily or by exclusion) before the statutory school leaving age, expressed as a proportion of all children

Source: Post-Primary Pupil Database, Department of Education and Science

Environment and Places

Definition: The number of children aged 11, 13 and 15 who report that there are good places in their area to spend their free time, expressed as a proportion of children in the same age groups

Source: Health Behaviour of School-Aged Children Survey, National University of Ireland, Galway

Health of the Infant at Birth

Definition: The number of births within each 500g-weight interval, expressed as a proportion of all registered live and stillbirths. This can be sub-divided into: a) healthy birth weight (between 2,500 and 4,000 grams); b) low birth weight (less than 2,500 grams); and c) high birth weight (more than 4,000 grams)

Source: National Perinatal Reporting System, Economic and Social Research Institute

Definition: The distribution of timing of first antenatal visit by trimester of pregnancy for all women delivering live or stillborn babies. Trimesters are as follows: a) 1st trimester =< 15 weeks; b) 2nd trimester = 15 - 27 weeks; and c) 3rd trimester = 28 weeks or more

Source: National Perinatal Reporting System, Economic and Social Research Institute

Immunisation

Definition: The percentage uptake of D3/P3/T3/Hib3/Polio3 and Meningococcal C3 vaccinations at a) 12 months; b) 24 months of age

Source: Immunisation Uptake Statistics for Ireland, National Disease Surveillance Centre

Definition: The percentage uptake of MMR1 vaccinations at 24 months of age

Source: Immunisation Uptake Statistics for Ireland, National Disease Surveillance Centre

Mental Health

Definition: The number of children referred to child and adolescent mental health services, expressed as a proportion of all children.

Source: Health Service Executive Statistics, Health Services Executive

Definition: The number of suicides among children in age categories 10-14, 15-17 and in total, expressed as a proportion of all children in the same age groups

Source: Vital Statistics, Central Statistics Office

Nutrition

Eating habits:

Definition: The number of children aged 11, 13 and 15 who report eating breakfast five or more days per week, expressed as a proportion of all children in the same age groups

Source: Health Behaviour of School-Aged Children Survey, National University of Ireland, Galway

Feeding practice:

Definition: The number of newborn babies who are: a) exclusively breastfed and; b) partially breastfed throughout the first 48 hours of age, expressed as a proportion of all newborn babies (to be developed further)

Source: National Perinatal Reporting System, Economic and Social Research Institute

Nutritional outcomes:

Definition: To be developed

Source: To be developed

Parental Time with Children

Definition: The number of children aged 15 who report that their parents: a) discuss how well they are doing at school; b) eat a main meal with them around a table; and c) spend time just talking with them more than once a week, expressed as a proportion of children in the same age group

Source: Programme for International Student Assessment Survey, Education Research Centre, Drumcondra

Participation in Decision-making

Definition: The number of children aged 11, 13 and 15 who report that students at their school participate in making the school rules, expressed as a proportion of children in the same age groups

Source: Health Behaviour of School-Aged Children Survey, National University of Ireland, Galway

Pets and Animals

Definition: To be developed

Source: To be developed

Public Expenditure on Services for Children and Young People

Definition: Public expenditure on education as a percentage of GDP (to be developed further)

Source: Tuarascáil Staitistiúil, Department of Education and Science

Quality of Childhood Care and Education

Definition: To be developed

Source: To be developed

Relationship with Parents and Family

Definition: The number of children aged 11, 13 and 15 who report that they find it easy or very easy to talk with their: a) mother; and b) father when something is really bothering them, expressed as a proportion of all children in the same age groups

Source: Health Behaviour of School-Aged Children Survey, National University of Ireland, Galway

Relationships with Peers

Definition: The number of children aged 11, 13 and 15 who report to having been bullied at school, expressed as a proportion of children in the same age groups

Source: Health Behaviour of School-Aged Children Survey, National University of Ireland, Galway

Definition: The number of children aged 11, 13 and 15 who report to have three or more friends of the same gender, expressed as a proportion of children in the same age groups

Source: Health Behaviour of School-Aged Children Survey, National University of Ireland, Galway

Screening for Growth and Development

Definition: The percentage of mothers of new born children contacted by a Public Health Nurse (PHN) within 48 hours of hospital discharge

Source: Health Services National Performance Indicators, Department of Health and Children

Definition: The percentage uptake of developmental screening at seven to nine months

Source: Health Services National Performance Indicators, Department of Health and Children

Self-esteem

Definition: The number of children in age categories 8-11 and 12-17 who report feeling happy with the way they are, expressed as a proportion of all children in the same age groups

Source: KIDSCREEN, Programme of Action for Children

Self-reported Happiness

Definition: The number of children aged 11, 13 and 15 who report being happy with their life at present, expressed as a proportion of children in the same age groups

Source: Health Behaviour of School-Aged Children Survey, National University of Ireland, Galway

Sexual Health and Behaviour

Definition: The number of births to females in age categories 10-14 and 15-17 and in total, expressed as a proportion of all children in the same age groups

Source: Vital Statistics, Central Statistics Office

Things To Do

Definition: The number of children aged 11, 13 and 15 who report to be physically active for: a) at least two hours; and b) more than four hours per week, expressed as a proportion of children in the same age groups

Source: Health Behaviour of School-Aged Children Survey, National University of Ireland, Galway

Definition: The number of children aged 15 who report that reading is one of their favourite hobbies, expressed as a proportion of children in the same age group

Source: Programme for International Student Assessment Survey, Education Research Centre, Drumcondra

Use of Tobacco, Alcohol and Drugs

Definition: The number of children aged 11, 13 and 15 who report to smoke cigarettes: a) every day; and b) every week, expressed as a proportion of children in the same age groups

Source: Health Behaviour of School-Aged Children Survey, National University of Ireland, Galway

Definition: The number of children aged 15 who report to have had five or more alcoholic drinks in a row at least once in the last 30 days, expressed as a proportion of children in the same age group

Source: European Schools Project on Alcohol and Drugs Survey, St. Patrick's College, Drumcondra

Definition: The number of children aged 15 who report to have used any illicit drugs in their lifetime, expressed as a proportion of children in the same age groups. This can be sub-divided by type of drug used

Source: European Schools Project on Alcohol and Drugs Survey, St. Patrick's College, Drumcondra

Values and Respect

Definition: To be developed

Source: To be developed

SOCIO-DEMOGRAPHIC INDICATORS

Child Population

Definition: The number of children under 18, expressed as a proportion of the total population

Source: Census of the Population, Central Statistics Office

Family Structure

Definition: The number of children under 18 who live in family household units with only one parent or primary caregiver resident, expressed as a proportion of all children

Source: Census of the Population, Central Statistics Office

Parental Education Level Attained

Definition: The number of children under 18 whose parents have attained: a) primary; b) lower secondary; c) upper secondary; and d) third level education, expressed as a proportion of all children

Source: Census of the Population, Central Statistics Office

Child Mortality

Definition: The number of deaths among children under 18, expressed as a proportion of all children. This may be sub-divided by principal cause of death

Source: Vital Statistics, Central Statistics Office

Children and Young People with Additional Needs

Definition: The number of children under 18 registered as having an intellectual disability, expressed as a proportion of all children. This can be sub-divided by grade of disability: a) mild; b) moderate; c) severe; and d) profound

Source: National Intellectual Disability Database, Health Research Board

Definition: The number of children under 18 recorded as having a physical or sensory disability, expressed as a proportion of all children

Source: Census of the Population, Central Statistics Office

Definition: The number: of a) children seeking asylum, alone or as part of a family; b) non-national children; c) homeless children; and d) traveller children, expressed as a proportion of all children

Source: Census of the Population, Central Statistics Office and Child Care Interim Data Set, Department and Children

APPENDIX 8

OVERVIEW OF MAIN DATA SOURCES

Title: Census of the Population
Source: Central Statistics Office (www.cso.ie)
Description: Population statistics including housing, employment, education and family structure.
Frequency: Every five years

Title: Childcare Interim Data Set
Source: Department of Health and Children (www.doh.ie)
Description: Statistics on children in care or at risk.
Frequency: Annual

Title: Education Welfare Board Database
Source: National Education Welfare Board (www.newb.ie)
Description: Statistics on children absent from school twenty or more days.
Frequency: Annual

Title: European Schools Project on Alcohol and Drugs (ESPAD) Survey
Source: St. Patrick's College, Drumcondra (www.spd.dcu.ie)
Description: European survey of the behaviours, knowledge and beliefs concerning cigarettes, alcohol, solvents and illegal drugs among 15-year-old children.
Frequency: Every four years

Title: European Union Survey on Income and Living Conditions (EU-SILC)
Source: Central Statistics Office (www.cso.ie)
Description: European survey on income, living conditions and basic deprivation.
Frequency: Annual

Title: Garda Annual Report
Source: An Garda Siochana (www.garda.ie)
Description: Crime statistics including arrests and diversions to the Garda Juvenile Liaison Programme.
Frequency: Annual

Title: Health Behaviour of School-Aged Children (HBSC) Survey
Source: National University of Ireland, Galway (www.nuig.ie)
Description: International survey of the health behaviours of 11-, 13-, and 15-year-old children covering areas such as general health, food and nutrition, exercise and alcohol consumption and children's perceptions of happiness.
Frequency: Every four years

Title: Health Services National Performance Indicators
Source: Department of Health and Children (www.doh.ie)
Description: Statistics on health and healthcare services including mental health, child and adolescent health and child care.
Frequency: Annual

Title: Hospital In-Patient Enquiry (HIPE)
Source: Economic and Social Research Institute (www.esri.ie)
Description: Statistics on hospital stays including date of birth, gender, marital status, medical card status, diagnosis, procedure and length of stay.
Frequency: Annual

Title: Housing Needs Assessments published in the Quarterly Bulletin on Housing Statistics.
Source: Department of the Environment, Heritage and Local Government (www.environ.ie)
Description: Statistics on families on housing lists and homelessness.
Frequency: Every three years

Title: National Intellectual Disability Database
Source: Health Research Board (www.hrb.ie)
Description: Statistics on those with an intellectual disability (mild, moderate, severe and profound) in receipt of, or on a waiting list for, specialist services.
Frequency: Annual

Title: KIDSCREEN
Source: Programme of Action for Children (www.hse.ie)
Description: European survey of the Health-Related Quality of Life of 8-11-year-old and 12-17-year-old children.
Frequency: Currently being piloted

Title: National Disease Surveillance Statistics
Source: National Disease Surveillance Centre (www.ndsc.ie)
Description: Statistics on infectious diseases and vaccinations.
Frequency: Quarterly

Title: National Perinatal Reporting System
Source: Economic and Social Research Institute (www.esri.ie)
Description: Demographic statistics including stillbirths, perinatal and maternal deaths, mother and father date of birth, nationality, occupation and marital status and basic clinical information including birth weight, period of gestation, type of feeding and congenital anomalies for every birth.
Frequency: Annual

Title: Post-Primary Pupil Database
Source: Department of Education and Science (www.education.ie)
Description: Statistics on pupil participation and retention rates.
Frequency: Annual

Title: Programme for International Student Assessment (PISA) Survey
Source: Education Research Centre, St. Patrick's College Drumcondra (www.erc.ie)
Description: International survey of reading, mathematics and science achievement of 15-year-old children.
Frequency: Every three years

Title: Tuarascáil Staitistiúil
Source: Department of Education and Science (www.education.ie)
Description: Statistics on schools and examinations.
Frequency: Annual

Title: Vital Statistics
Source: Central Statistics Office (www.cso.ie)
Description: Statistics on births, marriages, deaths.
Frequency: Quarterly